Diamond A Ranch
1970s

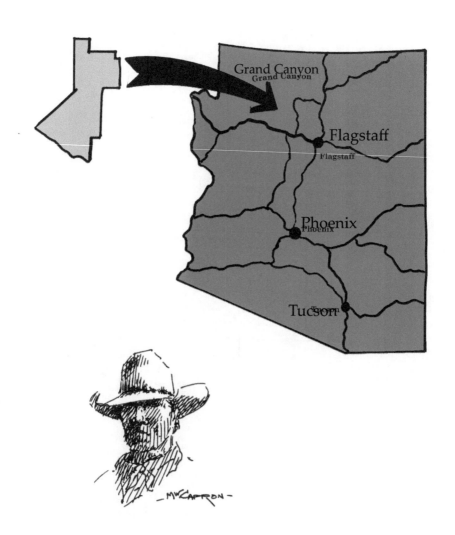

WAGON BOSS
A True Cowboy Story
By
Ed Ashurst

Illustrated
by
MC Carron

Ed Ashurst Publishing Company
Douglas, Arizona

Dedication

This book is dedicated to: Randy Rutledge, Pat Prosser, Barney Prosser, Cole Gould, Sam Gould, Beano Kimball, Jim "Strawberry" Dixon, Chip Dixon, Scott Westlake, Mark Westlake, Elmer McDonald, Josh Copeland, Al Smith, Truman Rustin, Snooks McDonald, Brad Meade, Barry Prosser, Butch, Jim Casebeere, Cole Moorhouse, Tom Reeder, Stacy Taliafaro, Cody Sawyer, Ben Benton, Bruce Barker, Shane Sanders, Slim Sandsness, Robert Hogue, John Hogue, Cody Cochran, Cody Dinsmore, Clay Ashurst, Everett Ashurst, Yates Dixon, Jim Marler, Jim "Baldy" Ivy, Kent Snedicor, J. D. Williams, Tom "Swede" Erwang, Jack Bowlin, Jim Bryant, Jim Fancher, Charlie Wascogamie, John McGrew, "Super" Dave Phillips, Kennon Allen, Jeff Osborn, Doug Nolan, Jason Mueller, Steve Webb, The Vampire, Margie Fancher, Willy "Rotten" Larsen, Floyd Martin, Rex Williamson, Jessi "the runaway," Eric "the Viking," Jake Bowser, Bradley Rogers, Daniel Pritchett, Ron Remington, Jim Dewey Brown, Mike McLaughlin, Stan Livingston, Jake, Bubba Smith, Devin Kanapily, Lee Pehl, Larry Don Leist, Kent Craven, Leo Ryff, Clint Halford, and Rick George. They rode for the fun of it, suffered much, and were rewarded very little.

Other Books By Ed Ashurst

Miracle or Coincidence?
Real Cowboys - Grand Canyon to Mexico

Table of Contents

꽃ⓒ

Acknowledgements

Lyrics from the song *Cowboy Pride*
Courtesy of Ian Tyson
Lyrics from the song *The Old Double Diamond*
Courtesy of Gary McMahan

Wagon Boss
A True Cowboy Story

Introduction

ne of my favorite authors is a man named Rick Bragg. Mr. Bragg was born into and is a product of dirt poor southern white trash who lived in northeastern Alabama. By some miracle or twist of fate Rick Bragg became a famous writer, and he won a Pulitzer Prize for reporting for the New York Times. The book of Mr. Bragg's that is my favorite is titled "Ava's Man" and is a biography of his grandfather whose name was Charlie Bundrum. To most of the world, Charlie Bundrum was a no-account poor man who was a roofer by trade and a maker of moonshine by avocation. But Rick Bragg's story of Charlie Bundrum and his family is a riveting tale full of the pathos of blood and guts living that make you feel like you are there, present and watching, as the story unfolds. Rick Bragg's most famous book is titled, "All Over but the Shoutin'" and is a tribute to his mother who picked cotton by hand and did other people's laundry for pennies to put food on the table. She didn't buy herself a new dress for eighteen years so she could afford to buy shoes for her three sons and buy lunchmeat so they would have something to eat besides government peanut butter. In the prologue in "All Over but the Shoutin'," Rick writes, "... dreaming backwards can carry a man through some dark rooms where the walls seem lined with razor blades." That is Rick Bragg's line not mine, but I wish I could claim it.

If three people witness an automobile accident and then are questioned by the authorities to describe what they saw, most of the time the authorities will get three stories that will be different. Sometimes separate stories describing the same event will be so different it will make one think that one or two of the three witnesses must be lying. We all see things from a different angle. Some of us remember better than others. Some people have a well-lubricated, selective memory.

I have tried to write fiction, but so far my success has been writing true stories. I write about my memories. I wrote this because I thought it was a good story. This is not an important book, but it is a real book, and the people in it are, or were, real people. The events I describe really took place, and as far as good storytelling goes, they are not exaggerated. Parts of it, I hope, are humorous, other parts perhaps disturbing, and in places you may become angry, perhaps at me. I don't have a problem with that.

This is my story, and it's written from the angle I saw it. If you were there and saw it differently, I encourage you to write your own book that includes your own version of what happened. I will buy a copy and read it, and I imagine I will enjoy it!

Beware as you read through the pages that follow, there may be some razor blades laying around. I hope that Rick Bragg would approve of my style.

Ed Ashurst

Foreword by Charlie Gould

Oh, Lord, how time has flown.

I am not now nor have I ever been a good cowboy. So it came as a surprise when Ed asked me to write this foreword! I guess friendship like love is blind.

I have known and worked with many of the good hands in this book, and also some of the "others" as well. I feel Ed is qualified, and very well able, to tell these stories about life in the "Big Outfit" world. Some folks try to make believe that all is rosy all the time: every day brings more chances for big time mistakes and wrecks—such is life on these ranches.

One friend said, "The three most radical, uncontrollable, unpredictable creatures in the world are cowboys, horses and cattle." So how could you possibly put all these together and hope for total, perfect harmony. Thankfully there are "Wagon Bosses" who mix all this together and come out (at least mostly) with smooth, well run wagons on this type of ranch.

Thank God for this life and the people and animals and cow country all over the West that make this ranching world exactly what it is now and has been, oh, these many great years!

God Bless You.

Charlie Gould
July 2014

Cowboyses and Corporations
Seem to naturally collide
And you come out the loser
With your durned old Cowboy Pride

End of an Era

ഇറ

*Diamond A Ranch, November 1972, A
few days before Thanksgiving*

The Diamond A wagon moved from Pica Camp north to Camp Sixteen fifty miles distance. Actually the Diamond A Ranch ran two wagons in those days. One of them was known as the upper wagon and was run by Burley McDonald; the other was known as the lower wagon, which was run by Mike Landis. The lower wagon was the one I referred to saying it moved from Pica to Sixteen. Tenneco Oil Corporation owned the Diamond A Ranch at that time, and they had decided to liquidate the Hereford cowherd that had run on the ranch for decades. Jimmy Gibson, who was the Arizona State Brand Inspector stationed in Seligman at that time, eventually wrote hauling papers for over seventeen thousand mother cows. Roundup would be over the day before Thanksgiving with the bulk of these cows being loaded and gone by that time; although a few remnant cows would still be gathered as much as a year later.

I was working on the lower wagon, or Mike's wagon as some cowboys called it due to the fact that Mike Landis was the wagon boss. The Diamond A had two other ranches leased besides the Diamond A proper: the Denny Ranch to the west of Seligman near the Grand Canyon Caverns, and the Sevens Ranch, which lay to the north of Ashfork. These two ranches together made up about eight and a half townships of country, and when you added that to the size of the Diamond A itself, the cowboys who worked for the big outfit had about fifteen hundred square miles to ride and gather cows on. Mike's wagon, which normally consisted of ten men plus a cook and hood, usually worked about half of what they called the top country around Big Chief, Black Mountain, Trinity, and Reed Cashion, as well as the Denny, the Sevens Ranch, and Aubrey Valley. Burley and his crew would gather and work everything north of that.

For reasons not known to me, the ranch manager, Jim Lowrance, ordered Mike to move his wagon to the far north end of the ranch and set up camp at Sixteen and gather the Bishop Pasture, a fifty-five square mile piece of country north of there that bordered the Hualapai Indian Reservation to the west and the Supai Indian Reservation to the north. The Bishop Pasture was the last pasture on the ranch to still have many cows in it, and we were to have them ready to load on trucks the day before Thanksgiving. Mike left me and a cowboy named Ron Harris at Pica to finish loading some trucks, while he and the rest of the crew moved camp. Ron and I finished loading those trucks about sundown and loaded our horses on a big truck the ranch owned, and we were chauffeured north to Camp Sixteen by a fellow who worked on the maintenance crew. Just before we stepped in the truck to go, I noticed a pair of chaps that had been left by mistake by a man on our crew named Joe Chavez, so I picked them up and took them with me. We got to Sixteen late after everyone else had gone to bed, so we set up our teepees and went to bed ourselves.

Early in the morning, about three, I was woke up by shouts of joy from Joe Chavez as he found his chaps that I had laid on the ground in the cook tent when we arrived in camp a few hours earlier. No one else was up except he and Rex, the cook, and Joe kept singing and acting happy as if he had just won the lottery. Actually, he was a moody individual who would descend into the depths of depression and vitriol and stay there for days, and of late had been a resident of that dark place, but seeing his chaps had raised him up. He was singing praises about what wonderful fellows Ron and I were because we had been smart enough to rescue the missing leggings. That was a fine switch because usually he thought of Ron and me as a couple of gunsel buttons that were wasting our share of that wonderful commodity known as youth.

I sat up in my bedroll and dressed starting with my cowboy hat and then my shirt, and when I started to open the flap or teepee door, I could feel that it was heavy with snow. I opened it and looked out to see about six inches of good heavy snow that had fallen after I had bedded down for the night. It was now clear and there was a huge moon in the sky.

Rex had fried a big bunch of steak off the round of a beef. He had rolled the steaks in flour before laying them in the frying pan, and as usual he produced a very large pan of gravy and another of biscuits with more coffee than you could drink. That was pretty much what the menu was three times a day. I have no recollection of Rex cooking roast beef, although there would naturally be some baked ribs occasionally, beings all the beeves we butchered possessed ribs. But my memory tells me that Rex had the ability to cut the rest of a beef up into slices that could be fried in a skillet. That was fine with me. I remember Rex making donuts one time, and they were better than any you could buy in town, but that only happened once or twice a roundup. I have no memory of a cake, pie, or cookies produced in his kitchen. Light bread, when he made it, was excellent, but that was maybe once every two weeks. The rest of the time it was steak, biscuits, and gravy. At least it was good steak, biscuits, and gravy.

After breakfast Mike Landis and his jigger boss, Cole Moorhouse, roped our horses and we saddled up and took off in a long trot, which was Mike Landis's signature trademark. It was eleven miles from Camp Sixteen to the farthest northeastern corner of Bishop Pasture, and we would be there before sunup. That morning is one of my most vivid memories because of the big moon in the sky reflecting off of the new six inches of snow. Somehow it was almost lighter than day because the reflection and brightness created abnormal contrasts to everything that came out of the ground. Every bush, fence post, or tree seemed easily noticed. Our shadows as we trotted through the snow were more noticeable than they would have been in the middle of the day. The crew, as I remember it, was made up of Mike Landis, Cole Moorhouse, Larry Leist, Ron Harris, Mike Pemberton, Dave Burt, Doug Kepkie, Joe Chavez, and me. A cowboy named Joe Burris had quit a day or two before.

In typical Mike Landis fashion, we made the eleven mile trip to the Supai Indian Reservation fence in record time, and it was still too dark to see real well. We lit a big dead juniper tree on fire and warmed up. No one on the crew owned any overshoes, and some didn't own a heavy coat, perhaps a vest and Levi jumper. We enjoyed the fire.

We gathered Bishop Pasture and deposited the herd of Hereford cows into a holding trap that ran out to the

west of the house and corrals at Sixteen, and about the time we got that accomplished, Burley McDonald and all his crew moved into Sixteen and set up camp next to us. The manager, Jim Lowrance, was a man who always liked to make a big splash and had decided that beings this was the last big shipping of cattle owned by Tenneco Oil in Northern Arizona, he should throw both wagons together and do it up right. Jim Lowrance liked his position as Diamond A manager, and he always had on a good pair of Jessie Bogle or Paul Bond boots, a starched white shirt, and a 10 X hat. His wife drove a big new white Cadillac. She was beautiful like Elizabeth Taylor and wore the biggest diamond ring I had ever seen.

Two days before Thanksgiving, the crews from both wagons, upper and lower, trotted out to the backside of the shipping trap and gathered the cows that we had put there from the Bishop Pasture. There were about three hundred fifty mother cows plus their calves, bulls, etc. We had enough men to butcher them before noon. As we approached the shipping corral, being perhaps four or five hundred yards away, Jim Lowrance, who had showed up after breakfast, driving all the way from Seligman sixty miles to the south, came loping out to meet us. "Get 'em runnin' boys! Get 'em runnin'!" He shouted and he began slapping his chaps with his bridle reins and squalling, riding into the flank of the herd. I thought it completely out of place to be making cattle run toward the scales and loading chute, but Lowrance was in a mood to put on a show, and we did as ordered.

We hustled the cows into the corrals and began separating the calves from their mothers and weighing and loading. There were a few calves that had escaped past the men working in the gate and were still mixed in the herd of cows. Someone ordered Ben Fancher, who was Burley's jigger boss, and me to ride amongst the cows and rope the calves that were there and drag them through a gate so they could be weighed with the other calves and loaded on trucks separately from their mothers. With as many men as we had, and no shortage of bosses, we made short order of the cutting, sorting, weighing, and loading; and we were through by lunch.

The only thing left to do now was pull the shoes off all extra horses that would be turned out to grass for the winter. Checks were written and given to all the extra cowboys who had been hired to go through the fall roundup and would now be laid off. I was among that bunch. A skeleton

crew would remain on the payroll to gather remnant and perhaps land a job with whoever would lease or buy the big outfit. It was the biggest in Arizona, one of the biggest anywhere. Its future was uncertain.

Jim Lowrance did not want to be known as being anticlimactic, so in honor of seeing the huge herd of Hereford cows go, not to mention Tenneco's Arizona cattle operation, he planned a big blowout to be held at the Salty Dog Saloon in Seligman on Thanksgiving Day. The Salty Dog was well named. Although it was a nondescript edifice made of unpainted cinder block, it was famous for blowouts, some large but most small. It had been the scene earlier, that very fall, of a shootout between two Diamond A cowhands who had been eighty-sixed out of its exalted interior. They positioned themselves out in the parking lot behind a 1962 Chevy Impala and shot a hole through the window in hopes of wounding the bartender who had thrown them out. A deputy followed them north to Mike's wagon, ten miles distance, but was unable to apprehend them, at least at that time.

The Diamond A manager invited every cowboy within a hundred mile radius to his party at the Salty Dog. The man who was considered to be the most dangerous hombre in seven counties showed up and started several fights. One well-liked old-timer from a neighboring ranch came to the party with his son who was about twelve years old. The old-timer gave his son a beer bottle and instructed him to hit anyone who came near him if a big fight broke out. The boy was told, "Hit 'em right between the eyes!" Luckily they got through the party unscathed. Some weren't so lucky. No one I talked to ever mentioned eating turkey and dressing.

With the passing of the Hereford cowherd that had been started by Kern County Land and Cattle Company and passed on to Tenneco Oil, an era in Northern Arizona cow-history had ended. When one era ends, another will rise and take its place. I was only twenty-one. I would be around to be part of the next one.

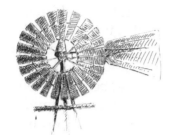

ഇൗരു

History

ഇൗരു

Ihe Diamond A Ranch has been the largest ranch in the state of Arizona for a long time. I have found no historical record of another block of land owned by one entity that is any larger but would not argue with someone who disputed my statement. When talking about the size of the Diamond A Ranch being the largest in Arizona, I have not compared it to the several large cattle ranches that lie within the boundaries of the San Carlos Indian Reservation; although, I think it is larger than those also. But in this I defer to someone who would have that knowledge, a thing I do not possess. The land inside the boundaries of the Diamond A Ranch in the years that I worked there totaled nearly eleven hundred fifty square miles, or close to it. I possess a map of the ranch made in 1971 that shows in detail the various pasture fences, giving the size of the pastures in acres. It also shows water pipelines, water storages, and pinpoints the locations of cow camps, railroads, and the town of Seligman. The map also shows the same details of the Denny Ranch to the west, and the Sevens Ranch to the east, both of which Kern County Land and Cattle Company were leasing at that time. The heading or title on the map, which is quite large, called it the Boquillas Cattle Company, which was what Kern County called its Arizona Division of the company. The ranches Kern County operated in New Mexico were called Victorio Cattle Company.

When I started cowboying in Northern Arizona, there were a good many old-timers who had worked on the Diamond A when it was known as the Three Vs. The Three Vs brand was a V placed on the jaw, another on the shoulder, and another V on the hip, all on the left side. Most old-timers just referred to it as the Vs, leaving out the word three. I worked with lots of these cowboys including Buck Smith, Whistle Mills, Coley Lyons, Jack George, Tracy Dent, Raymond Holt, Jep Stell, Pat Cain, John Andrews, and Lem Davis. I was also acquainted with Carl Welsh, Tom Dolan, Allie Scifers, Jerry Osborne, Rusty Criner, Marion Derenburger, and Slim Gilliam; all of whom worked on the outfit when it was known as the Three Vs.

There is very little written history of the Three Vs. All of the old-timers I knew would say that the Vs came into existence when a certain bank began foreclosing on numerous ranches in northwestern Arizona. I remember several old men talking about the Pacific Loan Company of California. Some men would just say the outfit was owned by a bank in California. To my knowledge, the best record that has been written is "Log of a Twentieth Century Cowboy" by Dan Moore. Dan worked on the Vs for several years beginning in 1926 and states in his book that the outfit was owned by the Pacific Loan Company of California. Dan Moore lists Tom Cavness as the general manager of the ranch, and a cowboy named Charley Hiler as wagon boss, or at least one of the bosses. He also worked for a rascal named Demas Yoder who ran one of the cowboy crews. Dan says in his book that Demas saw a lot of action in World War I, which gave him a drinking problem. Well, anyway, war or no war, Demas drank. I was acquainted with old men who knew and liked Demas, and they didn't mention the war being the cause of his various escapades. By all accounts, he was a very competent cowhand when sober. Actually, most of the time, Demas, and every other Three Vs cowboy, was too far from town and a saloon to stay drunk, so to remember him only for actions occurring on an occasional spree would be unfair.

Mildred Walker Perner wrote a book titled "Life with Old-Time Cowboys" that was a collection of her memoirs living on the Three Vs Ranch beginning in 1941. She married Phil Perner in August of 1941 and began living on the outfit. Her father-in-law, Ross Perner Sr., was vice president and general manager of the ranch at that time. The Three Vs Ranch, according to Mildred, was officially known as the Arizona Livestock Company and was owned by W. H. Waggoner who also held the title of President of the Arizona Livestock Company. According to her book, W. H. Waggoner was a banker by trade and had bought the ranch from Security First National Bank of Los Angeles. The Pacific Loan Company of California is not mentioned in Mrs. Perner's book. One thing is for certain, the Three Vs Ranch was originally put together as a result of a bank foreclosing on numerous smaller ranches, most of which were contiguous to each other. Most old cowboys I have been acquainted with would mention the name of the Pacific Loan Company of California, so I am inclined to think that they were the original operators of the ranch.

W. H. Waggoner was involved in the Three Vs operation early on and was probably an employee of the bank; although no one that I've talked to knows for sure what his original involvement was, or when it started. Dan Moore doesn't mention Waggoner in his book. In the early 1930s, probably '32, one of Tom Dolan's ancestors, whose name was Love, owned a ranch in the Sierra Blanca, Texas area, and W. H. Waggoner foreclosed on the Love Ranch. Mr. Waggoner took a liking to Tom Dolan and recognized his skill as a cowboy and told Tom, "I have a big ranch out in Arizona, and if you ever get a hankering to come out there, let me know."

Tom replied, "Well, you've put me out of business here, so I guess I'll follow you out there, right now." By this account, W. H. Waggoner was involved in the Three Vs Ranch at that time; although it is unclear whether he was still employed by the bank or had bought the ranch from the bank.

I talked to W. H. Waggoner's great nephew and his nephew's mother, who was a niece by marriage, and they both told me this story, W. H. Waggoner's first wife died in the late 1930s, and after a fair amount of time passed, he started courting a beautiful girl who was working in the Harvey House in Seligman. The girl's name was Frieda Swain, and she was the twelfth child of German immigrants who lived near La Junta, Colorado. Frieda ran away from home at the age of fifteen in 1925 because her father wouldn't buy her shoes to wear. He probably didn't have the money to buy shoes. She became a nanny in the home of Fred Harvey Jr. in Colorado Springs and eventually worked at several of Fred Harvey's hotels.

Frieda caught W. H. Waggoner's eye, and they married in August of 1941 (which by coincidence was the same time Mildred Perner married) at the Fred Harvey hotel in Las Vegas, New Mexico. After the wedding, they set out for Santa Fe where they planned to honeymoon at Fred Harvey's swanky La Fonda Hotel. In route between Las Vegas and Santa Fe, W. H. told Frieda that he had finalized the transaction to buy the Three Vs Ranch from the bank. According to family legend, Frieda demanded that W. H. Waggoner take her back to Las Vegas and have the marriage annulled because she didn't want to be married to a man who would be that far in debt. Evidently, Mr. Waggoner was persuasive in love as well as business because he got her settled down, and they stayed married until he died many years later. Frieda lived to be in her nineties.

When the Pacific Loan Company got the Three Vs put together, the eastern boundary ran along Highway 64 north of Williams for twelve miles, with Valle Junction being in the middle of that twelve mile stretch. The ranch encompassed almost one hundred percent of the Cataract Plains. To the north, it bordered the Supai Reservation, and to the east the Hualapai Reservation. Within its boundaries was most of what is now known as the Sevens Ranch, as well as all of the present day Diamond A Ranch. For a few years in the late '20s and '30s the Vs also leased the east half of the Hualapai Reservation and controlled that valuable asset known as Frasier Well, enabling them to pump water south into the Aubrey Valley.

Carl Welsh, a well-known Three Vs cowboy that I knew, told me he repped for the Vs in the Hualapai Valley, sixty miles west of Seligman. Bill Nelson, another old-time cowboy who spent most of his life near Peach Springs, stayed in a cow camp taking care of Three Vs cattle at Owl Springs ten miles south of Hackberry in Mojave County. Roy Olsen, who is a friend that I cowboyed with at the O RO in 1971 and who later became brand inspector in Seligman, told me he was acquainted with a couple who took care of Three Vs livestock at the Cienega Ranch, twenty-five miles south of Seligman.

In her book "Life with Old-Time Cowboys," Mildred Perner shows a copy of a map of the Three Vs Ranch that totals more than fifty-five townships, or the rough equivalent of two thousand square miles. This does not include any holdings that were leased or land owned by the company in places such as Owl Springs, the Cienega Ranch; or leases on the Hualapai Reservation. She states in her book that the Vs ran close to forty thousand cattle, fifteen thousand sheep, and several thousand horses. The sheep, for the most part, ran on the east side of the ranch under the management of the Grand Canyon Sheep Company, a subsidiary of the parent company that also owned the cowherd.

Dan Moore states in his book "Log of a Twentieth Century Cowboy" that the Vs ran twenty-five thousand cows. I know for a fact that the final brand inspection tally on the Hereford cowherd that was liquidated in 1972 was over seventeen thousand head. And they were running on far less country than the Vs had in the 1920s and 1930s.

Most of the Three Vs' holdings rested on what is commonly known as the Coconino Plateau. This plateau is a high, predominantly limestone cap rock that has numerous mountain peaks jutting upward from its base that were formed with basalt rock, or what cowboys call malpai, which is nothing more than molten lava that cooled when the parent volcano went to sleep. The Coconino Plateau is captured by the Grand Canyon to the north, the San Francisco Peaks and Little Colorado River Valley to the east, the western edge of the Mogollon Rim to the south, and Peach Springs Canyon to the west. Historically, the plateau has been a waterless place a great deal of the time. When you fall off the plateau in any direction, water has always been more plentiful, especially to the south. During wet periods the creeks and drainages, especially Cataract Canyon, had abundant water, but with the exception of a few springs, the water supply was not permanent. In one of the earliest accounts of white men exploring the area, a group of explorers, led by the famous mountain man Kit Carson, feared they would starve to death on a trip they made from the Verde Valley, across north of Fort Rock, to Peach Springs. They made the trek during a particularly dry time and found very little game to use for camp meat. When they got close to Peach Springs, game and survival were apprehended.

When white men began settling the Coconino Plateau, they began developing sources of water. For the most part, the men were cattle or sheep ranchers and the most successful method of water acquisition was building dams in the bottom of draws and canyons. Up until the 1930s or even the 1940s, this dam-building was done with teams of mules or horses pulling a dragline hooked to a Fresno, which is the equivalent of a modern day scraper. Some of the best dams on Arizona ranches were originally dug with teams and Fresnos; although they have probably been cleaned out or improved with modern heavy equipment. Wells were few and far between because the water table in most places was far deeper than the technology of the day could produce a dependable well from.

Today the Diamond A Ranch has several hundred miles of pipelines, and millions of gallons of water storages, with dozens of good water troughs in strategic places; and because of that, water is almost an afterthought. But most of this was not developed until the 1950s and 1960s. With the exception of the pipeline going south from Frasier Well and limited pipeline coming from Rose Well, the cattle on the Three Vs Ranch watered in dirt tanks. During dry times, which came almost yearly, keeping thousands of head of cattle located on a reliable water source often became a logistical nightmare. The northern tip of the ranch was sixty-plus miles north of the railroad where an emergency water supply might be rushed in with just a few days' notice. Far corners of the ranch were easily twenty or thirty miles from Rose Well, Frasier Well, Howard Springs, or some other constant water source. These wells and springs in themselves couldn't have supplied enough water for the entire herd, even if the cowboy crew could have gotten the cattle to that spot anyway.

On paper it sounds simple and easy, but for the men making the decisions in the early days of the Three Vs Ranch solutions to water problems were akin to waging large scale war. Contrary to what is portrayed in movies and television, even John Wayne or Clint Eastwood can't gather up a couple thousand cows with babies at their sides and move them thirty miles in a day or two. Any cowboy who ever spent much time on the Coconino Plateau can imagine the problems that arose during a hot April, May, and June after a dry winter. The amount of tired horses and men it took to keep thirsty cattle moved to water is a vivid equation to me, because I've spent a lot of time there. If it didn't start raining in July, like it's supposed to..., I can always conjure up a vision of too many dead carcasses. Cowboys and ranchers, large or small, don't like to talk about cattle dying of thirst, especially as a result of incompetence and neglect. But anybody who thinks there weren't a few that perished from a lack of water during some dry spells on the Three Vs never saw many thirsty cows on a hot June day. They will die. Without a doubt, many a Three Vs cowboy went to bed worried about a bunch of dried-out cows.

An Arizona rancher told me a story of how in 1915 he and an uncle were trying to keep a bunch of cows watered in a certain pasture during a particularly hot and dry June. They were hauling water in barrels in a wagon pulled by a couple of workhorses with the trail being five miles one-way. By making two trips a day, they were barely keeping their cattle from thirsting to death. Toward the last of June, it started clouding up, and after several days of promising clouds, it finally rained. The five mile stretch they hauled water went across three and a half miles of country owned by a neighbor who was also suffering from the drought. They were about half way across the five miles of wagon road and in the middle of their neighbor's pasture when a black cloud unloaded on them. It was a real frog-strangler and the mud became so deep the wagon wheels sank into the two-track road, and the tired team couldn't untrack it. The men were soaked but jubilant, and after enjoying the good rainwater bath, they emptied all the water out of their barrels to lighten the payload, which enabled the team to pull the wagon forward. They drove on with visions of a full stock pond and an end to their water hauling job. When they arrived at their pasture, they found it to be bone-dry. The cloudburst was heavy but didn't cover much country. Their water trough was dry and the water barrels were empty.

℘ ℭ

In the twenties, thirties, and forties, quite a few different men served as wagon boss on the Vs including Charlie Hiler, Demas Yoder, Pat Cullen, Arthur Haley, Kilo Pruitt, Phil Perner, Slim Gilliam, and Tracy Dent. Dan Moore substituted for Demas for short spells on several occasions.

In 1946 W. H. Waggoner sold a large portion of what had been the Three Vs Ranch to Marcus Rudnick, who was from Bakersfield, California. The outfit Marcus bought was basically the same block of land that is the present day Diamond A Ranch. Other parts of the Three Vs Ranch were sold to various people over a several year period. Marcus was heavily involved in the ranch's management, but I know of at least one cowboy who worked for Kilo Pruitt, who served as wagon boss for Marcus. When John Andrews first came to Arizona in 1947, the first outfit he worked for was the Vs, and Slim Gilliam hired him, so Slim must have been a wagon boss also.

In 1948 Marcus Rudnick sold the Vs to Kern County Land and Cattle Company, whose headquarters was in Bakersfield, California. Kern County had been operating big cow ranches in New Mexico, Arizona, and Oregon, as well as southern California for decades. They owned the Armendaris Ranch at Engle, New Mexico, and the Gray Ranch at Hatchita and Animas, New Mexico, and called their New Mexico division Victorio Livestock Company. They had the Little Boquillas in Cochise County, Arizona, and when they bought the Three Vs at Seligman, they started referring to it as the Big Boquillas. For a while, Kern

County also owned the huge ZX Ranch north of Lakeview, Oregon, as well as several ranches near Bakersfield, California. They referred to their Arizona ranches as the Boquillas Cattle Company.

Leland Larsen had worked for the Kern County Livestock on the Armendaris and Gray Ranches and had held positions of responsibility for a number of years. According to one account, Leland had moved to Mojave County, Arizona, and was working for Leonard Neal before Kern County bought the Vs. But other accounts say Leland was still working for the Victorio Division in New Mexico when the company bought the Vs. At any rate, Kern County Land and Cattle Company installed Leland as manager of their newly acquired Three Vs Ranch early on. It was also at this time that the Vs became known as the Diamond A Ranch or the Big Boquillas, beings Kern County started using the Diamond A brand instead of the Three Vs brand. When the ranch changed hands from Marcus Rudnick to Kern County Land and Cattle Company, the Three Vs brand wasn't included in the sale.

The Diamond A, which was an A with the crossbar bent downward creating a Diamond within the A, was placed on a cow's left hip.

For a short period of time, Kern County Land and Cattle Company made Leland Larsen general manager over all their ranches from New Mexico to Oregon. It's a long way from the Armendaris Ranch at Engle, New Mexico, all the way to the ZX at Paisley, Oregon. Few men in history have been responsible for that much ranchland and that many cattle. Leland was on the road a great deal of the time and really didn't like it. He caused a stir at the ZX when he found out there were some old retired cowboys who were still drawing wages, though they were not still working, and he put a stop to it, or tried to. The incident ruffled some feathers, and Leland was demoted back to managing the newly acquired outfit at Seligman. Perhaps Leland planned the whole situation because he didn't care for life on the road. At any rate, he still had a huge ranch to run, and he was happy and content to run the Big Boquillas.

The 1950s and 1960s saw huge changes on the Diamond A. Leland was in his element and had resources at his disposal and in two decades made huge improvements on the Seligman ranch. A pipeline was run from the wells on the railroad at Pica, which were three thousand feet deep, all the way to the north end of the ranch, fifty miles or more away. At a half dozen places, spur lines were run off this mainline, going fifteen or twenty miles in places. One line left the main pipeline and turned back to the southeast going by Keseha and continued down Chino Wash to within six miles north of Seligman. The old well at Rose Well produced water that had always been "gyppy," having a lot of gypsum and other minerals in it. The new freshwater line from Pica provided better camp water for Pica, plus several other cow camps to the north. The old Rose Well was utilized by running a new pipeline going east-northeast eighteen miles to the backside of Broken

Axle Pasture. This line became known as the gyp line. In this period during the '50s and '60s, millions of gallons of water storages were erected. Three of these storages—one known as Big E, another as B Tub, and another called Number Two—could hold a half million gallons each. There were dozens of other storages of various sizes. The water troughs installed during those two decades were almost too numerous to count. A well was drilled at the north end of the Aubrey Valley right on the Hualapai Reservation boundary that became known as Indian Well. A long pipeline ran south from Indian Well watering the northwest end of the Aubrey Valley. Another well was drilled on the southeast end of the Aubrey Valley and was named Chino Well.

Under Leland's supervision, hundreds of miles of fence were built creating eighteen large pastures plus a great many smaller pastures and holding traps. Dozens of water lots, branding corrals, and several sets of shipping corrals were built. Cattle were starting to be shipped by semi-trucks that could be loaded at places like Rose Well or Camp Sixteen, and fewer cattle were shipped by railroad.

Leland ushered the Diamond A Ranch into the twentieth century, perhaps it was several decades late, but he got it there, nonetheless. There were countless changes in the '50s and '60s, but the biggest change was water. Cattle were no longer held hostage by shallow dirt tanks that had been made with the mule-drawn Fresnos but instead were kept alive by a modern pipeline system that insured life whether it rained or not.

It all came with a price. Lots of old-timers I knew, who were in their sixties and seventies when I was in my twenties, lamented the coming of the endless water and barbed wire. Men like Carl Welsh, Buck Smith, and Raymond Holt talked about the Cataract Plains being thick with chamise brush (which is as good a winter feed as you can find) before the pipelines were put in. They said in the old days drought would force the gathering of the Plains at least some of the time, which kept the country from being grazed too extensively. Water and fence can keep cattle in place regardless of the availability of feed. Sometimes large numbers of cattle look better on paper than they do on the range.

A lot of good cowboys worked for Leland in the '50s and '60s, some of them working for the outfit for years. Elmer and Nellie McDonald migrated to Seligman to work for Leland almost immediately after Leland took over as manager. Elmer's brother Burley soon followed. Both of the McDonalds stayed on the outfit for decades. Alvin Wagner was another who went to work on the Diamond A, hiring on to work for Leland and staying for a long time. Allie Seifers, Tom Dolan, and Dob Ernest had been working on the outfit for years prior to Leland taking over and stayed on working for Leland. Tom Dolan ran the wagon for Leland for a good many years and might have held that position longer than anyone in the ranch's history. If he didn't have the record, he was close. If he wasn't wagon boss the longest, he was definitely one of the best liked by the cowboy crews who worked there.

Leland went back to the Gray Ranch in Hidalgo County, New Mexico, in 1969 to run that outfit; and Jim Lowrance took over as manager at Seligman. Jim Lowrance decided to run two wagons and made Burley McDonald boss of the upper wagon and hired Mike Landis to run the lower wagon. That was the way the outfit worked when I first saw it in the fall of 1972. At that time the Diamond A Ranch was a well-oiled machine. The fences and corrals were in good shape. There were many small pastures and corrals built at strategic places to be used as horse pastures and corrals by the roundup crew when they would camp at those spots. The camp houses and shipping corrals were maintained and functional. Perhaps the best thing that could be said about the ranch at that time, when I first encountered it, was the fact that there were men working there who were good hands, and they had been there for years, several of them for several decades. For the most part, the cattle were gentle and easy to handle by a crew of good cowboys.

ഇന്ദ

On Board

ഇന്ദ

Seligman, Arizona, Summer 1966

Leland Larsen was like a god in Seligman. He was a big man with a commanding personality, and he ran the huge ranch with lots of men under his charge. The Diamond A Ranch owned several houses in Seligman where they would house extra men who worked out on the ranch. Among those houses was a large home two blocks north of the main drag, which was actually old Route 66, that was always known as the ranch manager's residence. W.H. Waggoner had lived in the same house when he owned the Three Vs in the '40s, and Leland lived there many years. Jim Lowrance lived there when I was first around the outfit in the early '70s. I was to live in the same house at a later date, but I am getting ahead of myself. By today's standards the house isn't anything to brag about, but in its day, it was the finest in town.

Tom Dolan's son Jim had a close friend who was a town kid with aspirations of being a cowboy like Jim. Like all high school-aged boys he wanted and needed employment during summer break, and Jim kept telling him to hit Leland up for a job. The boy was quiet and a little on the timid side, but job opportunities were slim;

and with Jim's continuous encouragement that bordered on pestering, he finally mustered up enough courage to approach Leland for a summer job. The young man walked up to the front door in the middle of a warm spring day knowing Leland was probably home because the ranch truck he always drove was parked next to the house. He stood there for a moment looking around hoping no one was watching. Finally he rang the electric door bell.

He heard movement in the house and directly the door opened exposing the famous giant who lived inside. "Well, what can I do for you, sonny?" Leland asked as he looked down in a well-practiced, judicious manner.

The teenager stood there unsure of himself for a moment and then blurted out, "I ..... was wondering if I could get a job on the ranch this summer?"

"Yeah. Well, what can you do?"

"Nothin'!"

"You're hired! You'll fit right in around here!"

§ ∞ ∞

I was working on the Babbitt Ranch north of Flagstaff in 1992 and had been there a long time. We lived in a nice home at Spider Web at the CO Bar Ranch headquarters, and we liked it. I was the jigger boss, which didn't mean much other than that I led one side of a drive and was responsible for getting a little work done if the boss wasn't around, but I liked it there. I had great respect for the boss, and the outfit was and always had been very well run. That meant a lot to me. I had a whole mount of good horses that I had broke, several of which you could haul to a rodeo and compete on or pickup bucking horses, a thing that I enjoy doing. My two sons both had good horses to ride and the ranch would pay them to help work cattle during roundup. There was a real good roping arena a couple hundred yards from the house, which was something we all enjoyed. My wife was happy and enjoyed living in the country. We lived in a stable environment.

On the first of October of '92, my wife received a call from the new manager at the Diamond A Ranch who said he wished to talk to me. I was thirty miles away working cattle with the cowboy crew, but when I got home, which wasn't every night, I returned the call. "The Diamond A needed to hire a new wagon boss, and I had been recommended for the job," was the message I received from the other end of the wire. Was I interested? Of course I was interested. My old friend Bob Scott had told me twenty years earlier, "Any cowboy that claims he doesn't want to run a big cow outfit is a liar or a sorry S. O. B. Classify yourself." A job interview was scheduled with me and the party I was talking to on the phone agreeing to meet at a restaurant in Williams in the evening several days later.

The job interview, if it could be called such, was a conundrum lasting several hours. I thought I would be questioned but was asked nothing, yet I felt responsible for keeping up a similitude of a conversation; the most memorable part of which was consuming so much coffee I wouldn't sleep for several days. I was finally told the job was mine if I wanted it. I replied that I wanted to think about it for a day or two and would let them know.

With the job interview over, the manager, his wife,

and I said our goodbyes, and I started walking across the dark parking lot toward my pickup that was parked on the backside of the lot. I had my head down looking at the ground dodging potholes in the asphalt, which were hard to see beings it was very dark. I suppose I had my mind on a million things and wasn't concentrating on what I was doing. I passed between a car on my left and a pickup that turned out to be the manager's, and as I got near the pickup door, a large white dog with a black ring around one eye lunged from the inside and hit the window barking very loudly. The explosion from inside the truck took me by surprise as I did not see it coming, and I fell against the car and almost fell down. The dog was standing on the seat of the pickup and continued to fall back on its haunches and jump smashing his lips and huge canine teeth into the right side door window. I almost fainted. The loud and vicious snarling continued while I put the palm of my right hand against my bosom to check for a pulse. I heard a female voice giggling in the background and saw that the Diamond A management team was close behind me and had observed my cowardly behavior.

I chewed on the decision for several days. Finally one day while riding along trailing a large herd of Babbitt cows, I asked Bill Howell what he thought about the job. I had worked for Bill for fourteen years, and I knew he had been faced with several decisions in his life similar to the one I was trying to make. He thought about it for a minute or two and then said, "You don't have any guarantee it will work out, you never do, so you just have to decide if you want to try it. But if you do go over there, I'll tell you two things. Keep your work out in front of you." I knew him well enough to know that he meant don't ever get behind in your work, and I listened as he went on. "And when you get there, fire every @!#$%^&* on the outfit. Then if you want to hire some of them back, you can, and they will be working for you."

After several days, I signed on to take the job and made

plans to move to Seligman in about ten days. They wanted me to move into the manager's house two blocks behind the Black Cat Bar in the middle of town. This was the same house that W. H. Waggoner, Leland Larsen, and Jim Lowrance had lived in. The man I was going to work for, who was the current manager, was living in one of the cow camps, although he didn't really take care of the country adjacent to that camp, which was customary procedure for men occupying cow camps, but he didn't want to live in town at the "mansion," as some people referred to the old manager's residence, so I had to. My wife hated the thought of living in town and never got used to it.

Several days after I agreed to take the job, my new boss called and was quite agitated. Someone had used a case of dynamite and had blown up a metal water storage located four miles south of Rose Well. The water storage known as B Tub had the storage capacity to hold a half million gallons of water. The maintenance man in charge of that part of the ranch, an old gentleman named Al Edgar, had checked the water level in the storage late in the afternoon. Early the next morning, he returned to turn some valves on the pipeline near this spot where the storage had stood and found that someone had blown the structure up. The steel sides to the open-topped structure, which had stood thirty-some feet high, had been ruptured and rolled off the side of the hill it had stood on top of leaving a bare cement slab that had been the floor or bottom of the storage. When Al Edgar had checked the storage the evening before, it had held about four hundred thousand gallons of water. Now it was all gone. Law enforcement personnel who investigated the incident figured someone who knew what they were doing floated a case of dynamite out over the surface of the water on a wooden pallet and set it off. Several weeks earlier, they had fired the man who was running the wagon creating the job vacancy I was to fill. They also fired his best friend and right hand man who had been a demolition expert in the army. There was much speculation about that individual's guilt but nothing more than gossip resulted from these facts. A friend of mine, who was a law enforcement officer at the time, later told me they knew who the culprit was, but they did not possess enough good evidence to arrest anyone. It costs a lot of money to replace a half million gallon water storage.

I wouldn't get my family moved over to the mansion in the middle of Seligman for another week, but the drama had already started.

ෆ෩
First Day
on the Job
෩ෆ

We moved into the mansion on the northwest corner of First Avenue and Picacho around the 25th of October. One block south was a struggling business called the Seligman Grocery. One block south of that was a thriving business known as the Black Cat Saloon. The front door of the Black Cat opened up and deposited one into Chino Avenue, also known as Route 66: a fact that had been the demise of more than one drunk cowboy.

We were now, for all practical purposes, town-dwellers, or at least my wife was. That situation was to be a bone of contention for three and a half years. She was a ranch girl that didn't want to live in town, but she would sacrifice so I could have the big job. I could escape town life and spend my time working on the biggest ranch in

Arizona, and I actually spent very little time in the white house two blocks behind the Black Cat Saloon. Part of my agreement with my new employer was that I could work my two sons on the cowboy crew that I was now the boss of. I could work them at full cowboy pay all I wanted, so a great deal of the time my wife was left alone, incarcerated in the middle of a town she didn't want to be in.

My first day on the job, the manager and I headed out to the wagon so he could introduce me. The men had all been told that I was going to arrive and be their new boss. I remembered Bill Howell's advice to fire them all, but I sensed the man I answered to wouldn't back me up on that course of action even if I wanted to take it. I had been told during my job interview that I would be expected to straighten things out.

We traveled north toward Rose Well through Big Chief and Owen Dam Pastures, and I was told these pastures had already been gathered. We passed by Big E, D, C, B, and A, all being water troughs on the Fresh Water Line going north from Pica, and saw numerous cattle around each water. At C there were about thirty-five head, and I could see from the window of the pickup several big five hundred pound calves that were unbranded. The barbed wire water lots around each of the water troughs were completely down at every water in the twenty-three mile stretch from Pica Camp to Rose Well with the exception of Little E.

We got to the wagon, which was an old Chevy one ton with a flatbed. The bed had wooden sides and a canvas top. Set up on the end of the truck bed was a large chuck box. A very large walled tent was connected to the truck bed and continued on for thirty feet. There was an old iron woodstove on top of an axle that was set up a few feet from the chuck box. This stove on wheels had a pipe tongue with a trailer hitch welded to it that stuck out for eight feet or so, and someone could set on this pipe when the stove was set up inside the tent. When the crew moved camp this stove was turned around and hitched to the bumper of the truck. Several men were in the tent when we arrived, and I was introduced to the crew, some of whom I knew and had worked with. Randy Rutledge and Jim Casebear had worked at Babbitts a few years earlier, and I had fond memories of knowing them and was glad to see them. Truman Rustin was there with his silver hair, and blue eyes, and hands like a blackjack dealer in a Reno casino. His silver mustache matched anything Clark Gable or Richard Farnsworth had ever groomed. I knew a coyote in a fox's coat when I saw one. Pat Prosser was there, and I knew him to be a good hand. His brother Jeff was one of the best cowboys I'd ever known. An old Indian man slipped in and out of the shadows, and I don't remember ever being formally introduced to him. He was the horse wrangler.

A tall slender boy, perhaps twenty years old, set on the tongue of the woodstove picking "Fox on the Run" on his guitar and was doing a good job of it. His name was Jason Mueller. Sitting on his pockets on the dirt floor was a young Texan named Robert Hogue, and he was showing several men in the crew a new Beretta forty caliber pistol. The gun was being carelessly passed around between men and looked awfully loaded to me. I wasn't sure if I was tough enough to run this outfit and or not.

About the time I was honored with a turned fondling the new Beretta pistol, a tall cowboy-looking character, who spirited a walrus mustache and a big silver belly hat with a Tom Mix crease, lifted the tent flap and stepped inside. I recognized him as Jack Ballard; a man I had met on several occasions. He had come to Babbitts at least twice looking for a job, and I had visited with him for a while. I remembered him being in possession of a pornographic saddle. The saddle was made by a man named Dickie Foster in Tombstone, Arizona, and it had numerous naked women carved into the leather. Jack Ballard was a bachelor. He stuck out his hand and said

"Howdy, my name is Ron Remington." I shook his hand but was confused in my mind thinking I remembered him having a different name.

Almost immediately another young man with blonde hair and a boyish face shouted from the opposite end of the tent. "Ron Remington! Hell, last week you introduced yourself to that cow buyer as Jack Ballard!" The voice loudly proclaiming this oracle of truth was John Hogue, Robert's little brother. Several men snickered, and Jason Mueller stopped playing "Fox on the Run" as if the fox had been caught. Ron Remington, as he was then wanting to be known, calmly turned around without saying anything and exited the tent. He resembled Sam Elliott in looks and had Sam's well-practiced, I don't give a damn, expression.

Pretty soon it was time to catch horses for the drive the crew was going to make the next morning. The man who had been running the show in between the firing of the last official wagon boss and me, the next official wagon boss, walked out of the cook tent and headed toward a corral where the horse wrangler had captured the remuda. Most of the men moseyed along following the man, but several stayed seated in the tent drinking coffee. Some were napping in their teepees, and the general atmosphere was one of not caring if school kept or not.

As the men who wanted to participate walked toward the horse corral, the manager called me aside and told me he was leaving and going back to town. I sensed this was the official handing over of the responsibility. I had been given the keys to a company pickup and had been told that we needed to ship four loads of calves six days later.

The manager also gave me four other shipping dates within eighteen days after that, and he mentioned that the crew had not gathered enough calves to fill the first four trucks that were coming in six days. No other orders were given to me, and I was given no information about where any of these cattle that needed to be gathered were located. I realized the manager didn't possess this information and therefore couldn't give it to me. As he opened the door to his pickup he turned and looked at me and said with as much authority as he could muster, "This crew is yours. You run this outfit however you want to." Then he put the truck in drive and went south toward Seligman.

I looked around and noticed several more men crawling out of the cook tent, and several rubbing the boogers out of their eyes as they stepped out of their teepee tents. Someone down at the horse corral, I believe it was John Hogue, was hollering "HORSES" as loud as he could, beckoning all who wanted to play to come and announce what they wanted to ride the next day. I had

hauled several horses up from Seligman and therefore had the horse I was going to use the next day. I would pick some more out of the extras in the remuda as time went along.

I decided to exert no authority at this time, but instead I just observed what was taking place. It seemed obvious to me that some leadership was in order. A nice person would use the word guidance. I envisioned shaping red-hot horse shoes between a large hammer and much larger anvil. I figured I could start giving orders soon enough. Giving orders, heck, I didn't even know where the cattle were hiding. Maybe I should start asking questions rather than give orders. But I knew were some of the much-needed cattle were at because we had driven by them this morning.

We ate breakfast the next morning and then headed toward the horse corral to catch horses. Several men didn't get up until we left the cook tent and so they went to work without any coffee or breakfast. One of the first horses caught was a good looking dappled palomino, and John Hogue quickly hung his bridle off of him and took the lasso off of the palomino's neck and handed it back to the man catching horses. John hurried, leading the yellow horse over to where his saddle was laying and saddled the horse up. When he pulled his cinches up tight, he led the horse off a step or two and the horse started bucking and throwing a fit. "Ed! You sorry no good @#$%^&*! I'm telling you, I'm going to kick your sorry worthless hind end all over the place!"

I jerked my head around upon the mention of my name and stared at John Hogue who was continuing to scream. "Ed, you are the most worthless piece of crap I ever saw! I'm telling you, Ed, you gunsel piece of no good rawhide!" John was obviously proud of himself at the opportunity to curse loudly while mentioning the name of Ed in every sentence. He was grinning and watching me from the corner of his eyes. Several other men were snickering. "Ed!

I'm telling you, Ed." The horse continued to act up. "Ed! You're a worthless piece of crap!"

Randy Rutledge walked by me leading his horse and commented rather dryly, "That horse's name is Mr. Ed."

෨෬
Into the
Wilderness
෨෬

Ron Remington, as he was wanting to be called at that time, was a mysterious sort of character; a man that was hard to figure out. He was quiet, but not brooding, polite but not social, and was a good cowboy seeming, at least to me, to know where to be and when to be there. He did not talk about his past, and no one knew his history. I learned many years later that he had put in a stint as Red Steagall's tour bus driver in the days soon after Red had discovered Reba McEntire and the two were touring together.

When I took over as wagon boss, I knew nothing more of the man other than he had a reputation of being a kleptomaniac, specializing in the theft of saddles. My first instinct was to fire him because of the reputation that preceded him, but there was another character on the crew whose reputation as a scoundrel far exceeded anything I had heard about the man with several aliases. I couldn't pick on one without dealing with the other, so I did nothing, deciding to see what played out. I noticed right off the bat that Ron seemed to dislike getting out of bed in the morning, and that was going to have to change if we were going to get along. But this bad habit was cured by himself, and within several days of my appearing, he started getting up earlier than anyone else. He made a hand and seemed to be the most positive man on the crew.

We were camped at Rose Well, on the west side of the creek, with the wagon being set up close to an old cedar picket corral where we would keep our horses penned, waiting for the next day's ride. Cowboys had their saddles laid on the ground against a long stretch of

pickets that were six feet high or higher. Most of the old cedar limbs, which was what the pickets were, had knots; and in several places, inches of side limbs that had been chopped off when the main shaft had been saved to be used in the fence. These knots and little fingers sticking out made perfect hooks for a cowboy to hang a bridle or pair of chaps from. There were forty yards of fence with more than a dozen saddles on the ground, and all kinds of regalia, such as bridles, hanging from the cedar knots. Each man had his spot and cowboy code required you stay out of another man's space.

I had a real good Scott Dieringer saddle that was flower carved, a pair of elk hide chaps that I had made myself, a snaffle bit that Twister Heller had given me twenty years earlier, and one curb bridle. The latigo headstall on the bridle was homemade with bridle reins I had cut myself, and none of it, save the saddle, was anything to brag about. The bridle bit connected to the homemade headstall was an old Texas-style grazing bit with a medium high port and cheeks no longer than four and a half inches. It had a little silver on the cheek that was mostly worn off. There was no maker's name stamped in it anywhere. I can't remember where I acquired it; although it was surely in a trade with someone I had worked with years before. It wouldn't have fetched much in a saddle shop, but it was mine and I liked it.

I had been working for the outfit about a week when one morning, as we were saddling up in the dark, I couldn't find my bridle. I asked several men nearby if they had seen it, which they had not; so beings we had work to do, I put the snaffle on a hard-mouthed drive horse, and we went to work. I immediately suspected the local kleptomaniac who rode the pornographic saddle.

I contemplated my dilemma all morning, and come afternoon, I made an exhaustive search for my bridle but found nothing. I thought about searching the suspect's personal effects but knew this would be risky. What if nothing was found? What if the bridle remained missing but a six-shooter barrel pointing at me appeared instead? Demanding a search would be unwise, or so it seemed. I waited until suppertime when the cook hollered chuck and most of the men were lined up and filling their plates. I made sure Ron Remington was in line, and I announced rather loudly that I was missing a bridle and described it with detail. I didn't have any idea what was going through Ron's mind but hoped when he realized that it was the new boss's bridle he had lifted, he might think it was prudent to return it.

Several days had passed without any mention by anyone about the missing bridle. Then one evening about sundown, immediately after we had caught horses for the next day, my gamble paid off. I was walking down the picket fence, and about the time I threw my rope down next to my saddle, Ron hollered at me from thirty feet behind, "Hey, Ed! Is that your bridle hanging there?" I turned and looked at Ron who was pointing at something hanging off of a cedar knot on the backside of a picket near where he was standing. I backtracked thirty steps, and sure enough, there it was, kind of hiding behind the offside of the fence. "By golly! I was just walking along and looked up and there it was," he exclaimed!

There was another mysterious character the crew kept talking about who didn't seem to be around. The manager had even asked about him to several members of the crew on my first day on the job when he brought me out to the wagon and introduced me to everyone as their new boss. The fellow's name was Robert, and he seemed to be related to someone on the maintenance crew. For some reason that had been unexplained, he had been AWOL for several days. About the third day I was there, we were leaving Rose Well in the afternoon trotting out into the Owen Dam Pasture, and when we were about a mile west of the shipping corrals, I noticed someone horseback following us a half mile behind. I pulled up and asked everyone in general, "Who do you suppose that is?" Someone answered my question saying that it was Robert. He was approaching in a slow jig, obviously not worried about catching up any time soon. I trotted back toward him and intercepted him a distance away from the rest of the crew. "Howdy, Robert, what's going on?" I asked.

"Oh, I don't know, just thought I'd come out and help gather some of these old cows I guess."

"So, do you work here?" I asked.

"Well, by golly, the last time I checked I was. So what's it to you?"

My selective memory has caused certain things in my past to become foggy, or sort of unclear, and what transpired between the phantom cowboy named Robert and myself after he asked that question is one of those foggy moments. However, I do remember quite clearly that several minutes later the rest of the crew and myself were again trotting west. Robert, however, was traveling east and had decided to seek his fortune elsewhere.

We were a couple days away from a shipping date at which I needed to produce at least four hundred of the ranches better five hundred pound calves, not counting any short-ages or dinks of any kind, which I knew there were plenty of. I had not been present when the crew started putting cattle in the shipping trap, and no one seemed to have an accurate count, but the general consensus was, we were short several hundred calves.

A selective memory isn't always what it is cracked up to be. It will at times block out certain unsavory or downright unflattering memories of events gone by. And then at other times it will, like a thing with a life of its own, refuse to perform as it is supposed to. To my knowledge there are no scenes in Clint Eastwood or John Wayne movies where the hero lives through a panic attack. I experienced one that afternoon.

I dropped the men off as we trotted and loped along the edge of the Aubrey Cliffs eight miles west of Rose Well. When I stopped and looked across the north end of the Aubrey Valley far below, I could look west six miles and see Robbers Roost rising up like a sentinel guarding Hualapai land. This should have been cowboy heaven, a thousand miles of ranchland and ten thousand spoiled cows that needed gathered. But for an hour or two, I couldn't see it. I became engrossed with the dark side of reality: A crew that was hoping I would collapse under the pressure while cursing their horses that bore my name; one thousand miles of fence that had been standing when I had worked there twenty years earlier that had all fallen down; a hundred good corrals and water lots laying in disarray leaving places thirty miles in distance with no place to pen a cow; a manager who had no idea where the cattle were running or even if they existed, and a crew that wouldn't tell me even if they knew, which actually they didn't. I started dwelling on the good horses, gentle cattle, and squared-away outfit I had walked away from a week earlier. I was like the children of Israel looking back across the Red Sea that God had just parted, remembering the leeks and garlics of captivity and wishing they could cross back over.

I rode along for a spell and then stepped off my horse to relieve myself, and suddenly felt like I was suffocating; my mind was drumming up thoughts of sinking in water. My thoughts of going under became so real that I could feel physical pressure around my chest, making me feel like I was in a vice. I stood next to my horse and held onto the saddle horn and for a moment thought I was going to fall down. I cannot turn this mess around, my mind reasoned within me. I felt as if I was sinking lower into some panic-driven manic depression, and with some perverted twist of human nature, I almost enjoyed the pain. And then with what might have been my last ounce of sanity, I realized I was going down a road where I shouldn't go. You had better get a hold of yourself, I told myself.

I began to realize a couple things. Number one: I hadn't really been acting like a boss. Number two: There was no one else on the outfit that was interested in the job, or they wouldn't have hired me. I had to give it my best shot and that meant starting to act like I knew what I was doing. If nothing else, run a bluff on 'em! They don't know what they're doing either. Start leading, go somewhere, develop a plan and some of the men will follow and the rest will fall by the wayside, and you can replace them. Do something! But don't give up. I got back on my horse and whipped him down the hind leg and started gathering cattle.

Traditionally, wagon bosses rope the horses for the crew at horse catching time, so when we got into camp that night, I roped horses for the first time since I had showed up on the outfit. The next morning, I led the crew out to where I thought we should make a drive instead of asking advice from the man who had been running things before me. That morning we made the best gather since I had showed up. I started developing a game plan for a month in advance. I started thinking instead of trembling in fear at the monster in front of me. I actually enjoyed myself at times.

The first shipping day after my arrival as the new wagon boss came, and we saddled up in the pitch-black darkness of predawn and headed out west of camp following the Wheat Pasture fence. There were three pie-shaped holding pastures running west of the shipping corrals at Rose Well. The Wheat Pasture was the one farthest south and it, as well as the other two, bordered the Hualapai Reservation on their west end. We traveled in a trot on the outside of the Wheat Pasture bouncing off the fence in the dark of night and entered into it through a wire gate six miles from camp.

By that time it was light enough to see a cow, and we split up and started gathering cattle, pushing them back east toward camp. Everyone in the crew had complained that Truman Rustin always rode straight to camp without gathering any cattle so I kept him next to me. This would be an everyday occurrence for a year and a half, and it seemed to work because he would work if he knew I was watching. I would find out the truth at a later date.

When we got to the corral, it was a little past sunup, and

we got what looked like enough cattle to fill our shipping obligation penned without incident. There was a very large water lot at Rose Well, probably four or five acres in size, and the cattle went in there first. When we got the gate shut, we started taking about half the cattle, about three hundred cows plus calves, and pushing them into a smaller corral. Off of this corral was yet another smaller corral that would feed a large crowding pen. There were no alleys in the set of corrals that a crew of cowboys could sort cattle in using the old "in and by" method. But instead there was a dodge gate, or dodge chute, which was a narrow chute with several smaller gates that needed to be operated by a man afoot standing on a block several feet higher than ground level. As cows, calves, yearling, bulls, etc. were prodded down this chute, a man, by using these gates, could cut cattle three different ways: cows one way, steer calves another, and heifers yet another. I had been around a good many dodge chutes and knew them to work fine, although it would not be my first preference as a way to sort. This particular dodge chute had a couple crowding pens feeding it with very high metal sides and large heavy metal gates, all of which were too heavy to open by a man mounted on a horse. There were also catwalks mounted along the high sides of the crowding pens enabling men to walk along and lean over and whip and prod the beasts that were captured within, and therefore direct their paths down the chute toward the man working the dodge gate.

All of this required a good many men to dismount and tie their horses up and either open and shut heavy gates or poke and prod the terrified beasts that were being funneled down through, what I'm sure the animals thought were the gates of hell, to whatever lay ahead of them. For the cows, it was being turned north onto the Cataract Plains for the winter, and for the calves, there was a ride on a semi-truck to greener pastures somewhere in California.

Shipping days have always puzzled me. It seems very good men with many years' experience who are usually calm and levelheaded, for some reason, lose both their composure and Christianity in preparing to wean, weigh, and load a bunch of calves on a truck. A spirit of frantic discombobulation will come over a crew when the owner of the cattle or his representative begins exhibiting extreme hypertension and chorea as a result of worrying about cattle shrinking an extra pound or two. Speed and swiftness in the task of getting the cattle sorted and weighed suddenly overrides all other human endeavors, regardless what they may be.

All cowboys I've known prefer to stay on their horses rather than dismount and work a gate or some other menial task. I had been instructed by the management that the outfit would not tolerate any unnecessary roughness or abuse of livestock. But suddenly we were in a frenzy to get the cattle coaxed through numerous solid steel gates and down dark corridors with men afoot with whips and electric prods, with management and cow buyers wanting them coming faster and faster. You can't put a cowboy afoot on a catwalk with electricity in his hand with someone screaming "More Cattle!" and expect him to not use the tools you have given him.

I soon observed the cows that we were trying to push into the smaller corral and on into the dark crowding pen pushing back at us in what seemed to me an abnormally strong manner. They were desperate to not be driven down the chute. There was tremendous noise, the clanging of heavy gates, men hollering, cursing the cattle they prodded down the chute. It seemed a better plan to open a gate on the opposite end of the corral and allow a man or two on good horses to allow the cows to escape going through a gate back the direction they came from, while at the same time keeping the calves from passing through the gate. A good hand on a good horse could have easily done this, but they wanted the cattle to all be forced down the chute and separated in that way.

Although I didn't like the way we were doing the

job, we did get the calves weaned and weighed in an acceptable amount of time. The calves weighed a little over five hundred pounds and everyone seemed happy. Four cattle trucks showed up on time, and we loaded them without undo complications and went down to the wagon and ate lunch.

We had a considerable amount of sorting to do on the cattle that were left over, which included, for the most part, the mothers of all the calves we had just weaned and shipped. There were, however, a few calves the buyer had rejected that needed to be sent south to Pica and sold to someone else. And there were quite a few young calves that needed to be branded and left with their mothers through the winter.

There was another issue that I wanted to discuss with the people I worked for. One of the owners had shown up at the shipping, coming from California, and riding up from Seligman with the manager early that morning. After we all ate lunch at the wagon, I asked the owner and manager if we could go out and look at the cows we had been sorting all morning. Nothing had ever been mentioned to me about cutting out and accumulating old cows that needed to be sold. All the cow outfits I had been around and worked on received a certain percentage of their income from the sale of cull cows. It was the accepted and natural order of life on a cow ranch that undesirable cows be sold and the herd managed so as the highest possible percentage of the cow herd would be productive and, as a result, profitable. I asked the two men if they wanted me to start cutting out any cull cows I saw and sending them south to Pica, which seemed to be the place where animals like that would be kept until they were sold. They acted like they had not thought about selling cull cows. They looked at each other in what seemed to be surprise. Finally I was asked, "Do you know what a cull cow is?" This question turned the table on me, and now I was the one who looked surprised. Well, I thought to myself, I sure as heck wouldn't have hired someone to run the wagon that didn't know what a cull cow was or at least have an idea.

We got in the manager's Ford pickup and drove out to where the cattle were penned. I was sitting in between the two men in the front seat. I began pointing out numerous cows that I felt should be sold for various reasons. Quite a few were very old, several had cancer in their eyes (a common problem in cattle), and several others were big, fat, and buffalo-shouldered, with no signs of ever having a bag, meaning the cows udder showed no signs of ever being swollen with milk, which would mean she tended to be a nonproducer. Nonproducers are dead weight and need to be sold and replaced with a female that will get pregnant and raise a nice calf to sell. The two men acted pleasantly surprised that I might know such a thing yet showed a considerable amount of skepticism that I might actually pull something like the culling of a cowherd off. I made the mistake of asking what they had been doing in the past. "Well, we haven't had anyone who could do such a thing," was the only reply they would give me, which gave me some food for thought because it wasn't true. There were several men on the outfit who could have accomplished the task. They wouldn't say it, but I guessed they just let the old ones die off. Later, I asked several of the men who had been working there, and no one gave me a different answer. Finally, after chewing their cud for ten minutes, I was given the green light to cut out cows that I felt should be sold and send them to Pica Camp. After visiting about shipping cull cows and future shipping dates, the owner and the manager left acting like they were happy with the way things were going.

We had about six hundred cows still being held in the corral, so the crew and I saddled up and sorted some of the cull cows I had talked about, putting them into a separate corral, and then we branded a good number of unbranded calves, probably twenty-five or thirty head.

We headed and heeled the calves to do this. All these cows were held overnight in the corral, and the next day we vaccinated them for Lepto and Vibrio plus gave them a dose of injectable Ivermectin. Good pour on Ivermectin hadn't been invented yet or wasn't widely used. There was no evidence of the cowherd having a Lepto or Vibrio problem, but I was told to vaccinate them anyway. By the time we had choused on those poor cows for two days, they were ragged with stress. When we got done with all the required torture, I counted them out the gate, turning them loose onto winter range on the Cataract Plains. I'd seen quite a few things, but I'd never seen a set of cows that just had their calves weaned off pull out and leave in such a hurry. There wasn't a single cow that turned around and bawled or looked for her calf. I never would have subjected a cow I owned to that kind of experience. An old corral made out of cedar posts and poles with an alley and a good gate or two and a couple experienced cowboys on cow horses is better than any dodge gate anywhere. Jabbing cows with dull needles for no reason is unacceptable behavior. A bunch of fresh-weaned mother cows that don't even turn around and bawl looking for their missing calves isn't progressive, it's stupid.

Watching the cows fight and try to push their way back through a crew of men in an attempt to escape the dodge chute with its clanging steel doors and cat walk full of electric prods and buggy whips made me realize why the cattle were so difficult to gather out in the brush. The cowboy crew on the Diamond A had been gathering the rough and tree-covered country, on what was called the top, making big drives with the crew scattered far apart. Mike Landis had gathered the top in this manner when I worked there twenty years earlier. The noise and men trying to force the cowherd into places they didn't want to go in the corrals was transposed out into the pasture, and I realized the cows were coming toward a crew in the trees, thinking they could escape from men by pushing against them rather than running from them. Drives, or circles as some men call them, were made with men being separated, sometimes by a half mile. The cows would sneak past the cowboys going the opposite way instead of moving out ahead of the crew like they were supposed to.

I started making the drives much smaller and tighter with men closer together and therefore missing fewer cattle. We used a holdup getting a bunch of cattle throwed

together in our first drive of the day and then using that bunch as padding to drive more cattle into, sometimes repeating the process again, making numerous smaller drives in a morning rather than one large one. It paid off, and we were gathering some snakey old cows and lots of yearlings and two-year-olds that were unbranded.

We managed to meet all the shipping dates through November, shipping somewhere over five thousand calves. The crew had shipped a good number in early October before I showed up. We moved the wagon to Pica about Thanksgiving and worked Last Chance Pasture and shipped several loads of cattle that were around Pica and officially ended the fall roundup around the third of December. A half dozen men on the crew had been hired when the wagon pulled out (as cowboys refer to it) to work through the three months of roundup and knew their employment was now ended with roundup being over. The manager came around and paid off all the extra men, one of whom was Ron Remington.

Most of the men had been given little or no time off for ninety days. There was much talk among the crew about what we would do with our days ahead. Several of us were wanting to take a few days off and go to Las Vegas and the National Finals Rodeo, and others mentioned going to Kingman, eighty miles to the west. Pat Prosser lived with his family at Pica Camp and was a steady employee, and he remarked to someone that he needed to go to Kingman and pick up several things he had ordered at a saddle shop owned by a fellow named Steve Sinn. Among these items were a new custom-made breast collar, some new latigos, and a new pair of stirrups. Ron Remington overheard Pat's remark about getting these things from Sinn's saddle shop and told Pat that he was going that way that very afternoon. If Pat wanted, he would pick the items up for him and bring them back to Pica the next day, saving Pat the hundred and sixty mile round-trip. Ron said it would be no trouble because, after a quick trip to Kingman, he planned on coming back by Pica and then going on east to Texas where he planned to spend the winter. Pat thanked Ron and said he would appreciate it, and to just tell Steve he would be down there soon and pay him for the items. Ron Remington went to the saddle shop in Kingman that afternoon and got the things Pat had ordered, telling Steve Sinn that Pat would be down in a few days to pay him. Pat and Steve never saw Ron Remington again.

About five days later, I saw Ron Remington in Las Vegas at a big trade show at the Las Vegas Convention Center. I spotted him from a distance in a very large and crowded room and thought he acted funny and then he disappeared without me being able to talk to him. I didn't hear about Pat's missing tack until several weeks later.

ഔ൧

The Lost U-Haul

൬ങ

With roundup over in the fall of '92, I planned on gathering remnant all winter. There were cattle scattered all over the top country in every pasture. Regardless what road I drove on, I encountered large numbers of cattle running in country that supposedly had been gathered during fall roundup.

We got some work done in December, gathering cattle in Big Chief, Trinity, and Black Mountain Pastures. Among those were several big steers that were full grown and at least five years old. But December was also full of other duties that led me and everyone else on rabbit trails doing other work, so I looked ahead toward January figuring to really do some serious cow searching after New Year's.

And then it started storming. We had a big storm around the 17ᵗʰ of December that dropped anywhere from six to twenty inches of heavy snow depending on where you were. Most of the top country in the triangle from Seligman to Rose Well and back to Pica got at least eighteen inches. And then a couple days after Christmas, it started raining. I don't recall how many days it rained, but it was several;

and after a few days, Chino Wash, which starts near Keseha and is the headwaters of the Verde River, came down running big enough to go under the railroad bridge on the west side of town. That hadn't happened in a few years and was considered a signature event, worthy of being marked on the calendar.

We had several men on the maintenance crew living at Rose Well, but no cowboy, and we needed to hire one. Sometime around New Year's, a young man, with whom I was acquainted, named John McGrew phoned the manager looking for a job. He mentioned that he knew me, and the manager asked me what I thought, and I replied that everything I knew about him was positive. I actually knew John's dad, Bill McGrew, better than I knew John and knew he was a top hand from the old school who was very well liked south of Prescott where he lived. John was married with a small child and had been working in Texas. He said that he needed a place to be pretty bad and would sure like to move into Rose Well at the first opportunity. I gave my blessing to the idea and was told that John and his family would be showing up any day. The manager told John to come on because he had a job waiting, and then he and his wife left for Phoenix on a trip they had been planning for some time, saying they would be back in a week or two.

John showed up early in the morning along with Maria, his wife, and a baby, who was only several months old. He was driving a little Chevrolet SUV, not much bigger than a Willy's Jeep, only less rugged. Attached to the rear bumper of the little Chevy was a U-Haul about the size of a Walmart grocery cart. What had not been stuffed in the U-Haul was crammed into the small rear seat of the Chevy. Maria was holding the baby.

It was a cloudy day as it had been every day for several weeks, with the clouds hanging low on the Aubrey Cliffs, Trinity and Mount Floyd. Occasionally a little rain fell. My wife and I had a small guesthouse in back of our house that the McGrew's could have stayed in, but John wanted to get moved to Rose Well, and for all I knew, the road would only get worse. The weather forecast called for stormy weather as far into the future as the weather people could see into their crystal ball. I got on the two-way radio and talked to one of the maintenance men at Rose Well, and he thought a person could get in there if they had four-wheel-drive. Jim Hagan lived at Pica and was head of the maintenance crew, and he said a person might make it, maybe.

I had not been up the road from Pica to Rose Well, a distance of twenty-three miles, in at least a week, so I wasn't sure about the road. John wanted to go, saying he would rather get moved in before it got so bad that they couldn't make it for a month. The final decision was up to me; and truthfully, I wasn't sure what to do, but it's my nature to put my head down and push forward, and so I decided to lead them up there. I had a brand-new, four-wheel-drive Dodge diesel pickup that I figured was surely invincible. Maria McGrew was a bubbly little blonde who would remind you of Gretchen Wilson's song "Redneck Woman." She was game for anything and could pack a baby on her hip as she did it. "All right! Let's go," I said and we went west toward Pica.

By the time we got to Pica Camp, it was early afternoon and still looking awful stormy. Jim Hagan again said he thought we might make it, but then again, maybe not. Again, it was up to me, and John and Maria wanted to go but were relying on me to have the wisdom to make the correct decision. We drove on.

Pica Camp was three miles north of the highway and in the middle of the valley. It was another four miles to the mouth of Road Canyon and the foot of the Aubrey Cliffs. After entering Road Canyon, the elevation rose for a little over three miles and finally topped out on a divide near a huge water storage known as Big E. It was easy going all the way to the top of this divide with a little mud, an inch or two deep, in the dirt road, but no reason to put a vehicle in four-wheel-drive.

We topped out at Big E, and I stopped and got out of my Dodge truck and looked around. There was a wet cool breeze and the clouds were only a hundred feet above us. It looked wet, really wet. John and Maria got out of their Chevy, her with the baby on her hip, and we surveyed the landscape. It was still at least sixteen miles to Rose Well. They were smiling and wanting to get moved into their new camp. I wanted to get them there. We agreed to move on; after all, so far we had experienced no hardship. We got back in our vehicles and set forth going downhill, with me in the lead. We were now in the Chino Wash, or Verde River drainage.

Things got wetter fast, and within a quarter mile, I had to stop and turn the hubs in on the front axle of my truck. When I got back in and took off, I looked in the review mirror and saw that John hadn't moved. He had stopped the Chevy when I turned my hubs in and couldn't get it moving again. I backed up and connected a long chain I had brought to the front of the Chevy. I noticed the Walmart shopping cart had some mud on it, mainly in front, but I could still read the U-Haul insignia on its sides. I got in, put it in gear, and took off with the Dodge diesel fishtailing a little due to its effort getting the Chevy moving. I figured when we got down the road a ways and came to a high spot we could probably take the chain off.

The mud got deeper, and the towing got slower, and the high spots we came to seemed wetter than the low spots. After a mile or so, I realized that I had made a very bad decision. Realizing I had exercised poor judgment made me fear another bad decision. I thought about stopping and trying to get turned around but knew that getting John and Maria's vehicle plus the U-Haul turned around was impossible. The mud became so deep and wet, I was afraid to even stop in the middle of the road.

I kept grinding ahead, a great deal of the time spinning my tires more than moving forward. The Chevy had become a great moving mud ball rolling along behind me. No windshield wipers ever invented could have kept the mud off the Chevy's windshield. Occasionally, John made the mistake of sticking his head out the window and yelling something at me. Immediately a flying mud ball would hit him between the eyes, and his head would disappear into the depths of the Chevy interior. I feared what might be being said between the man and wife I was towing into the center of the earth. My ears burned. I doubted my judgment, and in my confused state of mind, my right leg turned to stone in a pedal-to-the-metal position.

We plowed on at three miles an hour until finally at an hour past sundown the invincible Dodge was swallowed by a great cavernous soft spot in the left side of the road. The left headlight was even with the ground. I decided to face the music, and I stepped out of the Dodge thinking John

McGrew would exit the Chevy wiping dried mud out of his eyes and proceed to kick my arse. I also figured the redneck woman would remove the baby from her hip and support her husband's endeavor by attacking me with a brass table lamp or some other implement out of the back seat.

John got out of the mud ball that had long ceased to resemble an automobile, and stood there, and looked at me for a moment. He wiped dried mud out of his hair, and though he would later deny it, his jaw muscles were quivering a little. He grinned, "Where are we," he asked?

"We are at A."

"How far is Rose Well?"

"Another four miles."

It was sprinkling. We surveyed the damage and knew it would be impossible to dig the Dodge out with a shovel. I knew there was a backhoe at Rose Well and told them I would start walking and return with help. John insisted on going with me. The blonde with the baby on her hip was game to come along, but I talked her into staying, promising to return within a week. She smiled, and John and I took off walking north through the mud.

Around 9:00 p.m., we dredged into Rose Well, packing several pounds of mud on our feet, and thankful that the dogs announced our arrival. Had we just walked up and knocked on the door, we might have got shot because nobody should have been out on a night like that. I talked Justin, the maintenance man, into firing up the back hoe and gathering up some extra chains, and John and I climbed on the tractor with him and headed south to rescue Maria and the U-Haul.

When we got there, we started digging the Dodge truck out and had a good-sized cavern dug before we finally got it out to high ground. We all agreed that trying to do anything with the Chevy and U-Haul trailer should wait until some later date. John and Maria gathered up a sack of necessities and the baby and climbed onto the back hoe with Justin and rode to their new home. It was now starting to rain in earnest, and beings, with the backhoe's help, we had my truck turned around and pointed south, I headed for home. It was now almost one in the morning.

About six miles south of where I got stuck, I met Jim Hagan driving a huge Galion road grader. He had fired up the big machine to come looking for me and had another man on his crew following him with a four-wheel-drive Ford pickup. I stopped for a second and told Jim what all had transpired and then I put it in gear and got to moving again. It was really raining now, and the mud was getting deeper. Jim was going to turn the road grader around and follow me south to Pica. In the process of turning the big Galion tractor around, the earth swallowed it, and it sank all the way to the floor of the cab. Jim and his helper proceeded south in the Ford four-by-four. Jim had told me to go on, and I did so being afraid to stop for any length of time. The Ford pickup that had followed him did not have a two-way radio like mine, and I did not find out until the next day, but before Jim and his helper reached Pica, they twisted an axle in two on the Ford. They had to walk the last several miles into camp and got home about five in the morning.

I got into bed around 3:30 a.m. John and Maria arrived at their new home at Rose Well wet from rain blowing sideways into the back hoe that had a roof but no windows. Their little Chevy and the grocery cart-sized U-Haul were incased in a shell of mud a foot thick. The U-Haul did not get returned until sometime in February. The ranch's road grader was sunk past the axles half way between Rose Well and Pica, and a Ford truck had a broken axle. Everyone was mad at me except John and Maria who were glad to have a roof over their heads.

Chino Wash ran under the railroad bridge on the west side of Seligman seven times between New Year's and the 15th of March. An old cowboy named Bob Haley, who had grown up in Seligman, told me he had never seen water run under that bridge that many times in one year. Bob's father, Arthur, had been a wagon boss on the Three Vs.

The famous Arizona cowboy Dave Ericson has a saying about being a boss, "It's lonely on top!" I was feeling pretty lonely when I realized how stupid it was to drag John McGrew and his family to Rose Well in the rain.

୫୦୯ଓ
Branding Time
୫୦୯ଓ

For decades the main cowherd on the Diamond A Ranch had been moved south in the spring, from the Cataract Plains where they wintered, to the top country in the summer. Most of these were funneled through Rose Well, going south in the spring and north in the fall. Because of this, a large portion of the weaning and shipping were done there. There were, however, shipping corrals at Keseha and Camp Sixteen, as well as Pica, and Hoffman which was close to Seligman on the east side of town.

In the years prior to when I was given the job of wagon boss, a great many calves were branded at numerous branding corrals out on the Plains north of Rose Well. The wagon camped at places scattered all over the Plains and branded, and then later the cows would be drifted south to higher country. Lots of old-timers I knew who worked for the outfit in the 1960s and earlier would talk about the cows wanting to drift south so that several men could pretty much clean the Plains by themselves, working at it through July and August.

I was given no orders as to how I was to get the cattle moved, worked, and branded, or when. Early on, after taking the job, I perceived that if I came up with a plan, explaining how I wanted to gather the cows, where I wanted to move them, and when I wanted to execute my plan, I would be given the green light to do so, as long as the plan was a good one, or I could make it look like a good one. Through the winter, which was a long and very wet one and limited the type of work a man could do, I had a lot of time to come up with a game plan.

There were some tremendous obstacles, or so it seemed to me. The greatest of these was the fact that the majority of the infrastructure, as far as corrals and fences, had fallen down in the twenty-year period between 1973 and the early '90s. North of Rose Well was about five hundred square miles of country, and when I arrived in the fall of '92, there were five corrals in that area that would hold a couple hundred cows. Several of these had holes in them that we would need to block with a board or some other piece of refuse left laying around. Twenty years earlier there had been around two dozen good corrals in the same piece of country. From Rose Well to Black Tank there wasn't a single corral or fence that would hold livestock. The big water lot, corrals, and traps at Farm Dam were laying on the ground. The top country was worse.

Another issue that needed to be addressed was getting a good count on the cows. Elmer McDonald told me that the cows that ran north of the Aubrey Cliffs, which amounted to ninety percent of the ranch's cattle, had not been counted accurately in twenty years. Elmer had worked for the outfit a total of thirty-five years and retired that spring of 1993. He claimed the ranch recorded a death loss on paper of somewhere between five and ten percent at the end of each year in an attempt to estimate numbers. I was never given any numbers by anyone or ordered by anyone to come up with a certain number of livestock. It was hinted that a good accurate count would be a positive development but probably close to impossible to obtain. There was a huge amount of remnant on top, running in rough, brushy country, some of which hadn't been gathered in years, if ever. Because of the wetter than normal winter, we hadn't made a huge dent in gathering them. From what I saw that first winter I was there, I figured the number of remnant was a minimum of five hundred grown cattle, and maybe a thousand. Gathering the open plains north of Rose Well and counting those cattle would be easy, but a count would never be accurate until we got the top clean, and that would have to happen between November and April, so now in the spring of '93 that meant another year away.

Another problem for me was I had no experience dealing with springtime on the Diamond A working the Plains. Both times I had worked there before had been in the fall. I had heard lots of stories about gathering the outfit in the springtime, but I personally hadn't witnessed it. I had to rely on my experience on other ranches and other roundups. Mike Landis's wagon didn't gather the Plains; Burley's crew had always done that and I had never worked for Burley.

That winter of '92 and '93 we had several men rebuild the fence running east and west between Lower Sandstone, Midway, and Broken Axle Pastures. I planned on using this fence as a boundary to count through both spring and fall.

We threw the outfit together at Keseha around the 26ᵗʰ of March and gathered all the extra horses that had wintered south of there in Black Mountain. Then we moved out to Number Five on the Plains. There were several places called Number Five on the ranch: a water on a pipeline north of Pica ten miles, and another place twenty miles north of Rose Well. This Number Five, north of Rose Well, had a house and barn, etc., and the outfit tried to keep a steady man there all the time taking care of the country surrounding it. We shod the remuda there and then

spent several days drifting cattle south into Midway and scattering bulls that had been separated from the cowherd all winter. In a few days, we moved camp to Rose Well and gathered all the cattle in Lower Sandstone and trailed pairs up into Shafer and left several hundred dry cows in Lower Sandstone. Then we started gathering cattle from

Upper Sandstone and bringing them into Rose Well. We would make a big drive and throw a rodear together, north of the corrals at Rose Well about a half mile, and cut out all the dry cows and put them into Lower Sandstone. We would then bring the rest of the herd, which would be cows with babies on their sides, and put them in a trap on the south side of camp. By the time we got this done, it would be noon or later. We would leave the cattle in the trap overnight. Early the next morning while most of the crew went to the backside of the trap and started gathering it, I let any tight-bagged cows and bawling calves back out into Upper Sandstone figuring they would go get paired back up to their calves or mothers, whichever the case might be. I figured the rest of the herd would be paired up straight and safe to brand. I was hoping this method would cut down on the number of dogies or orphaned calves.

We repeated this process several times until most of the cattle in Upper Sandstone had been worked and the branded pairs turned south of Rose Well for the summer. Then when we were running out of cattle in Upper Sandstone, we would move camp back out on the Plains somewhere, sometimes Number Five, Number Two, or Hazen Hole, depending on where the most cattle were, and we would throw more cattle south into Upper Sandstone filling it with cattle again. Then we would move back to Rose Well and repeat the whole process another time. This same thing was repeated time and time again until we had all the cattle on the Plains gathered with the exception of Lower Sandstone where we had been depositing dry cows all spring.

We started putting dry cows into Lower Sandstone around April 1, and by the time we had the rest of the Plains gathered, it was the third week of June. In that two and a half month period, many of those drys had calved, and the last thing we did was to gather those cattle and brand all the calves that had been born in that timeframe. There were still some cows that hadn't calved in that herd, and we cut them out and left them in Lower Sandstone all summer.

There was lots of herd work: cutting and sorting, besides roping and dragging calves to the branding fire. We changed horses every day in the middle of the day and had a fresh horse to sort cattle on or whatever the afternoon might bring.

The first time or two we made a drive in Upper Sandstone and brought cattle down into Rose Well, we hauled our horses south on the main pipeline road to Number Two, which was on the far north end of the pasture, seven miles north of Rose Well. The cattle, which were scattered all over the pasture, would hear the trucks and gooseneck trailers and start trotting north. As we drove along, we could see cattle moving fast in the opposite direction we wanted them to go. By the time we got to our destination, most of the cattle were bunched up on the wrong end of the pasture, and we would have to trail them all the way back. It was impossible to split the pasture and try to get a portion of the cattle instead of everything in the pasture. On one particular day, we became bogged down with way too many cattle, and we had to pull up and regroup and let some of the cattle go. It was a mess, and some of the crew got bowed up about things not going smoothly. In the end, we got everything straightened out and got our work accomplished, but I knew I needed to change our method of operation. I asked several men who had been there if they had experienced the same problem in other years, and they replied, "Yeah, it always goes that way!" I wanted some advice but could tell I wasn't going to get any.

After several wrecks doing it the way it had always been done, I realized it was time for a change. We quit hauling out and left camp a little earlier and rode horseback way out to the side. I asked the crew to be as quiet as possible, and we were able to get out into the pasture without stirring the cattle up, and then we were able to gather the correct amount of cattle we wanted. The first few brandings we had, we ended up having a lot more cattle than I wanted to mess with in one day. At one branding we had more than six hundred calves, which was fine, but I wanted to average two hundred fifty to three hundred at each branding. With time, we got pretty good at judging where to cut a drive off and would get close to the amount of cattle we wanted, and things went smoother.

Around the 23rd of June, we had the Plains gathered with the exception of less than two hundred cows, all of which we ended up gathering in July. We moved to Pica on the afternoon of the 23rd and finished up the roundup there. There was a herd of Hereford cows that ran out in the Last Chance Pasture, north and west of Pica Camp. We gathered those cows, which totaled around nine hundred, taking three days to do it. All of the corrals in Last Chance had fallen down, so we branded outside holding the cattle in rodear fashion and roping the calves by the neck and dragging them to the fire. They had Brahma bulls running with those Hereford cows trying to raise F 1 replacement heifers, and beings it was close to the 1st of July, many of the calves were big and juicy. We flanked the smaller calves, but the majority were too big to be much fun to flank, and we roped them by the head and heels.

Through most of the roundup the crew consisted of fourteen or fifteen men, but around the 1st of June, we picked up several high school-aged boys who wanted to cowboy a little bit, and several were good young hands. On the last day of roundup, which was the last day of June, we had our picture taken with the crew totaling twenty-one men, which included the cook and horse wrangler. We had an old retired cowboy named Floyd Martin as a cook, and Charlie Wascogomie was wrangling horses. The crew, besides me, included: Everett Ashurst, Clay Ashurst, Truman Rustin, Jim Marler, Steve Webb, John McGrew, Jason Mueller, Cody Sawyer, Barney Prosser, Barry Prosser, Pat Prosser, Tom Reeder, Jeff Osborn, Al Smith, Cole Gould, Sam Gould, Randy Rutledge, and Stacy Taliaforo. We branded sixty-five hundred calves that spring.

ℬℭ
Sneaky Pete
ℬℭ

Flagstaff, August 1977

Sometime in the middle of the day, probably around one in the afternoon, Jean Ann told me it was time, the baby was coming. Actually our first child wasn't due for several weeks, but babies don't always cooperate and this one wanted to be born, or so my wife thought. We owned a half-ton Ford pickup, and we loaded up all the necessary stuff, although I can't remember what that was, and we headed to town. We were living at Spider Web, the Babbitt Ranch headquarters, thirty-five miles north of Flagstaff. It had been a dry summer, at least in a lot of places, and I remember looking at a huge thunderhead out toward Mesa Butte, twenty miles to the west, wishing it would rain. Darn, I thought to myself as Jean Ann indicated she was ready to go, now, I wish that baby would wait so I could watch that thunderhead build. A good rain doesn't happen around here every day.

We got to the hospital in the middle of the afternoon, and I walked with Jean Ann into the emergency room, and she told someone who looked important what was going on. They quickly took her down a hallway out of sight and left me in a waiting room with copies of Redbook and Better Homes and Gardens. I sat there a good while, but I can't remember exactly how long, maybe an hour, and then she reappeared. "They said it would be a long time so we might as well leave and come back later."

I argued. "Well, if they think its coming, why can't you just stay here?"

"I don't know, they just think I should leave and come back when the baby is closer to being born. They said we should go eat. Ha!"

It was still early enough to get in the ranch office in the old Babbitt building downtown, so I found a parking place across the street from the Monte Vista Hotel and katty-corner from the office, and I parked the pickup. I crossed

the street, walked west a half block, and went up the stairs and retrieved our mail. I didn't waste any time talking to Rocky or Bob, the bookkeepers, and hurried back to the pickup to take my wife home.

About the time I grabbed the door handle with my left hand while holding our mail with the right, I heard someone call my name. I looked up and saw Jim Dolan and Paul Gonzales coming toward me. "Hey, wait for us!" They were hollering. They had been down at the 66 Club having a beer or two and were headed toward the lounge in the Monte Vista Hotel to have another. "Let's go have a beer," Jim said. But I explained that I needed to get Jean Ann home. Jim argued, stating it would only take a minute or two to drink a friendly beer, and Jean Ann wouldn't mind. I stood there talking, determined that I wouldn't walk across the street to the Monte Vista no matter how much Jim pleaded. They had way too much of a head start for me to catch up. Paul said nothing but just stood there grinning and was obviously in that perfect state when the glow from the alcohol was burning at the perfect speed. Jim wanted to talk about horses and cows. I noticed Jean Ann give me a look. I tried to get away, but Jim wouldn't let me go. I couldn't insult my dear friend.

I don't remember if my wife told me to get going, or I got the information through osmosis, but I snubbed my cowboy friends and took ahold of the door handle and got in. Jim and Paul crossed the street answering the call of beautiful sirens who reside in the midst of cowboy heaven or some other mythical place. I could tell that my sweetheart was upset, maybe even scared; I was too dumb to be scared. There was a watery mess on the truck seat spilling onto the rubber mats on the floorboard that looked like water mixed with red wine. "My water broke; we need to go back to the hospital!"

This time they ushered us to the second floor where the maternity ward was, and my wife disappeared into some unknown place, and I went to another but much smaller waiting room. Before too long the sun went down, and beings I was alone and didn't know how to turn the lights on, the room got darker, and I went to sleep in a chair. Sometime later, I believe it was about nine, a nurse came in and told me, "Congratulations, you have a new son. You can come and see your wife now."

She looked tired. We talked and she told me there had been some trouble. The placenta had broken loose too soon and our son had lost some blood. Her regular baby doctor was on vacation and a new young doctor was on duty, and she felt like that was a blessing because he handled the crisis so well. I was nervous, not being use to hospitals. Perhaps it was because I wasn't use to being a father or having my wife lying in a hospital bed. A nurse came in and said, "You can come and see your son now, Mr. Ashurst."

I stood up and followed her down the hallway. I wasn't nervous. Actually, I had never been one to want children. It wasn't that I didn't want them; it was just that there was something in the equation that was missing. It was like not understanding algebra, not being able to figure out what the missing digit was. I wasn't guilty of not caring, but rather, I didn't know how to care. We reached a row of large plate glass windows, and on the other side of the glass were numerous incubators, several of which had babies in them. We stopped and the nurse said, "There's your son," pointing to an incubator directly below my eyes.

He had tubes stuck in his nose and arms held to his skin with tape. He looked fragile like very fine porcelain. All of a sudden, I felt faint, and I put the palms of my hands against the wall below the window pane bracing myself because I thought I was going to fall. I felt sick. In a minute my eyes began to focus again and I stared though the window. In that moment in time, I was transformed. For the first time in my life I understood. I wasn't just a dumb cowboy anymore: I was a father.

ℰↃ♋

Diamond A Ranch, early April, 1994

We had moved to Number Two, seven miles north of Rose Well. There was a barbed wire water lot, a smaller branding corral, and a holding trap to turn the remuda out in. We set up the wagon and cook tent inside the horse trap a hundred yards east of the branding corral. The afternoon we moved the wagon there, I drove into town and picked up my two boys who would help us for three days.

We had kept up horses the evening before in the branding corral, feeding them some hay. We ate breakfast early in the morning, and as soon as we were through, we walked to the corral, and I started catching horses for the crew. It was barely light enough to see. There were about fifteen of us. I roped Everett's horse first because he was a five-year-old that had not been ridden since November the fall before, and I figured he might act a little fresh. The colt's name was Sneaky Pete. Everett had ridden him a few times the fall before and had gotten along with him fine, but he was very green.

Everyone had laid their saddles and gear along the fence on the inside of the horse trap. I had hauled my kid's saddles out from town in my pickup that morning, and Everett led Sneaky Pete down close to the wagon and hobbled him close to my truck so he could reach his saddle easy. There were a dozen or more teepees set up close by. I caught my horse last, about the time Everett was getting Sneaky Pete cinched up tight. Other members of the crew were in various stages of getting saddled up along the fence between the wagon and the corral.

About the time I reached my saddle, Everett stepped on the bronc about a hundred yards away. He squeezed the horse's belly with his heels and the horse took a step and stopped and bowed up. He squeezed him again, and Sneaky Pete took a half step and humped up and stopped. He was pretty tight. Everett took the ends of his latigo reins in his right hand and swatted the horse down his right flank. Wwammpttthth, the colt turned loose with a tremendous expulsion of gas and headed toward the horse pasture fence a hundred feet away. He was traveling a jump at a time, about two and a half feet high, with his head down to the ground. Cachunka, cachunka, chchunka,

Everett's spurs were crashing into Sneaky Pete's gut, and the horse was squealing like he was being castrated all over again.

When he reached the fence, the bucking horse turned to the right toward the corner and branding corral two hundred fifty feet away. Men were along the fence trying to saddle their horses as Everett and the colt came straight toward them scattering men, horses and saddles. Cachunka, cachunka, cachunka, several horses jerked away from cowboys dragging their bridle reins. Someone hollered yeehaw and someone else cursed. Down near the fence corner was Jim Marler just trying to pick his saddle up as the bronc and bronc rider came toward him balling the jack. Jim didn't hear too good, and the bucking bronco was almost on top of him before he knew what was happening. At the last possible instant, he dropped bridle reins, saddle, and blankets and jumped at the barbed wire fence. He had on heavy shotgun chaps and a big coat. He wasn't young anyway, and gaining enough altitude to clear the fence was a bridge too far. His belt buckle landed on the top strand, and for a second, he teetered backwards his toes hitting the ground just as the colt was about to crash into him. He pushed off with his toes and turned upside down on the other side of the fence, his hands holding onto the top strand of barbed wire. His cowboy boots were straight in the air about six feet high, and his head barely off the ground. The bucking colt's hind feet kicked dirt into Jim's upside down face as he passed by. When that happened, Jim turned loose of his hand hold and crashed into the ground smashing the crease of his good black cowboy hat. He was pissed off for a week. I don't think Sneaky Pete ever bucked again.

ഇ൰

Bright Lights, Thick Smoke and Loud, Loud Music

ഇ൰

Diamond A Ranch, Winter 1993

On the far northeast corner of the ranch was a cow camp called Number Five. This place and many others were named with numbers that correspond to water storages and troughs on pipelines that traversed several hundred miles across the huge ranch. South of Rose Well the various watering facilities were named with letters in the alphabet, and north of Rose Well with numbers. Camp Five was fifty miles north of Seligman in a straight line, but by the closest road, which was dirt and not well maintained, it was sixty-five. If you went around by the Supai Highway, which went across the east side of the Hualapai Reservation and entered the ranch near Camp Sixteen, it was close to ninety miles to Seligman or one hundred twenty-five to Kingman. Camp Five was an isolated place to live. The nearest neighbor was Camp Sixteen, sixteen miles to the west.

There had not been a cowboy taking care of Camp Five for a few months that winter of '93, but in late January, the manager told me that he had hired a young couple who would be moving in there. The manager and his wife took off to Phoenix for a few days to attend the annual budget meeting, and while they were gone, the new cowboy, Jake, showed up at our house saying they were ready to move out to Five. They meaning a newly-wed, teen-aged-looking wife, Teresa; a two-year-old girl; and a baby boy in diapers.

The big boss had taken the keys to the company commissary that held the groceries under lock and key, and beings there was nobody else present trustworthy enough to possess that symbol of authority that unlocks doors, I was not able to stock them with groceries any other way than getting some from our own supply. My wife asked Teresa what she thought she would need to hold her over for a few days, but Teresa didn't seem to have a clue what she needed. She was more interested in telling about her recent deal with her father to get temporary custody of her children by agreeing to have an automatic-type birth control inserted under the skin of her arm, which she and Jake were thinking about cutting out because it was making her moody. My wife boxed up enough of the basic necessities to hold them over until a larger supply could be delivered after the manager returned from Phoenix with the keys to the commissary, while telling Teresa that they better not try a pocket knife surgery because they were moving to a very remote place and she just might end up bleeding to death. We both encouraged them over and over to stay in the guest house behind our house until morning to spare them arriving at a cold, isolated house with two babies late in the day, but they insisted on moving on as soon as the groceries we gave them were loaded. My wife fixed them a bite to eat for on the road or when they arrived, and I told them how to get to Number Five Camp traveling the long way around by the Supai Highway. I provided them with a map and specific directions.

Several weeks later on a cold windy day, I decided to drive around the winter country north of Rose Well, check on things, and talk to several of the camp men. I mentioned where I was going in a conversation with the manager, and he asked if I would mind delivering a load of groceries to Camp Five. I answered in the affirmative, and so early the next morning, he loaded me up with several boxes of victuals, and I took off in my new Dodge diesel pickup.

I traveled out west on Route 66 to Pica Camp and turned north up Road Canyon and over the divide at Big E and on to Rose Well. From there I went out the gyp line to Hazen Hole and then north to Number Five. I got to Five about ten o'clock in the morning. It was cold, and the wind was blowing making a windchill somewhere not far above zero. I pulled up to the yard gate and shut the engine off and got out of the Dodge truck. Teresa came out of the house, packing the baby in diapers, telling me Jake was out making the rounds, riding a horse and cutting ice. She didn't expect him back for three or four hours. I replied that it didn't matter; I would just unload her groceries and be moving on myself. I had plenty to do.

There were only three or four boxes to pack into the house, and in a minute or two, I was ready to go. I was headed out the door to go when she asked me if I wanted a cup of coffee. "Oh, I better move on," I replied. But she insisted it would only take a minute to make a small pot, and after all it was so cold. She hadn't shut up since I got out of the truck, and she obviously had a severe case of cabin fever. She had never lived out in an isolated place like this, and she told me so. I turned around and sat at the kitchen table while she made the coffee. The little two-year-old girl played on the tile floor, and the baby went to sleep on the couch where she had laid him with a bottle while I was carrying in the groceries. She told me about their old International pickup that was constantly breaking down and how before too long she was going to need to make a trip to Kingman. I hadn't seen an International pickup that was still running in ten years. "Do you know anyone that will give me a ride to Kingman," she asked? I replied that she and her husband would surely figure something out.

She rambled on and laughed and talked like we had been friends for years. I drank my coffee. I drink coffee that's hot, and I drink it fast. Before five minutes was gone, I was done with the coffee and got up to go. "Oh, no, there's another cup in the pot. Let me get it for you!" She stood up and walked to the stove. She was wearing tight shorts and a halter top that was tighter. She came back to the table bearing the small aluminum percolator and leaned way over to pour the coffee. As I looked at her stretching low over to my cup, from somewhere in that deep dark alley that lies between what could be and don't dare go there, a light in a small window showed and a still small voice said, "You better get outa here!"

I took a step backward toward the door while she stared at me with her big brown eyes; my coffee cup sat steaming on the table; the two-year-old squatted under the table picking up Fruit Loops that had spilled onto the floor and stuck them in her mouth; and within one minute, the tachometer on the dashboard told me the Cummins engine was turning over at 2100 RPMs.

After that Teresa started talking to every man on the ranch about giving her a ride to Kingman so she could do some shopping. Anytime anyone came around Camp Five for whatever reason, the subject would come up. Jake seemed to be fine with the idea of his wife going off to the big city with one of the other cowboys. She always used the excuse that the old International pickup didn't run very good.

Tom Reeder was staying in a small bunkhouse at Camp Sixteen helping Elmer McDonald who was about to retire. Several times through the winter, Tom told me he was thinking of taking Teresa to Kingman on a shopping trip. "Just to help her out," he would say. "After all, they don't have a good vehicle." He would always end our conversation by asking me what I thought.

"You do what you want, but I wouldn't touch that with a ten-foot pole," would always be my reply.

There was an old man living at Rose Well named Al Edgar; he was a member of the maintenance crew and took care of a hundred miles of pipeline on the ranch. Al was seventy-two years old in the spring of '93 and was a character. He only had two or three teeth left in his head and very little hair on the top of it. He stood about five feet eight or nine and wasn't packing any fat. He would get up extra early, about three o'clock, when the cowboy crew was camped at Rose Well, and start his pickup and let it warm up for an hour or two and maybe get up in the back of it and rearrange some tools, anything to make noise and wake the cowboys up. He was a hard worker who did his job but kept his nose out of other people's business. He didn't bother getting involved in ranch gossip or express his opinions about other ranch employees, but he was good humored and would visit and tell stories if you wanted to be friendly. I liked Al and thought he was a good man. He had been friends with Elmer and Nellie McDonald for years, as well as several other old-timers I knew including Johnny and Vi Sanders whom I had known years earlier when I worked at the Yolo Ranch. (Vi Sanders was a sister to Jimmy Gibson who was the brand inspector in Seligman for many years.)

Teresa began asking Al for a ride to Kingman as soon as she met him. Al took care of the pipeline that Camp Five was located on, and he drove by the cow camp on a regular basis. Several times though the winter, Al mentioned that the cowboy at Number Five had a good looking wife that wanted to go to town with him. He would laugh and tell me, "I don't go to town very often, and when I do, I stay for several days." Al told me that he told her, "I'll take you to town, but we're staying for a while when we go." I thought I detected a twinkle in his eye when he talked about it.

Finally about the 20th of March, Teresa convinced Al to take her to Kingman, which was over a hundred miles away. He had told her they would be spending the night at a motel where she could rent her own room or stay with him, whatever she wanted to do. They were off to the races: the toothless old waterman and the eighteen-year-old brunette with two little babies. They shopped, and Al hauled her around wherever she wanted to go. They went out to eat. And then it was time to bed down for the night. He had already told her how it would be. She chose to share a room with him, just to save money, of course.

Two days later, I gathered up my cowboy crew and camped the wagon at Keseha about fifteen miles south-southeast of Rose Well. We gathered the remuda that had spent the winter turned out in Black Mountain Pasture, and when we had them rounded up, we were going to move to Number Five, forty miles to the north. The night before we moved to Number Five, I stayed in town with my family at the mansion. I showed up at the wagon about four thirty in the morning ready to eat breakfast and then help tear the cook tent down and roll everything up and move camp.

I lifted the flap of the cook tent and stepped inside the big tent that was well lit with several Coleman lanterns. I was met immediately by Al Smith, a Texas cowboy who at the time lived at the Black Tank Camp with his family. Everyone else was sitting silently, sipping hot coffee out of porcelain-covered metal cups. "I need to talk to you alone—outside," Al insisted. We stepped out into the black night as I wondered to myself what in the heck this was all about. Al Smith was a good fella but was known for being melodramatic, and he kept up with all the ranch gossip and loved to share it. "Have you heard about Al Edgar and Teresa?" Al asked staring me in the eyes so strongly I could see the whites of his eyeballs through the pitch black.

"No. What about 'em," I asked?

"Well, Teresa is telling all the ranch women that Al raped her and molested her little two-year-old girl!"

I don't remember exactly what I said in reply, but I do remember wanting to hit Al Smith in the face with my right hand for repeating such crap. He was hyperventilating with excitement telling me the details as if he had been there: As Al Edgar and Teresa returned from Kingman, they stopped at Pica Camp and Rose Well where Teresa told the wives of several ranch employees that Al raped her and then abused the little girl. Al Smith was sure it was true and suggested I get the law out to the ranch real fast, if for no other reason than to protect myself, after all I now knew all the facts!

I told Al in a very low and quiet voice that Al Edgar was no child molester, and the whole story was a bunch of B.S. "Do you know what they do to seventy-year-old men that molest two-year-old girls?" Al Smith acted puzzled that I was not believing his juicy story. I told him that Teresa had been trying to get friendly with every man on the ranch, married or unmarried. "Hell, yes, Al Edgar probably tried to do something with Teresa, but he is no child molester!" And the conversation ended when I suggested he quit talking about it.

I couldn't believe the ranch manager hadn't already put a stop to this nonsense. I knew without a doubt he knew about it because the women Teresa supposedly told were constantly on the phone and two-way radio with the manager's wife. The whole bunch of them reveled in intrigue and any juicy tidbit of gossip they could imagine. The implications of accusing an innocent man of child molestation were astounding to me.

We ate breakfast and then prepared to move camp to Number Five. While the cook washed dishes and got his kitchen ready to load, we caught horses for four or five men to trail the remuda of a hundred horses north to Five. The men had already rolled up their beds and had taken their teepees down and had them piled up along with any extra gear, all of which was ready to load in a pickup. Having got the remuda on its way, those of us who weren't horseback trailing horses tore down the cook tent and fly, got everything loaded, and were soon on our way.

We pulled into Number Five where Jake and Teresa lived about nine thirty. Jake came out to greet us all and acted excited about working with the cowboy crew on the biggest outfit in Arizona. I got him alone and questioned him about his wife accusing Al Edgar of molesting his daughter. He said as far as he was concerned it was the gospel truth, and Al had raped his wife on top of everything else. I told him that Al Edgar was no child molester, but as far as being intimate with Teresa, I could believe that was true considering the fact she had come on strong to every hairy-legged man on the outfit regardless of how old they were.

We stood toe to toe. Jake was six feet one and twenty-one years old. I was five feet ten and forty-one. I told him, "There's only one thing worse than a child molester and that's someone who would accuse someone of being a child molester when they're not. Now you go inside your house and tell your wife to shut up, and if I hear one more word about Al molesting your little girl, I'm going to break every bone in your body." He moved his head back two or three inches, and his eyes got real wide, and I stood there and didn't move. Finally he turned around and stomped off to the house.

Five minutes later he came walking back to where we were setting up the large cook tent that was thirty-six feet long and twelve feet wide. "I quit!" he said.

"You do whatever you need to do, Jake, but don't be

tellin' anyone that Al Edgar is a child molester." He stared at me for a minute and then returned to the house.

When we got camp set up, we had several hours to wait around for the horses to arrive so we got some coffee and made small talk. "I-I I al-al-almost took th-that g-g-gal to t-town!" Tom Reeder announced out of the blue. We all heard just exactly what he was saying, but no one ever mentioned Teresa again.

௸
They Warned Me About Days Like This
௸

Spring 1972, Diamond A Wagon

Sometime in the winter of 1972, Burley McDonald was diagnosed with cancer and as a result of that was undergoing cancer treatment when it came time to start branding calves. So Jim Lowrance made Mike Landis wagon boss over the whole ranch with a larger crew then he had been used to and a lot more country to work. The outfit had corrals all over the ranch, but Mike and Jim put their heads together and decided they would brand everything outside, rodear fashion. They had a big crew, sometimes numbering twenty cowboys or more, and they roped the calves by the neck and flanked them accordingly. Mike loved it; it was Western, reminiscent of his days on the JA and Matadors in Texas. Sometimes they would hold a herd up outside using one side of a branding corral to throw the herd up against.

One morning they made a drive in the south side of the Rogers Pasture and throwed a small bunch of cattle together near Cooke Dam on the Trinity fence. When they got the cattle throwed together, Mike looked them over for a minute as they were quieting down, and he realized that there was only one calf to brand. That was not a problem because he had plans on making several more drives before lunch and knew they would find a bigger bunch as the day went on. They were mobile with a pickup to haul the branding outfit in, and someone to drive it. Mike told everyone they would brand the calf they had gathered and then turn the bunch loose and go gather some more.

Mike jumped off his horse, which was a big gray named Blucher, and quickly set up the branding outfit, which consisted of a propane bottle, branding pot, and a couple of irons. An old army surplus ammunition box held a bottle of blackleg vaccine and a vaccine gun. When he got the propane torch lit and was about to remount ole Blucher, he hollered, "Someone gets a shot, take it!"

There were twenty men surrounding the herd of cattle that numbered twenty-one. Everyone had a loop in his hand and a saddle that was cinched up. Truman Rustin was standing directly in front of a Hereford bull that was facing him and gently chewing his cud. When Mike hollered, "Someone gets a shot, take it!" Truman threw his best hoolihan and roped the bull, catching him deep.

The wreck was on with Ray Lambert taking the second shot roping a cow, and then it went downhill fast. Within seven seconds, every man on the crew had a critter roped with the exception of Mike who was just now getting the big gray horse in motion. He spied a critter getting away in the cedar trees and built to him, and just like a top hand, he had him roped in nothing flat; and he spurred ole Blucher dragging the critter back toward the pickup and branding fire that was surrounded by cows jumping around and bawling out on the ends of nylon ropes tied to saddlehorns.

In his haste, trying to figure out which cowboy had the unbranded calf roped, Mike failed to pay attention to the cow that was attached to his saddle, and she came hooking wanting to stab someone with her sharp horns. Coming out of his surveillance mode, Mike realized he and Blucher were about to be gored, and he spurred hard, which resulted in he and Blucher ending up in the branding fire. Blucher got the rubber hose, that was hooked to the propane bottle on one end and the burning torch on the other, wrapped around a hind leg and jerked the torch out of the pot. The hose was half hitched to the gray horse's left hind foot, and the fire, not unlike the blast from an F-16 Fighter Jet, set Blucher's hair on fire, especially his tail.

It's hard to be a boss when you can't see as a result of being in the center of a ball of fire and smoke. You don't know who to give orders to or what to holler at. No one could help Mike because they were all still attached.

Someone started laughing. Mike was coughing and gasping for air until Blucher stampeded in an attempt to escape the flames. The great rate of speed with which the gray horse traveled provided Mike with clean air to breathe and blew the flames out, saving Blucher's blistered life.

When roll call was made it was found that the unbranded calf had got away. Twenty men, twenty-one head of cattle. "Someone gets a shot, take it!" Well, in Truman's defense, he wasn't told what to shoot at.

ℰↃℭℛ

Diamond A Ranch, May 1993

Around the 1st of May, we moved camp from Camp Number Five, south, to a place known as Hazen Hole. There was nothing at Hazen Hole except a dirt tank, a water trough on a pipeline that originates from Rose Well about ten miles away, a barbed wire corral, and a small horse pasture. We got moved in the afternoon, set up the cook tent and our teepees, and caught horses to ride the next morning, which we kept in the barbed wire pen. We ate supper that our cook Floyd Martin prepared and settled in for the night.

The next morning we ate breakfast about an hour before first light and then caught and saddled our horses and took off at a lope and a trot and headed straight west toward the backside of the Broken Axle Pasture, ten miles away. Somewhere, three or four miles north of the southeast corner of Broken Axle, I split the crew up. I took about half the men south and Pat Prosser, who was my jigger boss, took the rest of the crew north, and we began making a drive back toward Hazen Hole where we planned to throw the cattle we gathered through a gate into a pasture called Midway.

One of the men Pat had with him on his side of the drive was his son Barney who was eighteen or nineteen years old. Barney was like all the other Prossers I've known, being an exceptional young cowboy who was well liked by everyone in the crew.

There were lots of cattle running in that country, and by the time we got halfway back to Hazen Hole we had perhaps five or six hundred cows strung out and moving in front of us. When we got about two miles from camp and the gate, which was our destination, I could look to the north and see numerous bunches of cattle coming down the slopes and headed in the right direction. Everything seemed to be going smoothly when all of a sudden I saw a man riding a dark-colored horse racing toward camp in a dead run. He was two or three miles away, but I could see he was pickin' 'em up and setting 'em down, so to speak, and moving fast. It was too far to tell, but from the color of the horse and the direction he was coming from, I thought it must be Pat Prosser. Camp was out of sight behind a small hill so I couldn't tell what was going on, but within a few minutes after the horse disappeared in that direction, my Dodge pickup came from behind the hill and headed back north, and whoever was driving was doing so at a much higher rate of speed than I approved of, and the dust was rolling. I wondered to myself, What in the world is going on.

About an hour later, as I was within a quarter mile of the gate, a helicopter appeared on the horizon and then seemed to be landing three or four miles off to the north-northeast. Some other cowboys, who were close to me on drive, started showing up, and one of them brought word that Barney was hurt real bad, and they were loading him on a helicopter ambulance. Everyone had an opinion: his horse had stepped in a prairie dog hole and turned over with him; or, he had got bucked off and kicked; one said he had an epileptic seizure, although he had no history of having epilepsy; one of the men closest to Barney on the

drive came running into camp crying and proclaimed that
Barney was dying for sure.

Finally, after another hour, we all saw the helicopter
take off and fly toward Flagstaff, one hundred miles away
to the southeast. A few moments later, Pat drove back into
camp in my truck. He was understandably in a hurry but
took the time to include his details to the other accounts of
what had transpired to create the wreck that had injured
his son.

Barney was the last man he dropped off, and things
went smoothly for several hours. Pat loped around a bunch
of cattle and turned them toward Barney, who was hot on

his heels flanking for him. Pat then saw another bunch a
quarter mile away headed the wrong direction and took
off in a lope to turn them. In doing so, he went over a hill
causing Barney to be out of his range of vision. Pat got
the cattle turned back to the south and into the drive and
was able to slow down for a few moments, thinking that
Barney would catch up with him shortly. After riding

along for a while, and Barney having not showed up, Pat turned and went back toward where they had last seen each other, thinking perhaps Barney needed help turning some cattle.

The cowboy Pat dropped off before Barney was Randy Rutledge. Within several minutes of Pat leaving Barney and running to turn those cows into the drive, Randy topped a ridge and looked several hundred yards ahead of him and saw what looked like a man sitting on the ground with his hat off and his horse standing close by. At first he didn't think much of the situation and just eased that direction, but the closer he got the more out of the ordinary things looked. He kicked his horse into a lope, and when he reached the sitting man, he saw that it was Barney, and he had a long and deep cut across one side of his forehead. The wound was not bleeding real bad, but looked quite serious. Randy jumped off and asked Barney if he was all right and what had happened. Barney didn't reply as he simply stared straight ahead, seemingly conscious but unable to think or communicate.

Within another minute or two, John McGrew showed up, and then suddenly Barney's eyes rolled back in his head, and he went into convulsions. The two cowboys were unsure what to do, and then Barney appeared to stop breathing. As they began administering CPR, trying to revive him, Pat rode up, having doubled back to check on Barney when he hadn't caught up to him.

Randy and John told Pat that Barney was in pretty bad shape, and Pat whipped his horse into a dead run heading for camp to get my pickup, which had a two-way radio. As soon as he was in the truck, he radioed the ranch manager, who in turn requested that a helicopter be sent to pick up the injured cowboy. Almost at once a helicopter took off from Flagstaff.

No one ever figured out what exactly happened to Barney, but the best guess was that his horse, for some reason, fell with him, and at some time during the wreck, he received a severe blow to his head. It took around two hours from when the wreck started until the helicopter landed and loaded him taking him to the hospital. His father, Pat, came back to camp and loaded up in his own company pickup and headed south to Pica Camp where he lived, which was about forty-five miles distance, with plans to go on to Flagstaff to be with his son.

The mood was pretty blue around the wagon as we ate lunch and listened to Randy and John relate what little they knew about the wreck that no one had witnessed. In their opinions, Barney had died three times, as he completely quit breathing while he lay unconscious waiting for the helicopter. Each time they pumped on his chest, trying to revive him, and then he would start breathing again.

Life goes on and staying busy was pretty good therapy for being worried about a friend; so we caught ourselves a fresh horse and saddled up, figuring to gather some more cows. We headed our horses out the corral gate and traveled about a hundred yards, and a sorrel horse named Superman started bucking with Tom Reeder. Tom couldn't ride a stick horse if it started bucking, and within two or three jumps, he was on the ground and not getting up very fast.

Somebody ran and caught Superman, and I rode over to Tom and inquired about his health. He was up but listing to the left pretty bad, holding his left arm, and his glasses were resting crooked on his nose. Tom was stuttering real bad and was having a hard time communicating, so we all pulled up and waited for him to get his air and figure out if he was going to live or die. Sometimes it's best to let the injured assess the situation, so we waited.

I had known Tom for years and I liked him. I looked at him now after being bucked off, and it didn't take me long to figure out he was sure-enough hurt. I got my Dodge diesel pickup and loaded him into it, and for the second time in three or four hours, I had a man headed to the hospital in Flagstaff. Only this time, I would make the delivery.

To my knowledge cell phones had not been introduced to the cowboy world, so I got on the two-way radio and told the manager I was headed to town with another injured man. While sitting at the Copper Cart Café in town gossiping, he had already told people I was hard to work for, and now he didn't sound happy, as if it was my fault. I didn't care, I was getting the cow work done, and all he was good for was answering the telephone, so I drove to the hospital.

About seven o'clock that night the doctor informed Tom that his shoulder and collarbone were broken, and he bandaged him up real well, and gave him a large prescription of pain medicine, and sent us on our way, telling us that Tom needed to stay immobile for a month or so, and his shoulder would heal in time.

Tom preferred painkiller that could be bought in a liquor store, so we purchased a supply of that along with the Percocet. While Tom was in the store acquiring these items, I communicated, via radio, with the manager and learned that Barney had been air-vaced to Barrow's Neurological Center in Phoenix and had been put on life-support in an intensive care unit. Pat and Debbie, his mother, were in route to Phoenix to be with him. The manager also informed me that he had hired two new hands, and they were spending the night in the guest house adjacent to my home in Seligman. I was supposed to take them to the wagon in the morning. Perhaps he thought they could replace Pat, Barney, and Tom.

Tom and I got to Seligman in time to catch a couple hours sleep, and then at 3:00 a.m., I got up and roused Tom and the new additions to my crew. One of these was a boy named Jessie who claimed to be eighteen years old. In fact, I learned later that he was fifteen and had just run away from home, which was somewhere east of Arizona. Jessie was a nice looking boy and was very quiet and polite. He was obviously under considerable stress, trying to act both knowledgeable and brave. The other man was named Eric, and he was proud of his nineteen years on this earth and didn't mind telling you so. He stood about six feet three inches and weighted two hundred pounds, opposed to Jessie's five feet three inches and one hundred forty pounds. Eric's hair was the color of carrots, and the bone above his eyebrows was at least an inch thick. Before the day was over, the cowboys, waiting for us at Hazen Hole, had nicknamed him Eric the Viking. We all loaded up in my pickup and headed north to the wagon, which by the road was some sixty miles or so distance. The doctor had ordered Tom Reeder to go home and rest, and beings his teepee was the only home he had, he went with us.

We got to the wagon about 5:00 a.m., and I introduced the new boys to the crew, who were all up drinking coffee; Jessie disappeared into a shadowy corner of the cook tent and said nothing, while the Viking made his presence known by dragging his size thirteen boots on the dirt floor, stirring up enough dust to choke everyone until they all went outside, except the cook who was frying breakfast and therefore held captive and getting madder by the minute.

As soon as we ate breakfast, someone wrangled horses so I could catch Jessie and the Viking something to ride. The crew had caught horses the night before but did not know that two new men were coming. I had only been wagon boss since the October before, and there were still some horses I didn't know, so I asked everyone if they knew of an extra horse that was sure enough gentle to mount Jessie on. Everyone on the crew was as new as myself, with the exception of Pat Prosser, who was in Phoenix, and Truman Rustin who had worked for the outfit off and on for years, so I relied on Truman's advice.

Truman was sixty years old with wavy silver hair and sparkling blue eyes. He resembled the movie star Richard Farnsworth. He was always clean shaven and neatly dressed, in spite of the primitive living conditions, and knew how to set his hat at the perfect angle in order to accentuate his virile profile. He was a lady's man, and of late had been visited by a certain good looking nurse from Prescott named Connie. He told everyone they were married, although that proved to be untrue. My wife met Connie, who was a very nice lady. One day the telephone rang at our home and my wife answered. A female voice on the other end said, "Hello, I am Truman Rustin's wife, and I would like to get a message to Truman, if that is possible."

My wife responded, "Hello, Connie, this is Jean Ann."

The phone went quiet for a long time and finally the voice asked, "Who is Connie?"

Truman believed in the old adage, "To thine own self be true." and his loyalties ended there. When I asked him about a gentle horse, he pointed out an old bay gelding named Teddy. He claimed that Elmer McDonald, who was a very good hand, but recently retired, had ridden him for years. He guaranteed me he was gentle, so I caught him.

For Eric the Viking, I roped a big glass-eyed paint named Patches. Patches had spent some time in a bucking string, but supposedly had quit bucking, but was a little hard to get on. The Viking assured me that he could mount anything that had hair, but as he put his bridle on him, I advised him to ease up on him and keep his spurs out of him. I turned my attention back to Jessie who seemed to be having trouble getting the kid horse bridled and saddled. For a saddle, he had an old flower-carved antique with a Bob Crosby tree and round skirts that was probably made in the 1940s. But his bridle was brand new, having a chrome-plated bit with JAPAN stamped on it. At first I couldn't figure out what was wrong and then realized that the reins were connected to the headstall end of the bit, and the headstall was connected to the reins end. The curb strap was upside down and attached to the wrong end. I ran to my truck and got some pliers and began tearing the bridle apart so I could reassemble it correctly, and while my back was turned, I heard a thunderous fart and turned around in time to see the Viking being launched into the stratosphere by Patches, the ex-bucking horse. The Viking's one point landing measured 5.5 on the Richter scale.

It was getting light, and I was getting mad knowing that the sun would come up and find me and my crew still in camp, a fact I did not appreciate. I noticed Floyd Martin, the cook, and Charlie, the Indian horse wrangler, standing outside the cook tent observing the goings on. The cook was slapping his leg and laughing hysterically, while the Indian was staring with typical Indian stoicism, wondering how a bunch of white skins who were so stupid could have possibly killed all the buffalo. I got Jessie's bridle straightened out and helped him get saddled up, assuring him that old Teddy was gentle. "Just get on and wait for the rest of us to get mounted, and we'll go gather some cows," I told him, trying to be friendly because I liked the little runaway who looked like Chris Shivers, the famous bull rider. I turned around to give Eric some riding instructions and realized I hadn't even gotten saddled. About the time I threw a blanket on my own horse's back, I heard a scream and turned to see Jessie hit the ground shoulder first and witnessed Teddy jumping and kicking through the community of teepee tents. I thought to myself, I swear I'm going to castrate that old silver-haired lady's man!

As someone ran and caught Teddy and another went and counseled the little runaway, I got saddled and witnessed the second launching of Eric the Fearless. The cook now lay in the dirt laughing, and Kawliga simply stared in amazement. I called a universal time-out and instructed Jessie and Eric to lead Teddy and Patches through the gate and not mount up until I gave them further instructions.

I led my horse through the gate and called Truman aside and, in a quiet voice, told him I was going to beat him until blood ran out of his ears if Teddy bucked with the runaway again. "When he gets on, you get a hold of his bridle reins and lead him around like he is your grandson, but whatever happens, don't let him get bucked off again!" He was mad but gave me a slight nod to the affirmative. I turned to the redhead with lots of bone in his forehead and told him to keep his spurs out of Patches. "We've got lots of work to do, and I don't have time for you to learn how to ride!" I insisted. The sun was now up, and though I was in a hurry, Patches had decided he was not going to cooperate. Eric the Viking had bravado but, certainly, no horsemanship skills, and Patches wouldn't stand still long enough for the clumsy redhead to get on. I asked Randy Rutledge to hand me his catch rope, which I put around Patches' front feet and instructed him to dally up and jerk Patches on his side when he tried to step away from Eric. I explained to Eric what was going to happen, telling him to act like he was going to mount up, and when the horse tried to whirl away, to just get out of the way while Randy laid him down. An application or two of that, and the outlaw would stand still.

We laid ole Patches out a couple times, and then I hobbled him with my pigging string, and I took Randy's rope off his front legs. I told Eric I was going to stand by Patches' head and hold on to the bridle reins while he mounted. I further explained that once he was mounted, I would reach down and unhobble the horse. Before proceeding any further, I explained in great detail that if he would get on, and hold his reins tight with his left hand, and hold the saddle horn with his right hand, and simply stand up in his stirrups, keeping his spurs out of Patches' belly, that the old horse would gladly walk off without trying to buck. I leaned forward until our eyes were only fourteen inches apart and said very clearly, "Eric, do you understand?" He assured me that he did. Right before I leaned over to untie the hobbles on Patches' front legs, I notice Jessie mounted on Teddy a few feet away. He was crying, and Truman's blue eyes were sparkling. The

Viking stepped onto the old paint horse's back as I held the bridle reins. "Are you all right?" I asked the redhead. "Remember, keep your spurs out of him; just stand up in your stirrups and let him walk off!" I leaned over and took my pigging string off of Patches' legs, and then the Viking threw his right hand up to the sun and lifted both legs bringing them down with toes turned out in a spurring motion that brought another large expulsion of gas from the backside of the paint horse, and within two jumps, Eric was slammed face-first into the middle of a hard dirt road.

This time he began to scream as if someone was skinning him alive starting at his scrotum. He lay on the ground and rolled over and over, wailing in agony, holding his stomach one second and his head the next. I had had enough of Eric and hoped he would die. To say I gave him a cussing would have been an understatement! I leaned over his writhing form and told him in great detail what I thought of his actions and, in very descriptive language, told him how stupid he was. And then suddenly, as I stood over him hoping we could soon have his funeral, he jumped up as if ready to run back to the line of scrimmage. He faced me, and with a great show of exclamation, he folded his arms, and threw back his head at a haughty angle, and loudly proclaimed to everyone present, "Well, I'm just an old boy trying to make a living!!!"

I stood in utter consternation! I was speechless. I was so completely taken aback after that performance that my mind went blank for a while, and I don't remember exactly what happened for fifteen or twenty minutes. Somehow or another we all got mounted, there were about fourteen of us, and started trotting west to where I wanted to start my drive. Clarity of mind came back when we were at the top of a hill, a mile or so southwest of camp. I looked back and realized that Jessie was a quarter mile behind and having a hard time keeping up. I asked, even pleaded with, Truman to take care of him and not let him get hurt. I sent half the crew with Randy, including Eric, whom I was sick of; and I took the other half, going north; and we began making a drive toward Number Nine, three or four miles away. I left Truman and Jessie in the middle.

Our morning gathering went well, and we managed to gather three or four hundred cows, and as they went through a gate into Lower Sandstone Pasture, we paired them out, making sure each cow had her calf with her and turning back those that were not straight. We did this as they were strung out and moving and managed to make fast work of it.

As the last cow went through the gate, I asked Truman where Jessie was. "Oh, he's all right," Truman replied. "He just doesn't know how to ride and he's moving slow." I looked out in the direction Jessie should be coming from and saw a horse and rider coming a quarter mile away. We started loping that way and soon came upon the runaway, who was riding humped over and leaning over the saddle horn. "Are you all right, Jessie?" I asked as I rode up next to him. His hat was pulled down on his forehead, and added to that fact, he was leaning forward; I could not see his eyes. He did not reply. "Jessie, are you all right?" I demanded. He didn't reply, and I leaned over trying to look into his face that he lowered even farther. I thought I detected a faint whimper. "Jessie, you need to talk to me, or I'm going to slap the crap out of you," I shouted! And with that, he slid off the right side of the horse and landed in a fetal position on the ground.

Holy smoke, I've killed the kid, I thought to myself, and jumped to the ground, and hovered over him trying to figure out if he was dying or crying. I asked questions, and he wouldn't speak. I could tell he was breathing but could not tell if he was conscious. "Jessie, talk to me!" I pleaded. I sat down on the ground, and picked the boy up in my arms, and held him like a baby. "Jessie, tell me, where are you hurt?" He wouldn't utter a sound with the exception of the occasional whimper. I finally resorted to threats of physical violence if he didn't start talking, which seemed to be the only thing that made him act rationally. I finally got him to say that he had a deep, agonizing pain in his abdomen.

About that time, Floyd, and Charlie, showed up in my Dodge pickup. Floyd had asked me that morning if he could use my pickup to go to Rose Well and get a couple of barrels of water for the wagon, and while he was there, he and Charlie could take a shower in the Rose Well bunkhouse. They were returning to camp, and when they stopped to see what was going on, I loaded Jessie and myself. When we got to camp, I unloaded the water, the cook, and the horse wrangler; and Jessie and I headed west toward Flagstaff and the hospital, some one hundred miles distance. For the third time in less than twenty-four hours, a man on my crew was headed to the doctor. Wow, I thought, what a rough outfit!

Going west from Hazen Hole, we passed through the Redlands Camp on Babbitts' W Triangle Ranch and traveled over at least forty-five miles of poorly maintained dirt roads before reaching the highway. Jessie curled up and lay tight against the passenger door, refusing to communicate. Every time I passed over a large rock or bump, he let go of a bloodcurdling scream that raised the hair on the back of my neck. I did not know if I should drive fast or slow, so I drove fast. The only time the boy responded to a question was when I asked him if he was dying, to which he offered a very faint, "Yes, I think so." I wasn't sure.

Around 1:00 p.m. I pulled up to the emergency room door of the Flagstaff hospital and ran in and announced that I had possession of a dying boy. Several minutes later I sat exhausted in the waiting room contemplating the romance of being the wagon boss on the biggest outfit in Arizona. I wondered why Bill Owen didn't paint a picture of me dressed in my cowboy regalia as I sat in a Naugahyde chair reading "Redbook" and calculating how much cannon fodder I had left to feed to the enemy as we charged forward.

Several hours later, a doctor in a white gown came out leading Jessie, who was moving. I saw no bandages. "How is he," I inquired?

The doctor pulled me aside and talked in a low voice, "He's fine."

"What? You didn't have to operate or something? No internal bleeding?"

"No, he's just pretty shook up and a little bruised, but he's going to be fine." The doctor turned around and disappeared into the bowels of the new building that was being financed by industrial compensation insurance.

We headed back to camp taking the same route back through Kendrick Park, Valle, and Redlands. I wondered how I should handle this situation, thinking my batting average had slipped several digits in the last two days.

The next morning we ate breakfast an hour before sunup, and after consuming lots of black coffee, I started out of the cook tent toward the corral where we had a fresh mount of horses waiting. I eased toward Jessie and told him I needed to talk to him in private. "Jessie, I need you to stay here and hood for the cook." I told him quietly.

"What's 'hood for the cook' mean," he asked?

"That means help the cook, like wash the dishes, and chop wood, and pack water, that sort of thing," I replied. I liked the kid, and if he wanted to run away from home, that was none of my business, but I didn't want to get him killed.

"I quit!" Jessi answered defiantly.

"What in the world are you quitting for?" I demanded.

"I am way too good a hand to be a hood!"

ഏരു
Trailing to Shafer
ഏരു

Diamond A Ranch, May 1993

On the east boundary of the Diamond A straight west of the SP Camp on the Babbitt Ranch was a pasture called Shafer, about a perfect township in size, and part of what was called the top country. It was a little rougher than most of the ranch, covered with brush, and filled with juniper and pinion trees. Because of its position in comparison to the rest of the ranch, it was the least accessible pasture, especially when trying to trail cattle in and out of it. Shafer was easiest to get into or out of with a herd of cattle by the northern route, coming from the direction of Farm Dam and a piece of country called Lower Sandstone. Starting at Rose Well and going east through Lower Sandstone to Farm Dam and then turning south through the Black Tank Mare Pasture, it was twenty miles. When I had worked at the Diamond A in the early seventies, there were several good pasture fences as well as several good corrals in that twenty mile stretch. When I went back to run the wagon in 1992, all the infrastructure had fallen down. From the northern boundary fence of the Shafer Pasture to the Broken Axle fence straight north was almost twenty-five miles and there wasn't a fence that would turn a milk cow that wanted to get to the other side.

Shafer had already been worked when I went to work there in October of '92, and supposedly it was clean with the exception of some remnant. There were rumors of a herd of old wild steers that no one had been able to gather. Several years earlier the ranch had hired a helicopter to gather the steers, but the venture had been unsuccessful. I hadn't been there to know what happened but was told that no one had really made an effort to stock the pasture in years. Instead, they would open the gates and let cattle drift in there as they pleased, but they never really knew how many were there. I also got the impression no one worried about gathering it too clean in the fall. I planned on changing that, but in the spring of '93, I wasn't sure how I could get it done, but I planned on trying.

There was a large herd of cattle that had accumulated in Lower Sandstone, some of which were remnant not accounted for the fall before. We gathered them, starting at Number Six a couple miles east of Rose Well, and drove east toward Farm Dam eight miles away. There were also two pastures west of Farm Dam: one called the Corner Pasture and one called the Farm Dam Horse Pasture. The fences on these pastures had been allowed to fall down so we gathered them also. Our drive took in close to fifty sections. We threw our roundup together south of Farm Dam a mile or so. I wanted to take nothing but cows and unbranded calves on south to Shafer, so we needed to cut out all the dry cows and turn them back north toward Farm Dam. The wind was screaming bloody murder, probably fifty miles an hour. There were fifteen of us altogether, so we had enough men to have two men cutting dry cows out of the herd at the same time. As we cut them, we just turned them loose and made them drift back to the north. We cut, and we cut, and we cut. The wind screamed, and everyone suffered from the blowing dirt. Randy Rutledge, who was a good hand, cut a dry cow out by my youngest son, Clay, and said, "I just had a vision!" Clay asked him what the vision was, and he replied. "This is hell and we're never going to run out of dry cows."

We threw the herd of cows and calves that were left, south, toward Black Tank, hoping to pick them up and move on to Shafer the next day. There was an old fence to keep the two herds separated, but it was falling down in a lot of places, so we put several miles distance in between the cows with calves and the dry cows that we had cut out; doing this before we went back to camp for the night. We were camped at Rose Well.

The next morning we made a drive starting south of Farm Dam and going south toward Black Tank. We throwed a roundup together close to the Black Tank Mare Pasture fence about a mile east of the camp house at Black Tank. We still had too many cattle, so we cut out some more dry cows and anything that looked like it couldn't make the trip on to Shafer. We needed to brand the calves in our herd when we got there, but there was no corral left in the thirty-six square mile pasture, and we were going to have to brand outside. Branding outside without the help of a corral was a lot more time consuming, so I wanted to keep the herd down to a maximum of two hundred fifty calves.

We got the herd trimmed down to the right size and drove them through a gate into the south side of the Mare Pasture fence and turned them loose. The cook showed up in a pickup with a lunch about the time we got this done, probably about noon, so we hobbled our horses and unsaddled them and ate while the herd of cattle grazed.

The cattle were what cowboys call "sticky," meaning they weren't wanting to move. They were all in fine shape but had been driven, worked, and sorted on for two days and were sick of being messed with. None of them had ever been driven up this way and were unfamiliar with the trail, and I wondered if we could get it done. I had doubts and was second guessing my decision to even try doing it.

I mentioned my concern to Jim Marler, who I considered to be a good hand and someone I would listen to. He suggested we leave the cattle where they were, in the Mare Pasture, overnight. He thought we should stand guard along the fence we had just put them through and perhaps build a fire every hundred yards or so to keep the cattle from busting through the sorry fence and going back to the north.

If we could get the herd of cows and calves strung out and walking, we could make it to our destination easy and make it back to camp before sundown. I knew that some of the men who had been working for the outfit for several years were grumbling about trailing a herd into Shafer from this direction for the simple reason they hadn't seen it done before. For several of the men, the simple fact that the idea was mine was reason enough to not like it. I also knew that no one, including me, wanted to spend the night right where we were. There was no guarantee it would be any better the next morning. I decided to go on.

We rested ourselves for ten or fifteen minutes after eating our lunch. As the cook got in the pickup to drive back to camp, I told him we would see him at suppertime. I hoped that wouldn't be midnight. After our short rest, we got back on our horses and started bunching up the cattle and trying to get them strung out and walking. We had two hundred fifty cows, almost all of which had calves, plus about forty bulls. It was now around one in the afternoon and pretty warm. The calves had all sucked and were uninterested in their mothers. The cows wanted to go to water, which in their minds was to the north, and they were not interested in their babies or in walking uphill to the south. The bulls were interested in the cows, which created more havoc. After ten minutes we had gone a hundred yards. We had four miles to go and we were getting nowhere fast. The crew was putting out no effort with the exception of two or three men. We were dead in the water.

I had seen Bill Howell do several things that at the time he was doing them looked totally outrageous, but he would somehow make them work. It was evident that if some drastic change didn't take place, this attempt at putting a herd into Shafer in this manner was going to fail. I had to try something. The cattle were strung out for about three hundred yards, but most of them were just standing still. I was in the drags. Without telling anyone what I was doing, I whipped my horse into a dead run and ran right up through the middle of the herd screaming and popping my shotgun chaps with my bridle reins. When I reached the front end of the herd, I turned around and headed back down through the herd toward the drags zigzagging from one side of the herd to the other screaming and slapping my chaps as I went.

At first the entire crew stopped and stared at me convinced that I had finally lost my mind. I think it crossed the minds of several of them that I might have a gun hidden and be planning to start shooting people. Their eyes bulged at my antics. Several men were laughing. The cows started bawling and looking for their calves. They, too, were shocked at my outrageous behavior. I started up through the herd a second time trying my darndest to be louder and crazier than the first time. Men started whipping and hollering at the flank of the herd and things started moving. As I made my way back to the drags a second time, the entire herd was moving, most of the cattle being paired up. Some of them were even trotting. The men, at least some of them, acted nervous, like they were working with someone who was dangerous. I returned to my place in the drags and told the cowboys on both sides of me to leave the drags to me alone and to get around on the side of the herd, and whip on the flank of the herd, and try and keep them moving. The cattle strung out and kept walking about two miles an hour, and we made it to the north Shafer fence by 3:15 p.m. We trailed the herd on another mile to a dirt tank called Indian Tank and turned them loose for the night. We made it back to camp and caught fresh horses for the following day and were eating supper a few minutes before sundown.

The next morning we were back at Indian Tank when the sun came up. We had turned the cattle loose in a pasture of thirty-six square miles, but it was a good spring, and there was lots of fresh green foxtail about four to six inches high; add that to the fact the cattle were tired when we turned them loose: they didn't scatter very far. We made a drive covering about four sections in the northeast corner of Shafer and gathered ninety-five percent of the cattle we had trailed in there the day before. We threw the herd up on the side of a small rocky hillside, hoping the rocky ground would help hold them still, and set up our branding outfit on the downhill side. We had enough men to hold the herd horseback, and about four of us worked on the ground: flanking, branding, vaccinating, etc. I put two men in the herd roping the calves around the neck and dragging them bouncing to the fire. We rotated every fifty calves or so giving everyone the opportunity to flank, hold the herd, or brand. No one had to work too hard, and we branded two hundred twenty-seven calves in about three and a half hours. Not bad for having no corral. Actually there wasn't a corral left standing anywhere in the vicinity; the closest one being at Keseha, ten or twelve miles to the west. They had all fallen down in the twenty years prior to that day.

ℰꙦ
Good Ones Like Dob and Bad Ones Like Blue Feathers
ℰꙦ

Diamond A Ranch, Early 1950s

Dob Ernest came from Texas during the Second Great War. No doubt Dob was a fighting man because he was born with a cleft palate that caused his speech to be severely abnormal, and though somewhat stocky and rugged looking, he suffered because of various health problems. He possessed a lower jaw that jutted forward in a perpetual, "Get out of my way, I'm coming through," attitude that defied all comers. The U.S. Army didn't take men they classify as sickly, but had they taken Dob and a few others like him, the war might have ended a year earlier. Dob learned to defend his deformities early on and never weakened. Dob would show up and work at the 3Vs, or Diamond A as it was later called, maybe staying for several years, and would then go back to West Texas and work for the famous Texas cowman Foy Procter, and then he would return, and ended up going back and forth several times.

Tom Dolan was always known as a top hand who was at home with rough men but had the rare quality of never losing his soft and humorous side. Tom liked people and Dob was no exception, and Dob probably sensed that his weak and vulnerable side was safe in Tom's presence. Tom could laugh at people's oddities without offending them. He didn't look down on people.

Tom and his family were living at Pica Camp, twenty miles west of Seligman, and Dob was living in the small bunkhouse that stood fifty yards south of Tom's house. Dob was eating his meals with Tom and his family and showed up early one morning as Tom sat at the kitchen table smoking cigarettes and drinking coffee, while Ruth Dolan cooked breakfast.

"Tahm, shumone shewed up on a horse laast night and caime inda bunkhowse and weentta bed, and hee's

over thdere ashleep rieght now!" Dob blurted out as he sat down.

Tom looked at Dob and wondered whom it might be riding through the country horseback. The only cowboy

Tom could think of that was traveling that way on a steady basis was Pete Keenan. (Pete was a good cowboy who was struck and killed by lightning at the K4 Ranch, forty miles south of Seligman, not many years after that.) Tom looked at Dob and asked, "So who is he?"

"I don know who e is."

"Well, who does he look like, Dob?"

Dob sat in his chair for a while contemplating the visage of the midnight intruder who lay in slumber fifty yards away. "Well, I think he looks like an ole heela monshter, I guess!"

ഏറെ

In those days the Diamond A had its share of rank horses, one of which had the name of Blue Feathers. Blue Feathers was part Percheron and was a stout bucker, the type most men would just as soon avoid. Tom Dolan was running the wagon, and Blue Feathers was among the extras, not being in anyone's string. One day Dob, who had never been a great bronc rider, told Tom he wanted to trade for the outlaw horse. Tom wasn't one to interfere in another man's business, so he approved of the horse trade even though he doubted Dob could ride one side of ole Blue Feathers. The wagon crew was working north of Rose Well, seven miles, and was going to change horses at noon. Tom was roping, and about the time he started to catch the first horse, Dob took the bridle off the horse he had been riding all morning and announced rather loudly, "Ketch me ole Blue Feathers, Tom, and ketch him right now!" Tom roped Blue Feathers and led him out, and then Dob hung his bridle on the outlaw's head and jerked Tom's rope off and stomped over to his saddle with Blue Feathers in tow. Tom continued catching horses for the rest of the crew, but before he could finish, Blue Feathers

had bucked Dob off three times. After the third trip to the earth, Dob unsaddled Blue Feathers and led him back into the rope corral and quietly said to Tom, "Ketch me ole Heavy, I guess." He never got on ole Blue Feathers again.

Dob suffered from a condition he referred to as dropsy. Perhaps he had diabetes, and quite possibly he didn't even know what he had. Men like Dob weren't prone to seek medical help or follow the doctor's orders should they be privy to such a thing. He retained water, especially in his hands and feet. The condition worsened as he grew older, and at times he suffered miserably. Periodically, when he was suffering the most, he would leave his cowboy boots on for days, fearing he would never get them back on if he took them off. In spite of all his frailty and deformities, he was no slacker. Not being able to work and make a hand was probably the only thing he ever feared. Finally the swelling and pain got so bad he weakened. He went back to Texas, his kidneys failing and night closing in. He was a good one.

℘℘℘

Diamond A Ranch, Fall 1992

When I moved to the Diamond A in the middle of the fall roundup, there was a cowboy working with the wagon named Randy Rutledge. Randy and I worked together several years earlier at Babbitts where he went through a spring roundup. He was a wiry hundred and sixty-pounder that was as tough as a sixteen-penny nail and wasn't afraid to be his own man, which is a nice way to say he didn't care what anyone else thought. Randy broke lots of horses in a variety of settings, including a spell as an assistant to Pat Perelli. He traveled to Australia with Mr. Perelli, assisting him in the production of horse-breaking clinics. While in Australia, he left Perelli's organization, and put on some clinics of his own, and also worked on a big ranch or two. Later on he had the opportunity to spend some time with Tom Dorrance.

Randy had a horse in his string that was five or six years old that was a really good looking bald-faced red dun. He called him Dill. I noticed that Randy rode Dill more than any of his other horses, sometimes to the point of blatant persecution. He mentioned to me that Dill had an attitude and worked best if he was used hard. He rode him with a tight rein on one end and a very sharp spur rowel on the other. He could and would do anything on Dill, including rope big heavy cattle, and always seemed to have the dun horse in control, even if it was of the heavy-handed variety.

When the wagon pulled in that fall, Randy stayed on, and I camped him at Pica where he started about fifteen colts during the winter. I liked Randy's style of colt-starting because when he got done with one the horse knew what a man on his back was. He never tried to sneak a ride on a colt. He started a dirty-gray five-year-old he named

Powder Face that I took when he was through with him, and I rode him the whole time I was there and I liked him.

Another colt he started was a freakish-looking little bay mustang, which he named El Capitan, that had come off a neighboring ranch. El Capitan never grew to be fourteen hands high but was an inch or more under. He had a big hatchet-shaped head, which might have been as big as his stomach, that was perched at a high angle at the end of an abnormally short neck. He had high withers, probably the only perfect aspect of his confirmation. His belly was large, probably too large for his short-bodied length, and came to an end with a hindquarters no better looking than any mediocre Mexican mule you ever saw. The most impressive thing you noticed from a view at his south side was his tail, which was full and drug the ground. A great ranch with a reputable horse program like the Four Sixes would have shot him at birth and buried him in the middle of the night in hopes the neighbors or media personnel never got a chance to lay eyes on him.

Beings El Capitan was among the oldest of the broncs he had to start, Randy started him and Powder Face early in the winter. I talked to Randy on a regular basis and asked him how his colts were doing, and before too long, he was bragging on El Capitan, telling me what a great horse he was. At first I just laughed, thinking surely he was pulling my leg. I couldn't imagine a good cowboy liking such a grotesque looking specimen. By the time February rolled around, Randy was using El Capitan to rope and snub the younger broncs on, giving poor old Dill an occasional day off. As spring grew closer, El Capitan obtained a spiritual presence similar to a revolutionary general in a banana republic. He always caused a vision of Pancho Villa to come to my mind. Randy would mount him and ride off with his spurs no more than twenty inches off the ground, and the "Captain" would stick his hatchet head upwards, with his nose tucked, and prance off ready to do battle with whomever wanted to mix it up. He had presence.

Randy worked all winter starting colts and stayed through the spring roundup, which started the 1st of April and lasted until the 1st of July. He had told me when we started branding calves early in the spring that he was going to leave when the spring branding wagon was over. Randy was a hard worker, tough as a cedar knot, and very loyal to me; I hated to see him go. Truman Rustin had been watching Randy ride Dill for two roundups, making the horse look dependable all the time, with the horse never showing any outlaw traits. Beings he knew Randy was leaving, he asked me months in advance if I would put Dill in his string when the fall wagon pulled out after Labor Day weekend; and I promised him I would.

ℴℴ

The fall of '93, we pulled out the day after Labor Day and set up a camp at I Tub in Reed Cashion Pasture. I Tub lay in a side canyon close to the main Chino Wash drainage, six or seven miles north of Hoffman Camp and Seligman. We worked for several days shoeing the remuda. El Capitan was an extra in the remuda, and nobody was asking for the ugly hatchet head, even though Randy repeatedly bragged about what a good son of a gun he was. I put him in the string of a new cowboy whose name was Rick George.

After sundown on the second day we were camped at I Tub, I walked one hundred fifty yards away from the wagon to a water lot and a big thousand gallon water trough. The water was clear and clean looking, and I planned on washing my hands and face and was packing a towel with me. We had to haul clean camp water for the wagon, and with a big crew, we would go through a lot of water, and I was trying to cut down on the water hauling chore. I hadn't noticed Jimmer Fancher and Cody Cochran sitting off in the distance enjoying a friendly storytelling session. I rolled up the sleeves of my shirt and cupped my hands, splashing water on my face. "Ed, wait! ED, STOP, STOP!" I looked up and saw Jimmer and Cody running toward me saying, "Don't wash in that trough. Truman just came down here thinking no one would see him and dunked his bare hind end in there and washed his hemorrhoids!"

"PPPsssssssTTTT!" I went to spitting and coughing. I'm going to kill that old coyote, I thought to myself. The amount of humor Jimmer and Cody enjoyed at my expense made me wonder if it was quick thinking, rather than slow reactions, that made them let me get started washing before they stopped me.

The first day we actually gathered any cattle that fall, we made several drives in the south half of Reed Cashion Pasture, using a holdup for padding and moving it to several locations, making drives into it, accumulating a larger herd with each drive. Finally, when it got close to noon, we ended up near a big dirt tank called Quarry Tank in the bottom of Chino Wash, and very close to the Thirty-Six Pasture's northern boundary. We had about two hundred head of cattle gathered. I had told Charlie to trail the remuda down there and day-herd it until we got there. (The horse pasture at I Tub wasn't very big and I figured the feed might be getting a little short, and it would be a good chance for the horses to graze elsewhere; and besides the old Indian needed something to keep his mind occupied.) The cook, Al Smith, was also going to show up with some lunch; and when he appeared, we took turns holding the herd and swapping off with someone to grab a quick bite of groceries.

After everyone got a chance to eat something, we used the same rotation system to catch ourselves a fresh horse to ride all afternoon. As the cook drove back to the north toward camp, I started catching horses. When a man got a fresh one, he would saddle up and lope out to the herd and trade with another cowboy who would lope in, unsaddle, turn his tired horse loose into the bunch, and tell me which horse in his string he wanted to ride that afternoon. Two of the last men to come in and change horses were Truman and Rick George. Truman called for Dill and Rick called for El Capitan; neither man had been on his horse before, and like most of the other horses in the remuda, they had been turned out all summer and were fat and fresh. I caught my horse last, and then Charlie Wascogamie started the remuda north, up the creek, following the tracks of the cook.

I was just pulling the latigo tight on my front cinch when Truman and Rick stepped on their horses almost simultaneously. I was not expecting anything to happen with Rick and El Capitan; but I suspected Truman had misjudged Dill, and I would never have put the horse in his string if he hadn't begged me to do so. As I buckled my flank cinch, I watched Truman, who was sixty years old, lead Dill down into the creek bottom, amidst a pile of smooth river rocks the size of basketballs, and mount up. From seventy feet away, I could tell the red dun horse was as tight as the rawhide on an Indian's tom-tom. He took a step or two and literally exploded. Poor Truman never knew what hit him, and he came off hard the first jump and landed on his hands and knees in the boulder pile. There wasn't any one of Dill's four feet closer to the ground than three feet, and the second jump, the horse turned his neck completely around, and his eyes, which had turned red, looked straight at Truman; and with his left hind foot, he let loose with a kick that came within an inch of slicing Truman's head off like a razor.

While all this was going on, Rick George had stepped on El Capitan off to my right, and the little potbellied hatchet head had took to him bucking and crashing into

some juniper trees. I was too busy to see much of El
Capitan's tirade as I was trying to watch the mutilation
of poor old Truman. But a second after Dill's attempt to
decapitate the silver-headed ole rounder, I heard a great
sound of juniper limbs breaking as the Captain crashed
through a thicket with Rick's saddle horn hanging up on
the limbs as the horse bucked forward. Rick was already
on the ground. Truman, in spite of his age, got right up
and dusted himself off, but I could see he had a mighty
worried look in his old Sinatra-blue eyes. I walked over
to Rick who had leaned himself up against the trunk of a
tree. "Are you all right?" I asked.

"I think I'm going blind, I can't see very good."

"You think you're going blind?" I was hoping for more
details.

"My eyes are kinda' cloudy, like they are not focusing
right."

"Okay. Sit there and take it easy while we catch your
horse. I got on my horse and loped off to catch El Capitan
who had stopped a hundred yards away. Cody Cochran
had caught Dill for Truman and was offering to trade
horses with the old man, who didn't have to think about it
very long to accept the offer.

El Capitan was pretty proud of himself, having
scratched up Rick's saddle, and broken one of his bridle
reins. Rick remained seated on his pockets in the dirt with
his back against a tree trunk. "You feelin' better?"

"I don't feel too bad, but my eyes are fuzzy. I can't see
real good, like everything's still fussy."

We were a long ways from the wagon, at least three
miles, and had a couple hundred head of cows we needed
to get moved before sundown; so I hoped Rick's eyes
would start working soon. He looked all right to me.

"How about we trade horses? My horse is gentle; you
can ride him, and I'll ride El Capitan this afternoon. Maybe
your eyes will get all right if you just poke along."

"Okay, I'll give it a try." Rick agreed. So we proceeded to change saddles and horses. I got on El Capitan and whipped him down a hind leg, and he bogged his head and stirred up some dust for a second or two. At one point, I'm sure all four of his feet were three inches off the ground: a lot of show and noise, but no real action. Finally we were all mounted with Rick on my horse, Cody Cochran on Dill, and me riding El Capitan. (I'll have to say that the little hatchet head was a neat feeling little horse, very quick on his feet; and in spite of his smallness, you felt like you were horseback.) After ten minutes, Rick said his eyes were almost normal.

Dill got passed around that fall, Truman didn't want any part of him after the first go-round so Cody Cochran rode him for a while, and got along with him, but didn't really like him. Another cowboy named Cody Dinsmore traded for him and rode him most of the fall. Cody Dinsmore was a pretty good bronc rider and could ride Dill when he bucked, but he didn't like the dun horse either and grew weary him. The horse seemed to get sourer and sourer.

That winter when we got caught up on the cow work, we put Dill in a bucking chute that I had erected in the roping arena at Pica. Everett was winning the bronc riding in the Arizona High School Rodeo Association and always wanted some practice. When the chute gate opened, old Dill blew out of there like an atom bomb, and for about four jumps, he bucked as wild as anything I ever saw. There was no part of his body closer to the ground than four feet each jump. He didn't really kick high behind, but got incredible altitude, twisting and sunfishing; and then on the fifth jump, he turned his head back and looked Everett square in the face unlike any move I ever saw a horse make except when he did the same thing, honing in on Truman's head just before he tried to slice it off with a hind foot. (I'll swear his eyes were red when he turned his head back like that.) When he looked back to the left it threw a lot of slack in the bronc rein, which Everett held in his left hand. With nothing to lift on, the cowboy came off. We loaded Dill in the chute a second time, and he made an identical trip with Everett riding him five jumps.

After that initiation as a rodeo horse, Dill was hauled to a half dozen rodeos in the next year, and he bucked some kids off but seemed to get weaker every trip. In December 1994, he was hauled to the bucking horse sale in Las Vegas that was held during the National Finals Rodeo. He was bucked there at the sale and made about an eighteen point trip, and Cotton Rosser bought him. A year later, we heard through the grapevine that after being bucked at a half dozen rodeos, good old Dill quit bucking altogether. He just didn't want to be worth a darn for anything. I always thought that maybe Randy Rutledge might have been a better hand than anyone thought. He was the only man that got any use out of Dill.

El Capitan's fame rose, although slowly at first. Rick George rode the old hatchet head a few times that fall but never said much about him. A year later a good young cowboy named Scott Westlake came to work, and I gave Capitan to him. From the start, he loved him and babied the hatchet-headed freak like he was Cutter Bill or Smart Little Lena. Scott still talks about the horse to this day and always with affection. You can't always tell a horse or a man by looking at them. Come to think about it, El Capitan kinda' looked like an old "Gila monster."

Mike Landis

Mike Landis ran the wagon at the Diamond A for four years. The last roundup for which he was wagon boss was in the fall of 1973. I worked for Mike the falls of '72 and '73, and he was always very good to me.

Mike was raised in Kansas on a farm by what he called "stern" parents who believed in hard work as well as other hardships. When he was about fifteen years old, he ran away from home and went south to Texas determined to become a cowboy, though he probably had no idea what that meant. His bus ticket and money ran out at Marathon, Texas, where he found work on a ranch north of town called the Hess Ranch with Leonard Mountain being in the middle of it. The year Mike landed at Marathon was probably 1946.The Hess Ranch, at the time, was being run by an Arizona cowboy named John Gould. (John raised two outstanding cowboys: the oldest named Skeet, and the younger one named Charlie. Charlie and I have worked together, and he is one of my favorite people.)

Mike bounced around Texas for a few years, learning the cowboy craft, and worked on both the upper and lower Matador Ranches and was with the JA wagon in the bottom of Palo Duro Canyon when well-known Texas cowpuncher Boots O'Neal first went to work there, being just a kid several years younger than Mike. In time Mike branched out and ended up in northern New Mexico at Vermejo Park and then on to Globe, Arizona.

Somewhere about here, being now in the early '50s, Mike received a draft notice from Uncle Sam who had gotten himself entangled in a fight in a place called Korea.

Mike ended up enlisted in the U.S. Air Force and made it through boot camp. He was not accustomed to being restrained and encumbered with responsibility and routine, and when the Air Force gave him some leave time after finishing boot camp, Mike decided to go AWOL, and he became a fugitive. He bought himself a couple horses, saddling one and packing his bed and a change of clothes on the other, and rode horseback from Arizona to Idaho where he landed a job taking care of some cows in a cow camp way out in the middle of nowhere.

Mike stayed in that cow camp for about nine months and never went to town or had any outside communication. An old man owned the outfit and cattle that Mike was taking care of, and he took a liking to Mike and brought out from town whatever things Mike might need to survive. One day the old fellow showed up at the cow camp and stayed longer than usual visiting, and at the end of a long conversation, he looked Mike in the eye and asked him, "What are you running from?" He leveled with Mike, telling him that no young man stays hid out in a camp for months, refusing to go to civilization once in a while, unless he's running away from something. He promised Mike that he would keep it to himself if he would confide in him, and so Mike told him about being on the run and absent without leave. The old-timer convinced Mike to give himself up and face the music.

After turning himself in, Mike was sentenced to Fort Leavenworth, Kansas, having to remain in the prison stockade the same amount of time that he was AWOL. And then upon serving his time in prison, he was to serve his entire tour of military duty. While at Fort Leavenworth, he and all the other inmates (who were all military prisoners like himself) were marched out of their cells and made to stand at attention for several hours in the middle of the day. He did this every day he was there. Mike knew the date his time would be up and was naturally looking forward to the day this period of his life was to be over. On the last day, he was standing in formation with close to five hundred other inmates when he noticed a guard in a tower on the prison wall aiming a rifle at him. The guard (who, he was told later, had went insane) shot and killed the inmate standing next to Mike on his left.

The Air Force sent Mike to the island of Okinawa where he was stationed most of the time he was in the service. While on Okinawa, he won the bronc riding in a serviceman's rodeo some soldiers produced. He was awarded a small trophy buckle for the win that he wore the rest of his life.

Mike met a Japanese girl there on Okinawa named Haru, and they married after a short courtship. Haru was from a small island off the north coast of Japan and had come to Okinawa because of the availability of jobs that were there. She didn't speak English, knew nothing about cowboys, or America at large, or Mike Landis in specific. She didn't have a clue what she was getting herself into.

When Mike's time serving in the U. S. Air Force was up, he returned to the United States mainland with an honorable discharge in his hand, and Haru in tow. He immediately fixed himself up with a cowboy outfit, which consisted of nothing more than a bed and saddle (dishes, clean sheets, and some furniture were not on the A list) and headed for Nevada. Mike found a job on a big ranch near Ely. He went to work for a fellow named Earl Prosser who was running an outfit near Lund, south of Ely. Earl and his wife Beth had several daughters and three boys (Earl and the boys all worked at the Diamond A in later years).

Mike and Haru moved into a cow camp called Forest Homes that was six miles or so away from the headquarters of the Moon River Ranch where Earl lived with his family. Haru was a beautiful little Japanese doll that increasingly found herself in a world so foreign she was overwhelmed. Mike took her out of a society always crowded with humanity, most of which she could communicate with, into the depths of the sagebrush desert where communication no longer was an issue. There were few to communicate with. Mike wasn't a big talker and never learned much Japanese. Haru had heard about wild Indians in the American West who raided ranches and ravaged women, and to complicate things further, soon she was pregnant and had little knowledge how to deal with that development.

Beth Prosser reached out to help Haru. Beth was one of those wonderful women whose grace and kindness were nourishment to many people. It proved to be a lifesaver for Haru Landis. Many times Mike would have to take her to the headquarters to spend all day with Beth, whom she knew would protect her from the Indians. The fact that it was 1954 and the Indians had settled down fifty years earlier meant nothing to her. Then when the baby came, she was short of milk, and attempted to bottle feed, but almost starved the little girl to death feeding her strawberry soda pop. Beth figured out what was going on and taught her about cow's milk and got Haru and the baby lined out on the path to success. Mike and Haru named the baby Beth. She grew up to be drop-dead gorgeous and a nice girl. She took after her mother.

One day Beth took Haru into Ely to do some grocery shopping. While they were pushing their grocery carts down the aisle, a woman came toward them pushing a cart, and she appeared to be Japanese. When she and Haru bumped into each other, they exploded into a conversation that lasted for an hour. Beth thought they would never get away. Beth taught Haru how to speak and read English. She also gave her a Bible written in Japanese.

Mike worked for Earl Prosser for six or seven years and then got a job running a ranch in the hills north of Kingman, Arizona, called the Quarra Ranch. While he was at the Quarra, he became good friends with Leonard and Johnny Neal, and they were good friends with Leland Larsen who managed the Diamond A for many years.

Johnny Neal was married to Leland's daughter Patsy. When the Diamond A needed to hire a new wagon boss in 1970, Leonard and Johnny recommended Mike for the job, and he got it.

The man who had been wagon boss before Mike led drives riding a Honda motorcycle; going from that extreme to Mike Landis was akin to taking a bite of sauerkraut and then tasting good chocolate fudge. By this time in his life, Mike was a dedicated Westerner. He lay awake at night wondering how the old-timers would have done it. The best way wasn't best unless Charles Goodnight, Ab Blocker, or Bob Fudge would have approved. High on the list of old-timers' priorities were getting up early and speed. Breakfast was almost a late dessert after supper, and if there was no moon, Mike caught horses when it was pitch-black, and a man who couldn't get saddled and mounted quickly was looked down upon with derision. Then Mike and crew would trot, and after you had trotted a long while, you would trot some more, hurrying to find a dead juniper tree on the backside of nowhere so you could light it on fire and wait for daylight that would finally come, a couple hours later.

He liked young guys, especially if they were cowboy-minded, and they tended to like him because when working for Mike there were plenty of opportunities to ride hard and be wild. If the wagon was camped at Hoffman, where Mike, Haru, and their two girls lived, he would pitch his teepee and stay in it to show solidarity with the crew.

When I first met Mike in 1972, he had a new Jerry Franklin saddle made in Ontario, Oregon, built on a Will James tree. It was basket stamped with round skirts and a full double rigging. He owned several very nice Eduardo Grijalva spade bits and a couple pair of beautiful silver-mounted spurs made in Mexico. I traded one pair out of him and used them for years. The pair he used at that time had eight-point, two-inch rowels that he had sharpened with a file, and they were as sharp as needles. He spurred a horse very little, and I never saw a drop of blood from a spur on one of his horses. He believed in the old adage, "A dull spur and loose curb strap have ruined many a horse."

The crew in 1972, when I first met Mike, was made up of young men, which was consistent with most of the crews he ever had. Old men tended to think he was wild and too fast. Perhaps they wanted a little extra sleep. We picked up a camp man from time to time who would work with us while we were in their country. Lloyd Hogdes was working with the crew when I threw in with the outfit. Later on we worked with Alvin Wagner and Raymond Scott. Lloyd, Alvin, and Raymond were all very good men and were easy to work with. The crew had a good attitude, or so it seemed to me, and treated Mike with respect.

Mike was a character, always coming up with a theory about the way old-timers did things. He decided that old-timers wore their Levis unwashed and put them on and continued to work in them until they were wore out. The fall of 1973, he donned a new unwashed pair of Levis the day the roundup commenced and wore them every day, without washing them, until roundup was over. Without a doubt, Louis L'Amour would have approved.

I never saw Mike in anything but a good pair of custom-made Jessi Bogle boots. Jessi Bogle made the best boots that I ever saw. He wouldn't make you a pair without personally measuring your feet. I gave Mike a very nice pair of rawhide reins and a romal one time, and he tried to give me a pair of Jessi Bogle boots that were brand new, but I wouldn't take them. They were a little tight for me and would have cost a half months wages.

Mike stood about five feet eight or nine inches and weighed about one hundred seventy. He had a head that was too big in proportion to his torso, reminding me of pictures I've seen of Charlie Russell, but not as handsome as Charlie. He had lots of wiry hair that stuck out like wheat straw if he removed his hat, which was seldom. He had a strong lantern jaw that encased a mouth that was large and wide, full of a good row of large straight teeth. He smoked Bull Durham cigarettes. He wasn't smooth but he was original. Mike never drew a breath with any thoughts about being anything but a cowboy.

Baldy

Jim Ivy showed up in the middle of the fall roundup. I think it was 1993. He started calling me "Boss" the first day he worked for me, and I didn't like it. I think he knew the moniker Boss didn't suit me, but he kept using it anyway. He shaved his head on a regular basis and let it be known that answering to "Baldy" suited him fine.

It was evident from the start that Baldy was a worker and was willing to get down and dirty trying to complete any task set before him. He had a good attitude and a sense of humor, and in spite of the fact he kept calling me Boss, I took a liking to him.

Baldy grew up in Detroit in the midst of what he described as dysfunctional people and lived in a rough part of town. Early on in our relationship, he told me how he had been institutionalized and explained that meant he had been locked up in penal institutions: reform schools, county jails, city jails, and a stint or two in a federal pen. He said he spent a total of five years in various lockup facilities. When he was a young man, he had a partner and a business in Detroit selling Mexican imports from Nogales, Sonora. What was advertised on the outside and sold on the inside might not have been the same thing. One of his visits to an institution might have been a result of this business endeavor.

Baldy traced his ancestry back to Shanghai Pierce and Jim Bowie and grew up in the projects of Detroit hearing stories about cowboys and men of the West. His first forays west of the Mississippi to Nogalas, where he and his business partner crossed Mexican pottery and contraband, whetted his appetite for more. Finally, in the early '70s he made his way to Las Vegas, Nevada, and UNLV, which he attended for four years on a music scholarship. Living in Vegas and going to school can be an expensive business, so he divided his time between studying the guitar and driving a cab on the Las Vegas strip. Soon he became a legend at transporting a high roller from a casino to the airport or a high stakes card game on the other end of town. It was here, living in the fast lane, that he began shaving his head and became known as Baldy. He's been Baldy ever since.

About the time Baldy's music degree materialized, the shows on the Vegas strip began using canned music played on tape, and that town, along with every other city in America, was full of musicians drawing unemployment. Baldy continued driving cab, but the Vegas lifestyle with all its glitter became stale. He needed a change so he headed to Northern Nevada. He got a job feeding cows and doing rosinjaw work on several different ranches. He worked on one outfit near Hidden Pass in the Ruby Mountains, east of Elko. He migrated south near Duckwater, west of Ely, and along the way began getting chances to get horseback.

Baldy moved south to Mohave County, Arizona, and landed a job on Don Laughlin's ranch, southeast of Kingman. Don Laughlin owned a big casino in the town, named after him, in southern Nevada. Baldy was "roughing it" working on Don's ranch herding cows and was able to acquire some personal assets, which included a large marijuana patch and a pet mountain lion. The government frowns on people who invest resources on marijuana gardens and caged mountain lions. The State moved in on him for the lion, but the heavy-hitters came from the federal building in Phoenix. They came, twenty-six DEA agents in all, armed with, among other things, six helicopters. Baldy took to the hills running, and when the DEA got a chopper close enough, they dropped a repelling line down to get agents on the ground. Baldy took the rope attached to the chopper and started tying it to a cedar tree. The chopper pilot understood the negative outcome this might create, and he backed off, but they eventually got Baldy anyway. He was outnumbered. The State took his mountain lion and the Feds sent Baldy to prison.

Baldy showed up with the manager early in the morning on a day we were shipping. He looked like a man who would dig post holes with his fingernails if that's what it took to get some employment. We had already gathered the shipping trap when Baldy showed up, and we were ready to start separating the cows and calves. I had not kept up a horse for an extra man because I didn't know one was going to show up, so Baldy was going to have to work afoot. I took him back to the crowding pen behind the dodge chute and instructed him on how to run a large metal gate. Truman Rustin was on a horse preparing to push cattle through the gate, and I introduced Baldy to Truman. Truman shook Baldy's hand, and with a self-righteous smirk on his face declared, "What have you been doing, Baldy, besides time?"

Baldy didn't answer the question but instead looked at me and said, "Ed, I'll be real honest with you. I'm on parole and I got to have this job. I'm not going to cause you any trouble. I promise, man; I'm willing to do whatever you need me to do!"

Truman pulled the finely greased and polished hairs in his gray mustache and stared innocently off into the distance. I answered Baldy, "I don't care where you've been or what you've done; if you'll just do your job, you

and I aren't going to have any problems."

For several days we had lots of work to do around the corrals such as vaccinating cows and branding calves, and I kept Baldy afoot. He was forty-six or forty-seven years old, but he was a go-getter and would bail into whatever obstacle lay in front of him. Flanking calves, or pushing cattle up a chute, or chopping wood for the cook, it didn't matter, he laid into the task with gusto. He finally told me, "You know, if you would give me a horse, I'd be more help." I cut him a string of horses, and he started riding with us. He rode like he flanked calves or chopped wood, full throttle with rocks, chips, and manure wildly flying about in his wake. He was no slacker. Once a month he would bring an affidavit for me to sign saying he was gainfully employed as a cowhand on the Diamond A Ranch, and after I signed it, he would mail it to his parole officer in Kingman.

Baldy was a stout man weighing around one hundred ninety, and looked tough enough to survive an institution, which was what he called the various jails he had visited. He was wearing cowboy clothes that fit as if they had been worn and stretched a size too big. His felt cowboy hat had been rained on and subsequently baked in the sun until all the life had departed; it hung limply around his bald head and was pulled tight with a stampede string. His saddle was a cheap factory affair that looked like it had been run over by a stampede of Kansas-bound longhorns. But the crown jewel of his cowboy outfit was a pair of rawhide split reins that he had braided himself. Added to the homemade reins was a rawhide reata seven-sixteenths of an inch in diameter that he had braided. It was at least seventy feet long, and a man who was sick couldn't have swung it. In places hair was still visible on the strings.

I gave Baldy a sorrel horse named Zephyr. I had ridden the horse myself a few times and knew he was somewhat gentle, especially considering where he came from. He was a Double O mustang with China Lake ancestry. Zephyr stood fifteen hands but weighed only nine hundred fifty pounds. His head was abnormally long for his size, and the bridge of the nose was as sharp as an ax. Perhaps, that was why he was named Zephyr; when he ran his hatchet head could split the west wind. Zephyr had no depth in his girth, or belly, and even a short-legged man felt like he was riding a pole or rail.

One morning when we were camped at I Tub, Baldy mounted Zephyr, who was acting a little humped up. Several other horses went to bucking a little, and there was a considerable amount of whooping and hollering. Zephyr got caught up in the moment and started bucking and stampeding. The corral at I Tub sits in a narrow canyon with very steep sides. The small holding trap located there, which the remuda was turned out in, ran up the hill on the north side of the canyon. Zephyr was gaining a little altitude as he ran along. Baldy was staying on and seemed to be having no trouble getting the horse covered, so I wasn't worried about him. And then we heard a crash and realized it was the sound of wire stretching and old cedar posts breaking. Several of us ran over toward the sound of the accident, which was part of the way up the side of the hill. From two hundred yards away, we could see Zephyr down on his side, and when we got close, we could tell the wire in the fence was tangled around the

horse's legs keeping him tied down. The only part of
Baldy that was visible was part of his leg and a cowboy
boot. The boot was turned backwards going the complete
opposite direction of his leg. It appeared the bone in his leg
was broken completely in two, and his foot hung loosely,
being connected by nothing but skin. Someone wondered
out loud, "You suppose he's dead?" We had heard nothing
and could see nothing but the mangled leg. And then a
waving hand appeared from underneath the horse and a
voice said, "I'm under here guys!" He started laughing.

We cut Zephyr loose and got him standing without
injuring Baldy, and as we did so, the cowboy boot we had
seen fell off revealing a healthy leg. The boot, which was
a size too big, was almost off his foot allowing it to twist
and turn backwards, making us think his leg was broken.
Good old Zephyr wasn't even cut real bad.

A couple weeks later, we almost lost Baldy. We were
camped at Keseha and it had come a big storm and the
creeks and draws were running. I had driven down to
Seligman to pick up Everett and Clay so they could work
with us for the weekend while school was out. Baldy had
a habit of working on various projects in his teepee before
he went to sleep at night. He had a propane torch and a
small piece of railroad iron, and he built a pair of spurs
one time, hammering on metal while everyone else tried
to sleep. He usually had an old cowhide around camp
that he would braid rawhide gear out of such as reins or
reatas. There was no telling what might be going on in
his canvas tent. On this particular night, which was cool
and wet, Baldy had his lantern burning in his teepee when
everyone went to bed, which wasn't unusual. Barney
Prosser walked by Baldy's tent, heading out of camp to
relieve himself after everyone else had turned in for the
night, and he heard strange noises coming from inside
Baldy's teepee. It sounded like wheezing or faint groaning.
He spoke to Baldy, although the door to his teepee was
zipped shut, but Baldy didn't respond. Barney called to

Mike McLaughlin, whose teepee was nearby, and Mike jumped up and walked over next to Barney and hollered but got no response. Mike then got the canvas teepee door open and found Baldy comatose and lying on top of his bed. Thinking fast, Mike drug Baldy outside so he could get some fresh air. Mike realized that Baldy's teepee was deficient of oxygen because of the burning lantern and no ventilation, and Baldy was suffering from carbon monoxide poisoning.

Soon everyone in camp was up and wondering if Baldy was going to come back to life. Scott Westlake and Chip Dixon took off in a pickup to drive to Pica, nineteen miles away, so they could phone someone and get an ambulance coming. After they left, Baldy came to but was feeling very bad, so Brad Meade and Yates Dixon loaded him in Brad's pickup and headed down the hill towards Pica, about thirty minutes behind Scott and Chip. (Brad was the Keseha camp man and lived there with his family at that time.) Brad and Yates delivered Baldy to Pica before the ambulance got there, so they, along with Scott and Chip all headed to Seligman with a deputy sheriff leading the way with lights flashing.

I got a call before they got Baldy into town and was told what had happened and agreed to meet everyone in the parking lot of the O. K. Saloon on the west end of town. When we all congregated at the O. K., a local paramedic ordered Baldy to be taken to Flagstaff in an ambulance so the doctors there could check him out more thoroughly. He was still looking and acting very sick. At the Flagstaff hospital the emergency room doctors tested Baldy and said the carbon monoxide level in his blood was dangerously high. They also said that if someone had not found him when they did, he would have soon died. They kept him in the hospital overnight with plenty of oxygen to breathe and the next morning said he was good to go back home.

The manager's wife, who held the keys to the commissary, drove up to Flagstaff to pick him up, thinking she would do a big grocery shopping while she was in town. When Baldy left Keseha in Brad's pickup, nobody had the presence of mind to think about dressing him. So there he was in the hospital with no boots, no hat, no coat, and no shirt except a dirty undershirt. The clothes he had on were the ones he had been working, sweating and living in for a number of days (which is the way it is a great deal of the time around a cow camp, regardless of who you are). For some reason Baldy's clothes were always loose fitting and the loosest thing of all were the socks. It seems the Commissary Commander didn't consider him to be of enough value for which to purchase a clean tee shirt or a pair of two dollar slippers; so there they went, the two of them, the Commander and Baldy, off to the new and cavernous Sam's Club located on Butler Avenue in Flagstaff. He pushed the shopping carts around Sam's Club in his dirty jeans and undershirt that was on the dark side of dirty and hanging out because for some reason he had taken his belt off the night before. Perhaps, he had intended to put on clean jeans in the morning. His wool socks fit so loose that he walked them half off with the toes dragging along behind like a tow sack. But Baldy was handy because after a night on oxygen he had plenty of strength to push the numerous shopping carts needed when you are feeding thirty or forty people.

Being quick of mind in all things, he saw that he had a rare opportunity. Everyone was always talking about various types of groceries they wished the company furnished, but didn't. Baldy positioned himself behind the Commander as she walked down the aisle thinking about what she should purchase. When she wasn't looking, he would slip in a few jars of Smucker's Strawberry Jam to go with the Best Buy Grape Jelly, which was all she would ever buy. He managed to hide a few packages of Pecan Sandies and Oreos, as well as a good brand of bottled and stuffed green olives. In the paper aisle, they stopped as she pondered the huge cases of cheap toilet paper. After a moment she turned and looked him in the eye and asked, "What the hell do you guys do with so much toilet paper out there?"

Baldy, who always addressed a member of the fairer sex as ma'am, answered, "Ma'am, I don't have a clue!"

Baldy was delivered to the wagon that evening, and we all sat around roaring with laughter as he told of his escapades as a high grader in Sam's Club. The Smucker's Jam, Pecan Sandies, Oreos and green olives never made it to the wagon, but thankfully the paper did.

Later that fall when we were camped at Rose Well, we had a big branding. We had a big bunch of cattle in the picket water lot, probably five or six hundred cows plus calves. There were a good number of calves to brand including some big ones weighing close to five hundred pounds. I put the branding fire off to one side, thirty or forty yards away from the edge of the herd. We had a lot of men, including several who were expert ropers.

A couple men were roping the unbranded calves around the neck and dragging them out toward the branding fire, and several others were heeling them and stretching them out so we could brand and vaccinate them. Baldy was riding Zephyr, and he was heeling calves. Someone came out with a big bull bouncing along on the end of thirty feet of tied rope. I believe the man who had the calf roped around the neck was Chip Dixon. Baldy moved ole Zephyr into position and cut loose with a big heel shot with his heavy homemade reata. The lope missed, and beings it had been a big one, there was a lot of reata laying on the ground. As Baldy coiled up the reata so he could build another loop, Zephyr was ringing his tail and slinging his head. The horse slung his hind end around and his hind legs brushed against the heavy reata causing him to spook and jump. Baldy held his rawhide reins loosely in his left hand along with fifteen or twenty coils of reata, and in order to pull the slack out of his reins, his hand drifted out to the left. Beings his hand was off to the left of Zephyr's neck the horse turned to the left causing the reata to tangle in the horse's hind legs. This caused a chain reaction beginning with the horse spinning faster and the tangling getting worse, and Zephyr began slinging his head up and down, and because Baldy's hand was left of the horse's neck the head slinging sent the right rein over the top of Zephyr's head and now both reins were on the left side of the horse's head and neck. Now the stomping, head-slinging, kicking, and spinning began to intensify, and Baldy was obviously getting dizzy. I was working on the ground doing the branding, and I panicked thinking Baldy was fixing on getting in a sure-enough wreck. "Drop your rope! Drop your rope! Baldy, drop your rope!" I screamed. Trying to follow my advice, Baldy dropped his rope but in the process dropped both bridle reins also. Zephyr was now as free as a west wind and came out of his head-slinging spin and stampeded into the large herd of cattle. Baldy had become very dizzy and was holding onto the saddlehorn with both hands but leaning way off to the side of his horse, first to the left, and then the right, and then back again, like a man who was very drunk. He resembled the character Kid Shellen riding while drunk in the movie "Cat Ballou." Somewhere a man was laughing, and someone else hollered "yee haw." I was standing by the branding fire with my hands up to the sides of my head trying to hide my eyes and plug my ears at the same time. I didn't know whether to laugh or cry. Zephyr came to a stop in the far corner of the big corral surrounded by bawling cows. Baldy was weaving dizzyingly but was still astraddle the ugly horse.

Baldy would help you do anything and was not given to complaining. If he was asked to clean the toilet in the Rose Well bunkhouse, he would do it, and would do that or anything else with a good attitude. If you treated him good, he would act in kind. He was always very loyal to me.

ഇᏜ
Cole Moorhouse
ഇᏜ

Diamond A Ranch, October 1, 1973

Tenneco Oil Corporation dispersed the Hereford cowherd in the fall of 1972, and in 1973 they leased the outfit to some people who ran steers on it. The main player in this endeavor was a gentleman from South Texas named Pebo Coleman. Those of us who helped gather the cattle that fall of '73 were told that the new management had turned out thirty-three thousand steers. Some people claimed there were as many as fifty-two thousand turned out, but I think thirty-three thousand was a more accurate count. I know there were too many. It didn't rain real good that summer, and the cattle didn't gain real well. Perhaps, the fact there were a dozen steers staring at every blade of grass sticking through had something to do with it. The cattle were predominantly Mexicans, thousands of which were old-style horned Corrientes that are so rare these days. The Diamond A could have supplied roping cattle for every roping event in the Southwest.

Bob Scott and I came down from Northern Nevada together, where we had spent the summer, and went to work on the lower wagon, or Mike's wagon, as it was called. We shod the remuda at Hoffman around the last day or two of September. Mike Landis was wagon boss and Cole Moorhouse was his jigger boss. The crew also consisted of Wayman Vessels, Doug Kepke, a couple young boys from California, and Bob and me. At the start there were nine of us. Rex Williamson was cooking.

I had asked Mike to put a horse named Prisoner in my string. Prisoner was a wild Indian horse that Dave Ericson had caught at seven or eight years old and had broke him to ride. Prisoner stood about 14.2 hands and might have weighed nine hundred seventy-five, perhaps even a thousand on his fattest day. He was sort of wild acting and snorty but was a quick-footed going machine. The first morning we gathered cattle, after spending a day or so shoeing the remuda, we were going to make a drive in a pasture called Thirty-Six directly east of Hoffman Camp. We ate early, as we always did at Mike's wagon, and it was nowhere near daylight when we stepped out of the cook tent and headed toward the corral to catch horses. There was no moon and it was exceptionally dark.

Mike Landis had ridden Prisoner for several roundups before this one and, beings the horse was fresh, was wanting to give me advice on how to get along with him. He suggested that perhaps I should get on him outside the corral gate, and step on him, just letting him go, heading out into the middle of Thirty-Six. In his opinion, Prisoner would want to run more than buck if I turned him loose and let him race out into the wild blue yonder. I could catch up with the crew before they reached the east boundary of the pasture, six miles away. The cowboy code was clear that a man didn't just take off any ole direction when leaving camp, but instead got behind the boss and followed his lead. But beings the boss was suggesting I take a wild ride into the night air in order to get along with a fresh horse, I was all for it.

Mike caught Prisoner first, and I got saddled before everyone else, and beings I had his blessing, I led the bay horse out the corral gate and slipped up on him. I had him pointed northeast, and when I was up, I just stood up in my stirrups and let 'er rip; and we were running full blast across the rocky flat. It was very dark and I could barely make out the horizon in any direction. The morning lights of Seligman were several miles to the west, but Seligman wasn't much of a town, and they weren't very impressive. Prisoner and I covered about a mile in short order, and then we slowed down to a lope and kept going for five or ten minutes. We began to rise in elevation, and I knew we were climbing a hill somewhere in the middle of the pasture. I pulled up in hopes of figuring out where the crew was. I could hear horses traveling across rocky ground somewhere to the south, and then I saw a flash from a spark made from a horseshoe striking a malpai rock. They were a mile and a half or two miles to the south and heading straight east. I took off and started loping toward the sight of an occasional spark. I traveled for a few minutes in what I thought was the right direction, and then when I could tell I was on a high spot, I pulled up again to listen. It was still as black as the bottom of a well. I could hear horses in the distance and still over a mile away. And then I saw a small fire off to the right, a considerable distance behind the sound of the horses, probably a mile or more. I pondered the fire but continued to listen and could plainly hear horses trotting across rocky ground, and a good distance to the left of the fire and getting farther away. I thought perhaps the crew had decided to stop and build a fire real quick to warm up, but that seemed out of place because it wasn't very cold and the fire looked as if it was built after the horses were long past it.

I could hear the horses and they were leaving me behind, so I took off in a run and forgot about the fire. I caught up with the crew when they were about five miles straight east of Hoffman and about a mile from the Sevens Ranch fence. It was finally beginning to show a little light on the eastern horizon, and I just fell in behind the crew and said nothing. A few minutes later, we pulled up against the fence on the backside of Thirty-Six, and someone finally had the presence of mind to notice that we were missing Cole Moorhouse. Mike Landis asked if anyone had seen Cole stopping or having a hard time keeping up. No one had noticed anything. I told how I had observed what looked like a small fire a mile and a half or so east of camp. No one else had seen the fire that would have been straight behind them as they traveled east.

It was decided that we would go ahead and split up and make a drive back into Hoffman, and that perhaps Cole had simply gotten sick and had gone back to camp. Whatever happened would be found out soon enough as far as Mike Landis was concerned, so he gave Bob Scott the duty of leading one side of the drive, which would have been Cole's duty. Mike led the other side, and we split up the way he wanted and started gathering steers back into camp, six miles to the west.

Soon after I had let out of camp in a run, letting Prisoner

use up his excess energy, the rest of the crew had started west in a high trot. Cole and Mike Landis had been in front side-by-side with the rest of the crew following. About a mile and a half from camp, Cole had veered and stopped, stepping off the big black horse he was riding to relieve himself. The wagon boss and crew had kept moving at a brisk pace not thinking anything about Cole's pit stop. The stop only took a minute, and Cole was remounted and took off in a lope to catch up. Just a few yards after Cole stepped back on his horse, the animal stubbed his toe against a large malpai rock or stepped in a badger hole and went down hard. The fall addled Cole momentarily, but worse than that, it severely injured his back. He always had a pocket full of matches and quickly built a fire out of dry rabbit brush and turpentine weed. He hoped someone in the crew would notice the fire and realize he was missing. I was the only person who saw it from a mile or so to the north, but I traveled toward the sound of moving horses rather than the fire.

He laid by the fire for a short spell and realized he was on his own. He could barely stand up, the pain in his back being very great, but he started back toward camp. A great deal of the time, he crawled on his hands and knees, that mode of traveling being less painful than standing. The black horse had abandoned him for the house as soon as he got up. It didn't matter; Cole told us later that he would not have been able to get on the horse anyway. When we got back to camp three or four hours later trailing three or four hundred steers, he had just crawled into the cook tent. The cook had already sent word that someone needed to notify Cole's wife JoAnn to come up from Prescott, where she lived, and take him to see a doctor.

Cole had been having back pain for years, but the accident that morning finished him off, at least for the fall works. The doctor told him after looking at the x-rays that two discs in his lower back were severely ruptured, and he was going to have to undergo surgery. It would be a number of months before he would be able to ride again.

Cole stood about six feet and probably a hair over, and in those days he was thin as a rail. After that fall, you could pick him out of a crowd by the way he stood, being continuously leaned forward three or four degrees, with his posterior jutting backwards just a touch. He was a cousin to the famous Texas cowboys, Tom and Bob Moorhouse, and resembled Tom a lot in the face but stood quite a bit taller. He always wore a hat with about a three or three and a half inch brim, rolled up narrow on the sides, and pulled down low in front of his eyes. I only remember him wearing one black hat, usually having on a silver belly. He smoked cigarettes, usually Bull Durham, and had a permanent squint in his eyes so common among those of his type, acquired through years of gazing through smoke. He talked with a slow Texas drawl and his words to many cowhands younger than him were considered equal to that of a sage. He was independent in the manner of working men such as cowboys and others close to the earth, living below the poverty line. He was true to someone he considered a friend but easily offended by those he mistrusted.

ℰℴℭℛ

In the fall of 1971, I was working for the O RO Ranch; and along about the first of November, we were camped at Number Two, a windmill four or five miles west of the Oaks and Willows. Among the O RO crew that fall was a short little man named Lem Davis who was probably around sixty years old. He stood about five feet four, and at his age had become pretty stocky built. Lem told stories about riding the rough string on the Three Vs in the 1930s. When I worked with him in 1971, he was riding a brand new flower-carved, form-fitter saddle made by Bob McCray in Flagstaff.

About six months earlier, Lem had been working as roundup cook for the Babbitt outfit north of Flagstaff. One night Cole Moorhouse and a couple of other Babbitt cowboys came back from town pretty oiled up. For some reason or other, Lem and Cole got into an argument, and they got to wrestling around. Cole was probably pretty drunk, because sober he would have knocked Lem out with one punch, but alcohol on Cole's part and old age on Lem's part made it a comical affair, that was until it got ugly. I think Lem might have grabbed a butcher knife, and Cole grabbed a large metal spatula. In the battle that ensued, Cole sliced Lem's ear with the sharp edge of the spatula, and forever after it was told that Cole had earmarked Lem with a sharp knife. Having completed the job of earmarking the cook, Cole then locked him in a ten by ten room adjacent to the kitchen that was used as a commissary. To top things off, Lem then got sick with the type of sickness that makes a mess. When the boss found out, he fired Cole and several others that were present.

One evening, that fall of '71, while the O RO wagon was at Number Two, Buck Smith, the jigger boss, went home, which was a place he had not been in a number of weeks. The crew was up drinking coffee and eating breakfast when Buck arrived back at the wagon. Lem and about half the crew were sitting in the cook tent when Buck stepped inside and said good morning. I was one of the men inside the tent. Lem was seated on a wooden milk crate eating a bowl of stewed prunes and had just put several large prunes in his mouth when Buck stepped inside. After his good morning, Buck said, "Ole Cole Moorhouse came by the house last night and asked for a job." Lem's eyes lit up like someone had jabbed a 110 volt hotshot in his shorts, and he spit a prune pit across the tent that hit a water bucket on the top of the wood stove leaving a dent in the galvanized metal bucket. He ran outside through the tent flap heading to the bushes, obviously suffering from the same sickness that had afflicted him in the Babbitt Ranch commissary. Buck Smith stopped in midsentence with a, "what the heck is eating you," look on his face as Lem raced to the bushes. After Lem was out of hearing range, he finished his story. "I told Cole we had a full crew and didn't hire him, but thanked him anyway."

℘)Cℛ

Once in the fall of 1972, when I first worked with Cole, some of us, including him, were passing a bottle of VO around while squatting in an eight by eight canvas teepee tent. I was the youngest of the four. After tipping the whiskey bottle upside down, he commented how he judged a man by the size of drink he took. He handed the bottle to me, and I drank hard and long, making sure the bottle was upside down long enough to prove that I was no slacker or coward.

ℰ❯ℭ❰

Diamond A Ranch, June 1994

The ranch manager showed up at the wagon one day while we were camped at Rose Well branding calves. He approached me with an arm full of paper leaflets consisting of a half dozen sheets of white paper stapled together. He instructed me to hand one to each man on my crew, which would have been fourteen men. I looked at one and saw that they were titled "Company Rules," and as I leafed through the pages, I could tell it was someone's idea of how you should mandate common sense as well as self-righteousness. Each page contained a list of rules that all employees were to follow such as "Don't drive company vehicles too fast, Don't flush the toilet more than twice." The manager left as soon as he had deposited the rulebook into my hands for safekeeping. I suppose he didn't want to be part of the passing out of the hymnals. It's an old and expected practice that the priest should leave the dirty work to an altar boy.

The cowboys were sitting around in the shade of the fly waiting for the cook to holler chuck when I began passing the leaflets out. A response from the crew was immediate. There was a considerable amount of laughter mixed with an equal amount of cursing. Tom Reeder, whose problem with stuttering worsened when he was agitated, came to me holding the leaflet out with trembling hands. "Th-th-the- ther- there i-i-i-is for-for-fort-forty-sssen-sev-seven rrreasons fffofor mme ttto gggegeget fffififired hhere, bbbut nnot one rrrereason fffor mme ttto kkeep mmy jjjjob!"

The biggest rule was printed in extra bold print that said, "Absolutely no alcohol consumption will be tolerated." Undoubtedly that was where the stuttering and trembling hands originated.

Alcohol and the drinking of it have caused problems on just about every big ranch west of the Mississippi. The Diamond A was no exception. I had several drunks working for me at the time, and I had fired a man or two for being drunk and not making a hand. But I did not believe in legislated morality; and still don't, especially when it was mandated to some but not to others. The best way to make alcohol start causing trouble was to outlaw it, in my opinion. I refused to put up with drunkenness or drinking when we were working, but I wasn't going to tell a bunch of grown men what they could or couldn't do on their downtime. I wasn't going to start searching men's personal items looking for a hidden quart of whiskey.

A few days after we received our copies of the official company rule book, the manager told me he had hired Cole Moorhouse to be the camp man out at Number Five. Cole would also work with the wagon crew during the spring and fall roundup. The manager told me, "You know, you're going to have to watch him, he has a reputation for drinking too much!" What the hell did you hire him for, I thought to myself.

I had worked with Cole three different times, but it had been twenty years since the last time we were on a crew together. I had always gotten along good with Cole and considered him a friend. I had done a considerable amount of partying with him and had never had a bad word with him; I had heard that his drinking had gotten worse, but I had not really been around him much in years. I had quit drinking fifteen years earlier and had made a public confession of being a Christian, and I was sure he had heard. What little I had seen him in that period of time, he had seemed unfriendly. I remembered his statement about judging a man by the size of drink he could take. I had doubts about him wanting to work for me, but decided I wouldn't worry about it.

Cole came to work for me and was pretty quiet for several days. I suppose he was evaluating the outfit and everyone present. After a spell, he seemed to loosen up and started enjoying himself. He was a man other cowboys enjoyed being around. He had a sort of witty way of commenting on situations, all of which were spoken in a slow Texas drawl that could speak volumes amidst a scarcity of words.

In the fall of '94, a hunter, or someone, left a gate open on the drift fence between Lower Sandstone and Midway Pastures. We had a lot of cows in Lower Sandstone that we had not weaned the calves off of, and three or four hundred got through the open gate and drifted north. The gates in Midway were open on the north side, and the cattle were able to drift all the way to the northern end of the ranch. We had already weaned and shipped several thousand calves and let their mothers out north, so the big calves that got through the open gate were mixed with these. We needed the calves to meet our contract agreement with the people who had bought the calves, so the mix-up caused by the open gate created a mess.

I asked Cole to take some men and camp at Number Five, where he lived, and try to round up the majority of the big calves that had gone through the fence. I sent Chip Dixon, Barney Prosser, Ben Benton, and Steve Webb to help him. Cole's wife Linda Joe cooked for them. They worked hard for a week or so and got most of the cattle gathered, or at least enough to fill our contract. Cole and the other men really made a hand and helped get the outfit out of a bind. I was grateful.

Later that fall, after it started freezing at night, I cut down on the size of the remuda, down to five or six horses per man, and we started graining them. We made morrals out of burlap sacks and fed the entire remuda every night by hanging a morral with a couple coffee cans of grain for every horse. Even though we had turned out all the extra horses and cut the remuda down in size, there were still lots of horses to morral, probably seventy or eighty head. There were fourteen or fifteen of us on the crew, and we stood around the outside of the horse herd as they ate their grain, making sure they didn't wander off with a feed sack hanging on their head. There was a young man on the crew named Stanley Livingston who would not let the horses eat. As soon as we got all the morrals hung on, he would start wandering through the remuda taking morrals off. I had told him several times to leave the horses alone and give them a chance to finish eating their grain. One night we barely got all the morrals hung on when Stanley started pulling them off. Cole was standing leaned back against the picket horse corral fence smoking a Bull Durham cigarette. I hollered at Stanley, "Damn it, Stanley! What are you doing? Get over there and stand next to Cole and don't move until he does; don't do anything until you see Cole do it. Do you understand?"

Cole took a long pull on the Bull Durham smoke and said, "Damn, Eid! Whad Ah do to make you maad?"

I thought to myself, Nothing, Cole, you are just a man to admire. I never said one word to Cole about his drinking. I never gave him a copy of the company rule book. Cole made a hand the whole time he worked for me and never caused me any trouble and always treated me with respect. I'm thankful for that.

၈၁၈

The Code
of the West

၈၁၈

Mike Landis worked on the JA Ranch in Palo Duro Canyon in the late '40s. Every man I ever knew who was around that outfit in those days said it was one of the best cowboy outfits ever put together anywhere in the West. The JA wagon was pulled by a team of horses, and when camp was set up, a fly, or canvas tarp, was put up over the wagon and chuck box, which provided a little protection; but there was still plenty of open air. The cook cooked on a pot rack and used Dutch ovens; in other words, there was no woodstove. Coals from the fire were used to bake in the Dutch ovens or do any frying or boiling that was done. The cook built his fire where he wanted it, and he was boss of it. Any good and experienced cowboy from anywhere in the West knew there were certain practices of etiquette that should be recognized. The area between the fire, the chuck box, and the wagon belonged to the cook; it was his kitchen; and you stayed out of his way. Men who stomped around camp, dragging their feet and stirring up dust too close to camp and the kitchen, were looked down upon. I've seen many scenes in western movies, starring men like John Wayne and Clint Eastwood, showing men galloping up to the wagon and stepping off their horses within a step or two of the fire and chuck box. That would never happen around any cow camp I ever saw or heard of. Any decent wagon cook wouldn't have put up with a horse stomping and pooping right on top of his space. No wagon boss worth his salt would let his crew conduct themselves in that manner.

Mike told me a story about a loud-talking gunsel who showed up at the JA wagon while he worked there. The man talked incessantly and stomped around camp like a bull in a china closet. One day he made the mistake of traversing into the cook's side of the fire. He poured himself a cup of coffee and squatted low, with his Levi pockets resting on his gaudy spurs, and started telling a story that no one was listening to. He was crouched with his back to the chuck box lid that served as counter space.

The cook, who was a quiet man, not given to outbursts, noticed but said nothing as he stood calmly mixing biscuit dough. Presently, the cook walked over to the side of the wagon and got a shovel that he habitually used to pick up coals out of the fire to be placed under or on top of his Dutch ovens. He walked around the loud talker, who was squatted in his way, and with his shovel, he picked up one red-hot coal about the size of a chicken egg. The offensive man ignored the cook and continued talking. The cook deftly walked, with the hot chicken egg, around the man; and when he was directly behind him, he gently laid the burning ember in the low spot in the crease of the man's silver belly Stetson hat. The cook was so smooth the man never felt the extra weight on top of his head. Then the old cook silently walked back to the chuck box and started laying raw biscuits in a freshly greased Dutch oven. Suddenly the polished brass gates of hell flew open and the loud man screamed in torture at the demon that was trapped inside his sombrero. The cook never said a word, and Mike Landis claimed that was the only time he saw anyone on the wrong side of that man's fire.

ℰ❦ℛ

There are certain rules that have been common on all big ranches I've worked on from Elko County, Nevada, to Hidalgo County, New Mexico. You don't ride in front of a man, especially between him and a herd of cattle. If the boss drops you off between Bill and Steve when gathering a pasture, you are supposed to stay there and be between Bill and Steve when the cattle are throwed together at a rodear ground or corral. If you are holding up a herd of cattle outside, and you are between Bill and Steve, and a cow breaks out of the herd, and you chase her, you go back to your place between Bill and Steve when you put the cow back into the herd. If you chase the cow into the herd on the opposite side of the herd from Bill and Steve, you ride around behind everyone on your way back to your spot. To dudes and green kids this all seems too regimented and unnecessary, but to cowboys accustomed to the Code, it is accepted practice. The Code of the West was developed to create structure and order: there was a reason for its creation. The JA cook, who burned a hole in the loud man's Stetson, and subsequently his head, was responsible for feeding a large crew. He was also expected to be clean and on time. He couldn't do his job with someone stomping around in his kitchen. Had the man with the burned scalp decided to retaliate and threatened the cook in some way, the wagon boss and crew would have sided with the cook. It was the Code of the West.

ഌ☙

Boots O'Neal told me a story about his brother Wes, who ran the wagon for many years at the Waggoner Ranch near Vernon, Texas. There was a man working for Wes who was a good hand and employee but had a horse in his string that he seemed to be avoiding. Wes didn't say anything to the cowboy for several weeks but finally asked him why he wasn't riding the horse. The man replied that he wasn't riding the horse because he was afraid of him and knew the horse could and would buck him off. Wes told him in a matter of fact tone that the horse was part of his string, and he was required to ride him. The next morning after breakfast the cowboy quit. There was no anger or harsh words from either man. Boots said Wes even liked the man and hated to see him go but, in his mind, rules were rules; and the man was either going to ride the horse or go elsewhere. The cowboy understood as well and felt no animosity toward Wes. It was the Code, and the Code was upheld.

ഇൻരു

Cattle ranching, as an industry, is probably the most misunderstood business and profession there is, or at least that has been my observation. If an intelligent businessman and investor were to buy a hospital with the intention of operating it in a profit-making manner, he would not hire a cowboy or a truck driver to run it. He would hire a manager with some knowledge and experience in the medical and healthcare profession. A man who owns a large trucking company would naturally hire a manager with experience and training pertaining to trucks and the logistical intricacies of over the road freight hauling. But it seems cattle ranching is different. Any rich dude who has the money to buy a ranch is instantly a cowboy and cowman with the know-how to manage a cow herd. In their opinions, all it takes to be a cowman is a trip to the western wear store where a sombrero and a pair of boots can be purchased. Many ranches have suffered because of this fallacy. Old-time cowboys I've known have a saying that goes, "He was a piss-poor horse wrangler, so we made a manager out of him!"

Contrary to what dudes and gunsels think, there is an art to working cattle. To the untrained eye, things will happen, and go unseen or not understood, that have great implications concerning the success or failure of a piece of cow work such as gathering a large pasture, or sorting a large herd of cattle outside. Experienced cowboys of the old school understood and visualized the science of cow work, and they knew and lived by the Code, or rule book of correct procedure.

A good wagon boss has opinions about things like working a large roundup outside. He wants his herd of cattle thrown together at a certain spot. Perhaps, it is a place where the ground is soft and the cattle will move with ease. If he is shorthanded, he might put the herd of cattle in a rock pile to make them easier to hold. He positions his "cut" on a certain side of the herd, perhaps it is in a direction where he won't be cutting into the sun or wind. One thing is for certain, if he knows what he is doing, he will have opinions, and the Code was written and is observed to help him be successful in the art of working cattle. Contrary to what some observers of the West have written, the Code was and is observed to create structure in the workplace and not to promote romance or beauty.

I have worked with some modern cowboys and ranch owners who think that adherence to a code of conduct among cowboys during cow work is nonsense. I have witnessed big crews gathering pastures where men are riding around from one side of a drive to another, sometimes moving three, four or five men over, away from their original spot, to participate in whatever is going on over in the other person's territory. The end result of this is chaos and no one helping the person next to themselves. Strict observance to the old-timers' code of conduct condemned such actions.

One of the best and truly authentic cowboy books ever written is a biography of a man named Bob Fudge. Bob Fudge was reared in Lampasas, Texas, and went north to Montana with numerous trail herds. He worked for Ab Blocker and other famous Texas trail bosses. He worked for a spell on the huge XIT Cattle Company in Texas and then, for many years, for the same outfit in Montana. In his biography, Bob Fudge states that men were assigned a spot on a trail herd when it left Texas, heading north. The trail boss might put you on point, or the flank of the herd, or perhaps the drags; but regardless, you were assigned to that spot for the duration, which was over a thousand miles and four months' worth of riding. You didn't take any position you wanted; but instead, you went where the boss put you.

ℰℛ

Eph Fancher was an Arizona cowboy, noted for being a top hand, who was also short tempered, especially toward someone who was long on talk but short on skill. He told a story about working on a large cattle operation in the San Joaquin Valley in Southern California. Eph and a large crew of Californians gathered a sizeable herd of cattle in some fields and set about sorting them three different ways. They had lots of cattle, a thousand or more, and there was lots of cutting to do. Eph was accustomed to the method of working a herd where certain men did the cutting, while the rest of the crew held the herd in place. When they got the cattle thrown together, everyone began cutting. There were no designated cutters or designated herd holders; basically, it was a free-for-all with everyone doing anything they wanted and riding anywhere they wanted. The herd of cattle was continuously running and scattering, and the amount of mistakes that were made astonished Eph. All day long, he tried to do nothing but hold the herd together, while everyone else in the crew rode in and out of the herd at will. In Eph's mind, the whole affair was a debacle. In the evening, when the crew was unsaddling their tired horses back in camp, Eph overheard two of his comrades talking. One of them said to the other, "Boy, we had a nice day today, don't you think?"

"Yeah, I guess so," the other replied. "But it would have been a lot better if that S.O.B. from Arizona would have helped us!" Eph quit the next morning and went in search of a place where the Code was honored.

ℰℛ

I remember an incident that took place at the Babbitt Ranch one fall when the wagon was camped at Kendrick Park at eight thousand feet elevation. It was cold and horses seemed to want to buck at Kendrick Park more than some places. There was a buckaroo working for the outfit who hailed from Oregon whose name was Jerry. He was a pretty good hand and owned several nice bridles with silver-mounted Tietjen bits and rawhide reins and romal. He owned a brand-new Jerry Franklin saddle built on a Three B Tree that was basket stamped. We saddled up one afternoon after lunch and were going to go gather some cows on the side of the west San Francisco Peaks. Jerry had a horse in his string that was a real meathead, and the horse had Jerry buffaloed pretty bad. We all got saddled up, and Bill stepped on his horse and headed west in a lope with everyone except Jerry close on his heels. Jerry's horse was humped up and ringing his tail, and Jerry was shaking his rawhide reins and gently asking the horse to move out without bucking. "Bill! Bill! Bill, wait for me! Bill, hold up and wait for me!" Jerry was screaming at the top of his lungs and spurring his bowed up horse with the calves of his legs, making sure his spur rowels did not come in contact with any horse hide. "Bill! Wait for me!" I could have rode back and maybe helped Jerry get moving a little faster, but Bill never looked back. I was working for Bill so I kept moving. I figured the Code said Jerry and Bill's relationship was none of my business.

₮℞

In October 1994, the manager of the Diamond A hired a kid from the Bakersfield, California area. I don't remember what his last name was, perhaps I never knew; but he answered to the nickname of Willy Rotten. The story was that Willy Rotten was a moniker his parents hung on him for obvious reasons, and it stuck. Willy Rotten turned out to be a pretty good kid, especially when you considered the stories he told about his past. It hadn't been easy or pretty for Willy Rotten. He had no cowboy experience except working for a horseshoer in California, and a bit of team roping in an arena. At least he could shoe a horse.

Willy Rotten showed up about the same time we hired Margie Fancher to cook, they probably came to work the same day. Margie was Jimmer Fancher's aunt and had been around more cow camps and cowboy crews than a lot of men in my crew. She had been making a living cooking on ranches, resorts, and hunting camps for years. I knew she didn't put up with a lot of nonsense. I was hoping that we could keep her happy because the food hadn't been very good for quite a spell.

The first morning she cooked for us, she made pancakes and had fried up a lot of bacon. She had gone to the trouble of warming up the Log Cabin Syrup. When she hollered, "It's ready," men jumped up with more enthusiasm about breakfast than I had seen for a long time. There were six or eight men in line filling their plates in front of me. Willy Rotten was the man directly in front of me. When Willy Rotten stepped up to the stove lid where Margie had placed a big pan full of pancakes and another of bacon, he paused and considered the menu for a moment. "Margie, how about frying me a couple eggs?" Willy Rotten said.

Margie's head snapped back a little at his request, and her eyes opened real wide and started turning red. From behind, I considered slamming him face forward into the stove pipe. Margie turned around to grab a frying pan to fry the eggs. I informed Willy Rotten that it was customary around a roundup camp that you ate what the cook made and acted happy about it. Then Margie said it was all right, she would fry the little Californian some eggs. Then I said that was unnecessary because Willy Rotten didn't need any eggs. Then Margie acted mad at me for interfering. Willy Rotten took a pancake and moved off into a dark corner.

We were going to ship that morning and had six or seven miles to ride to get to the backside of the shipping trap. We caught horses in the dark and started trotting west. The cattle were in what was called the Wheat Pasture, and we rode up the outside of it on the south side. It was very dark, there being no moon. We could not distinguish a horizon or see more than a few feet and rode along very close to the barbed wire fence, which helped us keep our bearings. There were probably fifteen men horseback, and Willy Rotten was behind brooding over the fried egg incident. Brad Meade, never wanting to miss the opportunity to pour salt in someone's open wound, said rather loudly, "Who pissed on your cornflakes this morning, Willy?"

"NOBODY!" Willy Rotten snapped back. "But Ed sure took a dump in my fried eggs!"

ഐരു
Too Many Cattle and a Girl I Never Met
ഐരു

Diamond A Ranch, Fall 1973

Mike's wagon was camped at the Sevens Ranch down by the shipping corral, and we had been gathering Mexican steers in that area for a week or so. Alvin Wagner and his wife Hazel were living there in the old wooden-frame house and had been there for several years. Alvin was a good old-time cowboy who had been raised near the Texas line, out east of Tucumcari. He had been helping us gather the steers while we were there in his country. The last afternoon we were there, we trailed about twenty-five hundred steers from the holding pasture at the Sevens headquarters, to the west four miles, and put them in a small trap at a dirt tank called Six-Shooter. Alvin helped us trail the big herd to Six-Shooter. The next morning, we rolled up camp and sent Rex, the cook, along with the hood, Luis, to Hoffman Camp where we would camp for a day or two. The cowboy crew, which consisted of eight of us, trotted to Six-Shooter, gathered the small holding pasture, and pointed them southwest toward a gate in the backside of Thirty-Six Pasture, seven miles away. I'm sure Alvin would have been glad to help us, but beings we were moving camp, and therefore not working in Alvin's country anymore, Mike Landis didn't ask him to help. In Mike's mind, the old-timers who wrote the book on cowboy codes wouldn't have approved, so Alvin wasn't asked, and he stayed in camp and watched us trot away.

Six-Shooter Dirt Tank had a barbed wire water lot around it, and the holding trap was about five hundred acres in size. We gathered the trap, throwing the twenty-five hundred steers into the water lot, and then Mike Landis instructed Bob Scott and me to take the points and turn the herd toward Thirty-Six. "Let 'em string out boys. Let 'em string out! These ole Mexican steers will line out and walk like saddle horses, so let 'em string out! Don't stop 'em!"

Bob was on the left point and I was on the right, and we had our orders, and we let them string out. The country for miles in all directions was thick with juniper and pinon trees with gramma grass growing in between. Shortly after getting the herd out of the water lot, we were headed down a two-track dirt road that accompanied an underground coal slurry line that ran all the way from Kayenta on the Navajo Reservation to Laughlin, Nevada. The Kayenta coal fueled a big power plant at Laughlin. Bob and I were good soldiers and followed our orders allowing the Mexicans to string out and walk. After the leaders had traveled about four miles, the herd was strung out for at least a mile and a half. Up near the leaders, riding point, was almost boring because the steers performed just like Mike had predicted and walked along two abreast, a steer in each of the two tracks in the primitive road. It was at least a half mile to the man behind me on the flank, and everyone was having an easy day. At times I couldn't see the drags.

It was late October and deer hunting season. When I first saw the old Willys Jeep coming toward us, carrying a couple beer-drinking hunters, I thought nothing of it. They traveled slow, enjoying the scenery and the opportunity to drink Coors, and they moseyed into the front of the herd traveling in low gear. When the slow moving Jeep approached the two lead steers, the animals stopped and picked their heads up with ears pointed forward and looked with curiosity. When the vehicle was a mere twenty feet away, one steer stepped off the road to the right and the other to the left, and every steer behind them did the same. At first the situation seemed benign because nothing was going fast, and there was certainly no stampede. But the steers that had been walking for several hours started grazing, and all cowboys and stockmen know that a grazing cow brute walks as they graze. The steers were almost moving faster as they grazed than when they had been moving gently down the road. They fanned out and grazed in all directions, and the trees were thick. Being gentle was now a deficit instead of a positive attribute because the steers now wanted to eat, and the galloping and hollering and slapping of chaps by cowboys had no effect on them. They walked and seemed to disappear in the trees, and the crew was spread so far apart we didn't know where each other were.

I was riding a horse named K Bar, who at one time had been my friend Jim Dolan's practice bucking horse, and he was fairly tough, but not tough enough. I don't know how long we fought the scattered herd of steers trying to keep them together and deposited into the backside of Thirty-Six Pasture. We got the cattle put where we wanted them, but it was a nasty battle. K Bar didn't die, but he was never the same.

Later on that fall, Mike was instructed by Jim Lowrance, the Diamond A manager, to move the wagon out to Number Five in Last Chance Pasture on the north end of the Aubrey Valley. The ranch had three crews working. Besides Mike's crew, which I was a part of, Burley McDonald and his crew were gathering the north half of the ranch. Jim Lowrance had a third crew that he called his shipping crew, which consisted of four men and himself. The two wagon crews would throw cattle into a holding trap located near shipping pens, of which there were several around the ranch, and Lowrance and his shipping crew would gather the traps and load the cattle on trucks. At least, theoretically, that was what was supposed to happen. Actually, both wagon crews also did a lot of shipping and loading. There was an old Texan named Ernest Baty and a fellow my age named Larry Smith on the shipping crew, but I can't remember who else.

We gathered Last Chance Pasture when we first moved out to Five and put the steers into the Guilliam Pasture that was ten square miles in size, with old Route 66 Highway running along its south boundary. We put over three thousand steers into the Guilliam that we gathered in Last Chance. Last Chance was a large open piece of country with very sandy soil and is about a hundred and five sections, or square miles, in size. I suppose it took us two or three days to gather it.

While all of us on Mike's crew were doing this, Burley McDonald and his cowboys were working up on top and were camped at Owen Dam. Jim Lowrance had given Burley orders to put together a large herd at Owen Dam and then trail it down Crater Canyon, which emptied out into the Aubrey Valley a mile or two east of Number Five where Mike's wagon was camped. Mike had received orders to ride up into the mouth of Crater Canyon on the afternoon of a specific day and take possession of the steers Burley and his men were gathering and trailing down the canyon. The day after this connection was to be made,

Mike and all of us on his crew were supposed to trail the steers south and put them in Guilliam Pasture.

All of this sounded good in theory and looked good on paper, but sometimes theory and reality aren't related. Crater Canyon was a rough and steep piece of country cutting into the Aubrey Rim that rises a thousand feet off the valley floor. There are lots of trees and a considerable amount of brush, not to mention the rocks and cliffs in the canyon. Trailing a herd of cattle down that trail

could easily be done if the numbers and conditions were right, but Burley had accumulated a herd of twenty-five hundred or more steers, which were his orders. He, like Mike, had eight cowboys on his crew including himself, and the conditions and numbers weren't a good mixture. There was a big set of shipping pens at Rose Well six miles north of Owen Dam that were easy to get to, and there was much talk about the folly of not going that direction with Burley's herd.

Mike had been told that Burley would deliver the herd of twenty-five hundred steers to the mouth of Crater Canyon in the late afternoon, which meant in Mike's mind, three o'clock. From where we were camped, you could see the gaping mouth of the canyon a short distance away. A man could saddle his favorite horse and lope up there in five minutes. The canyon had great pinnacles on either side of its cavernous throat that rose up hundreds of feet like two sentinels guarding a dark tunnel shaded by pine trees and brush of every variety. We could have traveled that direction much earlier than we did beings we broke for lunch at eleven that morning. But instead of venturing forth into the bowels of the canyon in search of Burley and his crew, we lay around camp until two thirty in the afternoon. I suppose it was Burley's duty to hand over the herd at the very mouth of the canyon and not a mile or two up stream. Some men might have thought about providing a little assistance to the eight men on Burley's crew, but in our camp, there was no conversation with that flavor.

At half past two, we ventured out to where our horses were, and Mike hollered, "Horses!" which was the usual order to every man that he should announce in a loud voice what horse he wanted the wagon boss to rope and lead out to him. After saddling up, we rode east toward the canyon mouth. We arrived in short order and pulled up, staring into the dark hole before us, and wondered where the herd was. We waited, and for a period of time, there was silence and nothing to see except an occasional red-tailed hawk or crow. I suppose at first it was just noise, brush cracking, and rocks rolling, and an occasional holler from a man who sounded as if he was loading the last cannonball left, knowing the enemy would roll over him after his final shot was fired. And then they began to appear, steers everywhere from the very top of the canyon on one side to the very top on the other and everywhere in between. The canyon was a half mile wide at its mouth, and the leaders were spread out all over the width. The only thing keeping them contained was a rim rock at the top that kept them incarcerated below the rim.

Mike finally gave orders that it would be acceptable according to his code book to go forth and provide assistance. I took off climbing up the promontory on the north wall of the canyon, and somewhere near the top, I met Larry Leist, who was the point man on that side of the herd. One didn't need to ask to know that his horse was completely wasted. He had no idea where the man next to him was, he only knew that he and the rest of Burley's crew were outnumbered. I sensed that he was beyond being mad, and like his horse he was tired, and hoped that perhaps I could help him get shed of the steers. Steers were everywhere oozing down the canyon, moving slowly like cooling magma from a dying volcano.

Burley and his men could have treated us like we had treated them and turned and rode off toward their camp as soon as we appeared. But instead they stayed in their traces, working hard until the herd was completely out of the canyon and exposed by the openness of the valley floor. The task was now easy or was what Whistle Mills would have called "duck soup." We deposited the large herd through a gate into the same holding trap that held our remuda of horses. Burley and his men turned around and rode slowly, winding their way back up the canyon to their camp at Owen Dam. I heard later from Larry that Burley made them ride in a slow walk all the way, trying to save their tired horses, and they arrived late in the night. We were back in camp relaxing before sundown.

The plan was for us to take this same herd the next morning and trail them down and put them through a gate into the north side of the Guilliam Pasture, a distance of nine miles. While we were doing this, Jim Lowrance and his shipping crew of four men were supposed to be gathering the three thousand or more steers that we had just put in the Guilliam out of Last Chance, crossing Route

66 Highway, and taking them south a couple miles to the old railroad shipping corrals adjacent to the deep Pica railroad water wells.

Trailing the twenty-five hundred steers from our camp at Number Five to the Guilliam Pasture was an easy trip. There were no trees anywhere in the bottom of the Aubrey Valley, and the ground was sandy and easy going. The herd of steers marched down there like saddle horses, and we arrived at the gate early, around ten o'clock. We counted them in the gate as they passed by two and four abreast, and our task was accomplished. From where we were sitting on our horses on the north fence of the Guilliam, it was three and a half miles south to old 66 and a gate where Lowrance and his shipping crew were trying to cross their herd of three thousand. Interstate 40 had not been completed at that time, and all the traffic between Seligman and Kingman was still traveling on this stretch of Route 66. Lowrance had notified the highway patrol, and two officers had showed up to stop the traffic for Lowrance and his men so they could cross their steers over the pavement. The D.P.S. officers had traffic backed up a couple miles going both directions waiting for the Diamond A cowboys to get their herd across. We sat on our horses for five minutes and watched the rodeo taking place three and a half miles to the south. There was a mushroom-shaped cloud of dust rising five hundred feet in the air, and the steers were milling and running, and we could see men horseback running at breakneck speed trying to get the steers to take to the pavement.

I thought we might lope down there and help Jim Lowrance and his crew, but no one dared mention a comment or opinion. That would have gone against the Code. We watched, and Mike Landis rolled a Bull Durham cigarette and smiled as he took a long and satisfying pull of the hot smoke. With a big grin that exposed a mouthful of teeth he said, "Hell with that sorry @#$%^&*!!" He turned ole Sunday north and whipped him down a hind leg and loped toward camp with seven men following. It was the cowboy way. It was Mike's way, and we were working for him.

℘○℃

Diamond A Ranch, Spring 1994

A ranch with ten thousand mother cows will accumulate a lot of bulls. We wintered most of the bulls that would be turned out with the cows, running them on the plains in the Bishop Pasture north of Camp Sixteen. We pulled the wagon out around the twenty-sixth day of March and started working at Camp Sixteen, and the first chore was shoeing up the remuda. We worked at this a day or so and then gathered all the bulls that had spent the winter turned out in Bishop. We spent a day or two scattering the six hundred bulls that we had gathered. There is nothing more aggravating to handle than a bunch of fat bulls in the springtime after they've been separated from the cowherd for five months. I would rather trail eight thousand wild steers twenty-five miles than drive a hundred young fresh bulls ten miles.

One morning we left Camp Sixteen trailing about three hundred bulls southeast toward Supai Camp, seven miles away. We were going to put them through a gate into Midway Pasture and turn them loose. The bulls ran and fought and bellered and rode each other and then repeated the process all over again the entire seven miles. BBaahhh!! BBaah! Buuu Ba Mooh! It was like being sober and tied down in the Palace Bar amidst three hundred drunk cowboys and hard rock miners. Mooo! BBuahh! Baaah! Moooo! The cows we saw along the trail put a figure 9 in their tails and ran for their lives in fear of what lay ahead.

Four or five days earlier, a young boy had showed up from Texas whose name was Bubba. He was a handsome young man and appeared to have a considerable amount of talent but was obviously very green. By the way he acted, he had never ventured far from his home turf and was obviously having a bit of a struggle dealing with survival among a crew of the rough heathens that he now camped with. Bubba wasn't the only green hand in the crew, but for whatever reason, he soon found himself to be the odd man out. That fact, along with being a thousand miles from home, was a lonely proposition.

Brad Meade was among the crew, and four or five years older than Bubba, and was the type who exhibited no fear or pain, being over six feet tall and stronger than some of the bulls we were trailing. Brad got up every morning laughing and dreaming of some mischievous deed he might plot against someone weaker or smaller than he was. We were all weaker and smaller than Brad. We were all in harm's way and learned to be on guard when around him.

Bubba made the mistake of getting Brad's attention, similar to the way a packrat catches the eye of a diamondback rattlesnake. The other green hands in the crew egged Brad on, not because Bubba had wronged anyone, but they knew if Bubba was in the crosshairs, they wouldn't be; and so Bubba sat in the hot seat. The hot seat wasn't pleasant, and the only way to escape out of it was to keep your mouth shut and take your medicine until your antagonists were satisfied with whatever pain they had administered. Bubba made the mistake of not keeping his mouth shut.

We trailed the fighting and bellowing bulls to Supai and sighed with relief as we turned them loose amidst a herd of unsuspecting females who had made the mistake of lounging around that water hole. The bulls continued to fight and act stupid, and the cows got smart and ran like hades.

We turned back to the northwest and began trotting back to camp, seven miles away, two abreast. We moved along for several miles with me and Jim Marler in front and everyone else behind. Brad was somewhere in the back holding court, and as we traveled along, we could hear occasional outbursts of laughter and guffawing as one story after another was told among the crew.

Somewhere about halfway between Supai and the wagon, there was a great crashing sound of rocks rolling and thundering hooves, and Brad whipped his horse up alongside of me and said, "Do you know what that sorry Texan, Bubba, just told me?"

"Well no, Brad, what did he say?"

"He said that he had a sister back in Texas that could gather this sorry outfit by herself!"

I continued trotting along while struggling to keep a straight face. "Wow!" I replied.

"That sorry no good @#$%^&*!!! I'm going to go back there and kick his hind end!"

"Oh, Brad, settle down! Go back there and tell him that when we get to camp, I'm going to take him to Seligman and a telephone, and I'm going to get him to call her, and

I'm going to hire her to replace you." Jim Marler even grinned at that one.

"That sorry no good Texan! I'm going to whip his hind end!"

"Oh, leave him alone; he's just a kid." Brad retreated to the rear and we trotted on.

Man, I'd like to meet that girl. I muttered to myself.

෨෬
Wild Steers in Shafer
෨෬

Diamond A Ranch, Winter 1994

From the day I took over as wagon boss, I began to hear stories about the big steers in the Shafer Pasture. I was told that several years earlier, about 1989 or 1990, they had hired a man who was an expert at gathering cattle with a helicopter to come and fly and gather the big Shafer steers. I was never told the man's name, but he came from California and had a reputation for being good at doing this type of work. According to legend, he had been successful at locating the steers and driving them toward the cowboy crew that were present and supposed to be assisting him in subduing the wild beasts. The problem was there were no corrals within a dozen miles of where the cattle were running, and the country was rough, rocky, and brushy in every direction. There was also no shortage of water. When I had worked for the outfit twenty years earlier, there had been a real good water lot around the big Shafer Dirt Tank that almost always had water. There also had been a good picket corral off of one corner of the water lot that was big enough to hold a large herd of cows that could be used to brand calves or hold cattle. On top of that there had been a good holding trap that was probably four hundred acres in size. In the early '70s, we had camped the wagon there, and it was a fine setup and well maintained. In the twenty year span between 1972 in 1992 all of these facilities had fallen down, making them unusable. The helicopter found and drove the wild steers to the cowboys, but the cowboys were unable to hold 'em, or control them, horseback. There was no corral nearby in which to pen them, with or without a helicopter. The cowboys, for some reason, would not rope them; consequently, the wild steers remained in Shafer with a few spilling over into the Trinity Pasture that bordered Shafer to the west.

I had plans of attacking the wild bunch in January of 1993, but with all the rain we got between Christmas and the 1st of March getting around the top country was very difficult. There was water everywhere, and a great deal of the winter, it was so boggy a horse would sink to his hocks in the malpai country where so much of the remnant, like the big steers, was running. A winter like that makes remnant hunting difficult. We did manage to gather some remnants in Big Chief, Owen Dam, and parts of Black Mountain and the lower end of Trinity, but the Shafer Pasture remained untouched.

One day in the fall of 1993, when we were working in Shafer with the entire wagon crew, a man named Bruce Barker jumped a big bunch of steers while we were making a drive in the hills north of the Shafer Dirt Tank. He ran them for a good spell but could not control them and showed up at the holdup with no cattle but was very excited telling me he had seen at least fifteen huge steers in a bunch. He said every one of them outweighed any mother cow on the outfit and were all much taller. I did not doubt him, because I had heard the stories too many times from good hands that I figured were telling me the truth. I figured that it would be better to do battle with them at a different time, so we gathered the pasture as best we could with the wagon crew, promising myself I would be back at a later date.

The winter of 1993 and 1994 proved to be much drier than the winter before, and so around New Year's we set to work trying to catch the famous steers. Walt Robinson was a good cowboy and a friend of mine who lived on his family's ranch near Truxton, halfway between Seligman and Kingman. Walt had been raising Catahoula catch dogs and using them for a long time. I asked Walt if he had a good dog that he would sell me. He told me that he really only had one sure-enough good dog: a male he called Banjo. He wouldn't sell him, he said, but he would loan him to me if I promised to take good care of him and give him back if I got where I didn't need him. He also gave me a female that was a sister to Banjo, but he said he hadn't used her much and didn't know if she was any good. We called her Sister.

Sometime in early January, Jim Marler and I took our beds and several horses apiece, along with the two Catahoula dogs I had just acquired, and went to Black Tank Camp to spend several days hunting the big steers. Baldy was spending the winter at Black Tank, and I thought I would get him to help Jim Marler and myself on our wild cow hunt. I figured we would go at the project in spurts, working for three or four days at a time and getting the cattle we caught hauled out of there, and then leave it alone for a week or two letting things settle down. Then we would attack it again and keep repeating the process all winter if necessary, or until we had the country cleaned out enough we couldn't find any good tracks.

Black Tank Camp itself was north of the northern boundary of Shafer Pasture about three miles. The house and barn set down in the bottom of the canyon, perhaps a hundred fifty or two hundred feet lower in elevation than the black malpai rim rocks on top of the canyon rim. There was no shortage of malpai rock, pinion pine and juniper trees, as well as oak brush and lots of cliff rose. Where these items didn't manifest themselves there was an abundance of good gramma grass. In the spring, after a wet winter, which at best was occasional, there was plenty of foxtail bunch grass, filaree, and young tumbleweeds (all of which cows like to eat and thrive on). Now it was cold and everything was dormant making the wild cow hunting easier. A big cow, steer, or bull would be a whole lot harder to handle on the end of a rope when fat from eating green foxtail and tumbleweeds.

The first morning the three of us went up into Shafer was a cold one, probably about five above at daylight. There was a road leaving the Black Tank Camp climbing up a steep incline in the rocky canyon wall and heading south toward the Shafer Pasture. Like everything else on the tired old ranch, the road was in bad repair, being washed out right down to solid black rock making it almost impassable. I had Baldy and Jim lead my horse, and I put my Dodge diesel pickup in four-low and crawled out, pulling a sixteen-foot trailer at two miles an hour. Once we topped out, they loaded our three horses, and we drove south five miles to near the center of the Shafer Pasture. I stopped, and we unloaded our horses and the two dogs, mounted up and headed west on a faint two-track road. After we had traveled maybe half a mile, the dogs lifted their noses and stopped for a second, smelling something, and then they took off running down the road ahead of us. They were soon out of sight, so we picked up our pace a little and continued trotting along. Within several minutes, we could hear the two dogs barking around a half mile away.

The dogs continued barking, and before too long, we caught up with them. Banjo and Sister had three big steers held up that were standing with their butts together, staring out in three different directions, taking turns slinging their large heads at the hounds. One of the steers was an old Mexican that wore a very readable M brand on his hip, and a

7C on his left ribs. He was at least sixteen hands high and was a buckskin and white pinto color. He had no horns. Another of them was a solid reddish-brown muley and probably weighed a thousand pounds. The third steer was mostly black with a little white in his face and stomach. He was very big. The steers paid no attention to us at first, and we surrounded them staying about one hundred yards away.

We had no game plan, other than catching big steers. There really was no sense in talking; we would simply react to the events as they unfolded. It was obvious to me that once we started getting closer and putting pressure on them that the big steers were not going to cooperate. We were all cinched up. My rope was tied to the horn. After a moment or two, we slowly moved in closer to see what would develop; and sure enough, when we got within thirty yards, the steers broke and ran in three different directions. The big pinto went east between Baldy and Jim, and Baldy took after him. The brown steer bolted to the other side of Jim, and he was in hot pursuit going after him headed south. The big black steer headed west. The spot where this all started was actually a decent spot, located in the bottom of a wide draw. In the distance every direction except east, the country got rougher and thicker with vegetation; but close by, the pinion and juniper were scattered with good openings here and there.

I was mounted on a horse I had just started riding named Sandy that weighed one thousand pounds at most. I had only been on the horse one other time and knew almost nothing about him, but he seemed to be completely gentle and had a fairly decent handle on him. I had never tried to rope anything on him but was not expecting to have any problems. The black steer left there going full blast, and I had a hundred yards or so of open ground to close in on him. Within several seconds, I was on him, and I took about two swings and let 'er rip; and when the rope connected, the steer was off to the right several feet, which probably saved my life.

I have only been truly terrified when on a horse two times, and this was the first; the second came about twelve years later. My judgment of Sandy's reaction to being roped on was poorly conceived. When I turned loose of my loop, Sandy caught another gear that I didn't know was in his arsenal. In a mila-second, we were traveling at a terrifying rate of speed, and we passed the big black steer like he was standing still; but the truth was, he was running all-out. All of my life, I've heard of cowboys who are super quick and athletic enough to step off right before a horse was going to fall or some other mishap was about to take place. That's never been the case with me. I have been a fair to middlen' bronc rider at best; but if a horse was going to fall, jump off a cliff, or flip over backwards, I will ride them deep in the saddle every time. (I am now packing a considerable amount of metal because of my ability to ride a horse when he is going down.) As Sandy breezed past the black steer, he went to the right, and coming up fast was a very large juniper tree. In that instant, I thought I should step off, but in reality, that was never an option. My rope hit the juniper about midway between me and the steer, and I figured I was a dead man because I was sure the steer out-weighed my horse by several hundred pounds. It all happened in a flash, and I was expecting to get jerked down like a lightning bolt had hit me, but instead there wasn't even a slight jerk. The only thing I could figure was the rope hit a sharp snag on the tree trunk that cut it like a razor. Sandy ran off down the country a couple hundred yards where I got him stopped and coiled up what was left of my rope that was now fifteen feet long. The steer ran off down the country dragging the rest of it from around his neck.

I had coiled up and tied fifteen or twenty feet of an old rope behind the cantle of my saddle to be used as a neckin' rope. I got it and tied it with a square knot to the end of what was left of the rope tied to my saddle horn. I was back in business. For some reason, the two dogs had stayed with me and the black steer when the action had started, and now I could hear them a quarter of a mile away, barking to beat the band, so I loped that way. By now the dogs were getting aggressive and would grab an ear or nose and hang on for a second or two, but the steer would overpower them, and when I showed up again, he took off. We were now in thick brush, but the dogs were staying with him and tormenting him. I decided to bide my time and let the situation knock a little air out of him, knowing before too long we would come to a little better place to do battle. When we did come to a spot where the vegetation wasn't quite as thick, I got him roped for the second time. There was nothing spectacular about it because he had now slowed down. Sandy was winded and sweating, and as far as I was concerned, he was now a bona fide rope horse. By the time I got the big black steer wooled around and tied down, Sandy was sure enough bona fide. Under such conditions you learn real fast. I left the big steer tied down and went back to where we first encountered the three steers, thinking that Jim and Baldy would eventually show up. After waiting around for ten or fifteen minutes, they came riding back. Jim Marler had caught the steer he followed and had him tied down, but Baldy had been unsuccessful in apprehending the old outlaw he had chased. We were on a faint two-track road, so I sent Baldy back to get the truck and bring it up to where we were, and Jim and I left to lead the steers we had caught back to that spot so we could load them in the trailer. We had perhaps three quarters of a mile distance to get the steers back to that spot. The black steer was ready to go somewhere when I got back to him. When I let him up, he wanted to fight and butt his head into my horse's shoulder and my leg, but I dallied up close with his head right next to my knee, and we started moving. At first I just let him go any direction he wanted, just as long as he was moving; but before too long, we were going in the general direction of our agreed rendezvous and getting there wasn't too big of a problem with the exception of dodging numerous tree branches and saplings. I had made sure my hat was pulled down real tight. Jim got his steer there at the spot, and we got the steers loaded without incident, pulling them in by the saddle horn. We spent the rest of the morning hunting more cattle and found a cow or two and a couple yearlings weighing around six hundred pounds. By the middle of the day, we got back to camp and cooked ourselves some lunch. After lunch I took off to Pica, forty-five miles away, so I could deposit our catch in a corral that I was sure would hold them. I did not get a chance to weigh the big black steer until five days later, but when I did, he weighed fifteen hundred seventy pounds.

The next day we continued scouring the pasture, hunting remnant, preferably big steers. We were finding a few cattle every day that included a cow or two and several weaner-size calves or yearlings. We also found several unbranded cattle that were grown, or close to it, but did not find any more steers weighing over eight or nine hundred pounds for several days. Every afternoon I would go to Pica with the cattle we had caught to make sure they would be secure in a solid corral.

Our two dogs were working good, especially Banjo, and we were catching almost everything we found; but we knew, because of the amount of tracks present, that we had not found them all; and the country had lots of trees and brush, and plenty of hiding places. On the third day, we worked late only finding a couple critters, but always feeling like the big haul was just around the bend, so I didn't get started to Pica with our daily catch until a few minutes after sundown. When the road left Black Tank Camp, it traveled east for about a mile before turning north and eventually west toward Rose Well. At Rose Well it went south to Pica. I was pulling the gooseneck going east with an old barbed wire fence on my right, and when I was maybe a mile from the house, I saw two big steers just standing by the fence. Both of them weighed about a thousand pounds. They were pointed north and gave me the impression they had been traveling. I figured our continuous presence in Shafer had things shook up and maybe the cattle were going to change ranges, at least for a while. I got the pickup turned around and raced back to camp and jumped out and hollered at Jim and Baldy, telling them about the big steers I had just seen. I told them I was going to saddle up and try to catch one of them. Jim said, "Wait for me." So I told Baldy to follow us in the pickup and trailer. I had a bay roan horse I called Fooler in the corral. I saddled him, and Jim caught his, and we headed east at a lope. By the time we got to where the steers were, it was on the dark side of dusk, but the two steers had not moved. There was no sense talking so I whipped old Fooler down the hind leg and chased after one. It was dark enough that I just threw at a dark mass running in front of me, but Fooler could feel me cut loose with the loop, and when I did, he shut 'er down. The bellering commenced, and in the distance, I could hear tree limbs breaking and more bellering and crashing about, and I knew by the sound of things that Jim Marler had caught the other steer. When Baldy arrived with the trailer, we got the cattle already in the sixteen-foot gooseneck locked in front of the divider gate and jerked our new victims in the trailer with them. By the time we got this done, it was completely dark.

After catching these two steers in the dark, which I felt had left Shafer because of all the ruckus we had been causing over several days, I decided we needed to quit working in the area for a while. In my mind, I thought it best to concentrate on gathering remnant somewhere else and let the cattle in Shafer settle down and perhaps bunch up a little. It wasn't as if that was the only place we had remnant to gather. There were at least three hundred square miles in all of the pastures in what is called the top country, with remnant in all of it. Actually, at that time, no one even knew how many cattle were scattered throughout the top. You could drive around in a pickup and see cattle everywhere that had been ungathered for several roundups, and seeing a full-grown maverick from the cab of the truck was commonplace. So Jim Marler and I left Black Tank to work on remnant somewhere else with plans on coming back in a couple of weeks.

We returned to Shafer several more times in the next six weeks and were successful every day gathering something. Some days we got two or three and other days maybe eight or ten. We gathered several dozen cows, almost all of them branded, with big weaner calves following them. By the first week in March, we had caught and loaded about sixteen full-grown steers. Some of them were three or four years old and several that were as old as twelve or thirteen. We finally got where we were having trouble finding tracks. It was a dry winter, and the ground was powdery, which made accurate tracking easier. I felt like we were down to less than ten critters left in the Shafer pasture. We knew of one big steer that was still in there for sure because we had seen him once, from a distance, but had never even gotten close enough to have given him cause to be alarmed at our presence. What else was there, we did not know.

There was an old man living in Seligman named Bud Layman who owned several airplanes and liked to fly. I got acquainted with him, and he offered to fly me around the ranch anytime I wanted to look around from the air. I talked to Bud and told him I would like to take him up on his offer. We left the ground right after daylight on a day that was supposed to be nice and warm with no wind. It was in early March, and it didn't take long, flying in Bud's Cessna, until we were over Shafer, which in a straight line was sixteen or seventeen miles northeast of Seligman. We flew in a grid pattern going back and forth over the township-sized pasture. We found one bunch of cattle, and from the air, it looked like a couple cows, three or four big calves or yearlings, and one big steer. They were in the perfect spot to be easily located again later in the day.

I decided to go the back way into Shafer, traveling along the road that went up through the west side of the Sevens Ranch by Garrett Tank and Bishop, and enter Shafer through a gate in the southeast corner of the pasture. I took a cowboy named Steve Webb with me. Jim Marler was staying at Rose Well helping the camp man there gather remnant in Owen Dam and Rogers Pastures. Steve and I had been loaded up and sitting on ready before Bud and I took off in the airplane to go scouting. By ten o'clock in the morning, we had the small bunch of cattle located, being mounted on two good horses. We agreed that one of us would try and keep the bunch together while the other one roped and tied a critter down. I took to the big steer first who was a big buckskin Mexican that was about half Brahma, having high Brahma-looking horns and a pretty good hump on his back. He stood sixteen hands and probably weighed fourteen hundred fifty. For all his size and looks, he actually went down pretty easy and without incident. We traded off, and Steve tied one down, and then I another. We made sure the bunch kept moving eastward, toward more open country that was more accessible from the road; and before too long, we had the whole bunch tied down. Next, we began jerking them into the gooseneck trailer, starting with the big steer that we tied by the horns to a front corner of the trailer. We loaded the steer, two cows, and two yearlings weighing about six hundred pounds in front of the divider gate and then ran out of room. We jerked another yearling in behind the gate and left him tied down and had one more to go. Things were going too smoothly.

We were backing the trailer up to the last yearling when we heard someone holler, and we looked up to see Baldy loping up from the distance. He had been prowling around and had seen us from several miles off and rode up offering to help. He was glad to see someone after being by himself for several weeks without seeing or talking to anyone. I asked him if he wanted to jerk the last critter in the trailer for us, and he said that sure he would love to. We were going to leave the yearling's hind legs tied together to keep them immobile while we loaded our two horses in with them, including the one that was also tied down outside. Baldy was riding a big Belgian-crossed horse called Moose. He was a blood bay with a white blaze face and four stocking legs. Moose resembled the

famous bucking horse named Kool Alley. We fed Baldy's long rope through the side of the trailer and around the yearling's hind legs. Steve and I were going to help guide the critter into the trailer making sure nothing went amiss. I hollered at Baldy that we were ready, and he spurred old Moose who hit the nylon with all his thirteen hundred-plus pounds of horse flesh. Baldy had forgotten to cinch up real tight, and his saddle turned sideways enough to pinch Moose in the withers, and he blew up and went to bucking.

The first jump threw Baldy out of the saddle, but he hung onto his rope keeping his dallies, and Moose went into a spin turning to the right. Baldy had let a lot of rope run across his slick horn, and after one revolution, he was getting wrapped up in the rope, and his right leg was between the rope and Moose's right flank, which had the man tied to his stirrup by the tight rope. Baldy's head was three or four feet off the ground and four or five feet away from the horse's flank soaring through space like a ball on the end of a string. Moose kept spinning in the same place, and for three revolutions, Baldy's head barely missed the heavy metal brush fender of the trailer on the left back corner. I had visions of a watermelon dropping on a cement slab. The horse was bucking and kicking, and with all this happening, Baldy's head kept getting in the way, so I found no place for a sharp knife to slice the tight nylon rope into pieces.

By some miracle, Baldy suddenly came loose, not unlike a stone released from David's sling. He was jettisoned through space, his body being parallel to the rocky earth, his head being exposed because his hat had departed several revolutions earlier. At the exact moment he was emancipated from his bondage to the Belgian horse, both of his oversized boots came off. They were now sailing through space along with other articles of his personage: the whole of which resembled space trash thrust outward in a spiral motion away from a galaxy that was eternally spinning out of control. The most fantastic piece of this scene was Baldy's dirty socks. As a result of all the tremendous energy produced by the dynamo that Steve Webb and I witnessed, Baldy's socks had been pulled off about halfway. The tops of the calf-high woolen stockings clung near the low part of his ankles with about eight inches of loose sock hanging limply in front of his toes. Upon reconnecting with planet earth, he immediately stood up and grinned and shouted, "I'm all right, Boss!"

In the excitement of the moment, I hollered, "Baldy, your socks are filthy!"

ഇൗര

Turned Loose and Running Wild

ഇൗര

The Diamond A horse program had become somewhat peculiar during the late '70s and '80s. One of the people I was working for wanted to raise bucking horses and had imported a Belgian stud to cross on Quarter Horse mares with hopes of raising buckers. The colts from the Belgian stud were sent to Jack, the company horse whisperer in California, who would give orders to some young boy who was working there and being discipled in the art of whispering and other secrets of horsemanship. When these colts, and others of various breeds, came back to the ranch at Seligman, they would have ten or fifteen rides on them and whatever respect of man they might have possessed at one time would be gone. It was my job to dish these out to anyone under the age of sixty who had the privilege of working for me. If the colts were still bucking cowboys off after a roundup or two, they would then be put in the bucking string. Several of these horses went on to have respectable careers as rodeo saddle broncs including three horses named Santa Fe, Snuffy, and Crunch. These three geldings were in the remuda from the time they were three to five years old. I saw Jimmer Fancher ride Snuffy lots of times and make a hand on him even though he hated every minute of it. There were several cowboys on the outfit who talked about riding him but, in truth, were afraid to get in the same corral as him. Pete Chinaretto rode Snuffy at the

Cowpuncher's Reunion when the horse was about ten years old, and it was one of the best cowboy bronc rides I've ever seen. On that particular day, any good judge would have given Snuffy twenty-one points, if not twenty-two, all thirteen hundred pounds of him. Mark Westlake made a ride on Santa Fe, when the horse was a three-year-old, that sticks in my mind. We were seven or eight miles east of Rose Well in Lower Sandstone Pasture. Mark called for him to ride in the afternoon, and he sure bucked when he got on him.

In the spring of ninety-five, Crunch showed up in a load of horses that Whispering Jack had sent east from California. He was three years old, and we took him down to the shipping scales and weighed him; he balanced the scales weighing thirteen hundred fifty. My son Clay asked for him, so I put the horse in his string. He bucked, but perhaps the most impressive attribute he possessed was his head, which was too large for a normal-sized headstall. A regular snaffle disappeared, rings and all, into his hippo-sized mouth. One afternoon the whole crew and I left the corrals and rode out into a large holding trap west of the shipping pens. There were fifteen of us horseback. We rode up on a ridge, west of the shipping corrals, about a quarter mile and passed a large metal water trough and then continued traveling west toward the backside of the trap, five miles away. I was riding a real good three-year-old colt that I had bought from my friend Larry Leist. Clay and I were partners on him, and he had put thirty rides on the colt and then turned him over to me. The colt's registered name, believe it or not, was King of the Breed, but we called him Jim; and he was very fast. (A year later, I sold him to Mel Potter who lived in Marana, Arizona.) After going about a half mile past the water trough, we rode up on a big bull elk that was still in velvet. He stood up and his belly looked huge; he had no doubt just drank twenty or thirty gallons of water at the water trough we just rode by. I was cinched up tight, and without hesitating, I took my rope down and took after the elk. Jim ran right up on him and I roped him around one horn. Clay was riding the hame-headed bronc named Crunch and roped his hind feet with the first loop. We earmarked and castrated him and then turned him loose. Two men in the crew, Scott Westlake and Kent Snedicor, had worked as professional elk hunting guides and said the bull would have scored over four hundred Boone and Crockett points. I remember blood oozing out of his velvet-covered horns.

Another of the owner's ideas was to cross the half Belgian mares with a little streak-faced sorrel Arab stallion. The colts produced by this cross were not liked any better than the Belgian-Quarter crosses. They would buck but generally were sneakier about it. One day a nice Texas boy named Cody Sawyer was riding a five-year-old bald-faced sorrel that was an Arab cross. I can't remember the sorrel Arab's name, but I remember Cody and myself riding down the road heading north from Big E. Cody had a habit of riding with very loose reins. Perhaps he had showed some cutters. We were clip-clomping along in a fast walk when the sorrel Arab blew up unexpectedly and slammed Cody, kidneys first, in the middle of the hard roadbed. Ouch! I thought to myself. That's why I hold my bridle reins a little tighter.

One winter day, Steve Webb, Scott Westlake, and I went to gather the Arab stud that was running near Chino Well with a band of those "good" Belgian mares. When we got close to him, the Arab laid his ears back and charged us. I had my rope down and was ready to whip him and fight back, but Steve was unprepared. The stallion almost succeeded in biting him in the shoulder and neck but satisfied himself by biting his saddle pad, which he pulled completely out from under Steve's new saddle. The saddle was made by Matt Plumlee,and was beautifully made with basket stamping, and had only been ridden two or three times. I held the stud at bay while Steve picked up his saddle pad and put it back under the new saddle. When we tried to corral the stud at Chino Well, he charged again grabbing the corner of the saddle skirts, almost pulling the saddle off of Steve's horse. The new basket-stamped saddle had permanent teeth marks in the leather skirts on the left side behind the cantle. He charged Scott and left permanent teeth marks on his brand new Don Butler saddle as well.

The greatest stud of them all was a big chestnut Thoroughbred that showed up on the outfit a little before I did. They crossed the Thoroughbred, who was big and leggy, with the Belgian-Arab cross fillies. Some of the offspring created out of this conglomeration had Hall of Fame potential, but there are many Halls of Fame, and it's still undecided which one the Thoroughbred cross colts belonged in. Having a good cowboy stud like Hancock,

Colonel Freckles, Smart Little Lena, or Driftwood wasn't in the management plan.

Sometime in the spring of 1994, seven 3- and 4-year-old mares got out of a holding pasture at Pica and into the Last Chance Pasture. It's twelve miles from Pica Camp going west to the Hualapai Reservation fence. From Pica going north, it's seventeen miles to the boundary at Indian Well. All of the pasture was open and gently rolling, sandy country. A horse can literally run for miles in Last Chance.

In July, six or eight of us set out to gather the seven mares. Chip Dixon and his son Yates, Scott Westlake, Clay Ashurst, Steve Webb and I got together at Pica to make a run at them. I think there might have been another man or two with us, but I don't remember who they were.

I asked Bud Lehman to take me up in his Cessna airplane so I could locate them and make a plan. We took off from the airstrip on the edge of Seligman, flew west to Pica and the Aubrey Valley, and soon found the mares standing head to tail switching flies right against the reservation fence about twelve miles west of camp. Within forty-five minutes after flying over the mares, I was back out at Pica and ready to ride. All of us were riding stout mature horses.

I stationed men about two miles apart between camp and the mares, thinking we would relay them, hoping to have the wind knocked out of them by the time we got them close to the corrals at Pica. I hauled my horse in a gooseneck trailer close to where the mares were waiting and started them south toward the Grand Canyon Caverns and the southwest corner of Last Chance. At the corner someone picked them up and kept them moving east along the southern boundary of the Last Chance Pasture. When the man next to me took them from me, I loped back to my truck and loaded my horse and started driving back toward camp, twelve miles away. I could see the mares several miles to the south still moving on. They were now getting even with the Guilliam Pasture and running east.

I drove fast so I could catch up and help in the final stretch going into the corrals. I had thought that by the time the mares had ran within a mile or two of Pica Camp, we would have them winded, and they would be easy to handle. About a mile or so west of the corrals, the mares started veering off the fence and trying to go north. I suppose they could see the corrals and houses and didn't want to go there, but for whatever reason, they ran off and left us, headed north into the center of the Last Chance Pasture. Several of us quickly regrouped and loaded our horses in my horse trailer and drove out in front of the mares making a second attempt at penning them. They whipped us just as bad the second time. When I got home that night, I got out my map of the ranch and traced the route I had seen the mares run that day and found that they had ran a minimum of twenty-seven miles, never stopping. A great deal of the time, they were running hard.

Several days later, we attacked them again, but we brought in reinforcements. Mike McLaughlin and Brad Meade joined the rest of us that had been defeated by the mares. We found the mares on the southwest side of Robbers Roost and ran them south to the spot where we had started them a few days earlier. The mares had already ran five or six miles when they got to that spot, and we continued on the same path around the south side of Last Chance and on into Pica. This time we were successful.

ℰℭ

Frank Banks, who ran the Babbitt Ranch for thirty-some years and was a legendary cowboy, ran and roped at least seven different mule deer bucks on the Cataract Plains. This feat, which is almost unbelievable to me, is documented by various witnesses who saw him do it; besides, Frank was no liar or storyteller. I personally have roped three elk and know others who have roped more than that. I know several men who have roped bears and a buffalo or two. I've also roped a few wild burros and horses. It's been my experience that roping a bull elk is a piece of cake compared to running and roping a wild burro or horse, especially in the summertime when it's been raining and the horses are fat from eating stout feed. An elk is like a cow and doesn't have the lung capacity that a horse does. Frank Banks claimed a deer was the same way.

ℰℭ

Another great horse program was started by Mike Landis when he ran the Double O Ranch in the 1980s. The Double O borders the Diamond A to the south. Mike was legendary for being tight with the Double O Ranch checkbook, so when he went to putting together a broodmare band, he bought some mustangs that had been roped at China Lake, California. He not only bought mares to breed, but studs, and geldings to ride. The Double O mustangs, as they became known, were famous for several decades. Mike liked them because they were "Western."

One winter day in about 1990, or thereabouts, my wife and I went driving south of Seligman, down the county road by the Double O headquarters. It was cold and very windy. As we topped the small hill close to what was known as White Mill, I spied a cowpuncher riding west toward Daggs, a waterhole and set of corrals four miles away. The Double O headquarters was the opposite direction, about three quarters of a mile. I wasn't sure whom the man on horseback was but thought perhaps it was Mike or someone I knew, and I was hungry for a visit with a cowhand. The man spied me as I had stopped my vehicle and was standing next to it waving, hoping he would ride back and talk a while. He turned his mount around and started back from a quarter mile away. I could tell he was riding a bronc that was skittish. After a moment, I could tell it wasn't Mike, but I thought it might be Frank Bryant, whom I had heard was working there. The cowboy could never get the bronc any closer than two hundred yards. The wind screamed, and we couldn't hear each other, so we tried to communicate with sign language. Every time he raised his hand, the bronc grabbed himself and stampeded the opposite direction. The horse snorted and balked when he looked at me and my truck, although I was two hundred yards off. Finally the cowboy gave up and rode off, his horse holding his tail stuffed between his legs and stampeding. He was a China Lake mustang that they had been riding for months.

Sometime after Mike Landis started his mustang horse program, the same company that operated the Diamond A Ranch leased the Double O Ranch and retained Mike as manager for a short while. They also inherited the China Lake mustangs. A pretty big bunch of two- and three-year-old horse colts were running loose in a piece of country called the E. L. Pasture. E. L. was very rocky and rough, and the mustangs became very wild. Finally a big crew was put together with cowboys from the Double O, the Diamond A, and a neighboring ranch called the Fort Rock. Eric DeWitt was the foreman at Fort Rock and proved to be the wild-horse-gatheringest hombre I ever saw. The first day we worked in E. L., Eric caught more horses than the rest of the crew put together. When all the wild mustang colts were gathered, they were sent to Whispering Jack in California.

When Jack got them trained, they were sent to the Diamond A wagon. There were several of these that wouldn't have made a good bag of dog food, but the one that sticks in my mind was a bald-faced bay named Broken O. If Broken O had actually been ridden by someone during his stay in California, it wasn't more than a couple rides; and if he was ridden, I'll bet he had a foot tied up and was ridden three legged. I was told that the colts were well started and ready to go to work. I gave Broken 0 to a rugged young man named Tom who had what someone thought was a Swedish last name so the crew nicknamed him Tom Swede. He looked to be tough as a nail and told me he was willing to ride young horses.

We were camped at Keseha when Tom Swede called for Broken O the first time. He put a stiff curb bit in his mouth, which was a big mistake, but it probably didn't matter. Tom Swede and Broken O were destined for disaster. He mounted the mustang, and the horse went ballistic: bucking and raring up and striking at his face. Tom Swede came off pretty hard, but he was either tough or had no idea what lay ahead, perhaps he was both. He mounted again. By the time we had ridden two miles, Tom Swede had been bucked down hard three times.

We rode up to a gate, and while we were slowed down enough to all pass through, Clay offered to trade bridles with Tom Swede. The bridle on Clay's horse was a lot less severe than the one Broken O was wearing. The two cowboys jumped off and made their bridle exchange real fast while the rest of us watched. We were at the exact same spot where Beaner had run off with me a year or two earlier, eventually breaking his leg. When Tom Swede got the bridle on Broken O, he mounted up and this time the China Lake mustang decided to go "all in!" The horse went crazy, scary crazy, bucking and running and striking at his face. He was moving fast and somehow the Swede was managing to stay on top until the mustang made a suicidal move, unlike anything I ever witnessed, especially when you consider he had already bucked the cowboy off three times and had been ridden at least two miles. He bucked and stampeded straight into a big cedar tree, at least ten feet tall, and somehow landed in the upper half of it. Limbs were snapping and breaking, and the horse still refused to cease kicking and fighting. Somehow Tom Swede crawled out of the tree alive but unattached from the insane horse that Whispering Jack claimed was broke enough to ride. Whispering Jack said us Arizona boys just didn't understand how to get along with a colt. Looking back on it now, it seems funny; but at the time, the incident scared me, and I was ashamed I had put a decent human being on a horse like that.

Scott Westlake rode more than his share of Jack's products. A particularly notable one was a bay named Gabby. That same fall, and only a day or two away from the Tom Swede/Broken O incident, we came riding into Keseha after a particularly hard morning ride. Scott was riding Gabby and had been for at least five or six hours, maybe longer. Scott could ride and get along with a bad horse as good as anyone I've been around, but Gabby tested his skill. We came trotting into camp and everyone's horse had lots of sweat stains all over them. When Scott went to step off, Gabby spooked at something that no one else saw; and just as Scott's knee was over the cantle, Gabby blew up and bucked him off hard. A day or two later, Scott had the horse in a small round pen there at Keseha. The round corral was only twenty-two or twenty-three feet wide. He saddled him up and tied him to a railroad tie that was one of many that made the corral fence. Immediately after tying the knot in the lead rope that was attached to the railroad tie, Scott started walking away, and Gabby threw a fit and set back hard. The pressure applied to the railroad tie by the lead rope caused the railroad tie to break and come loose at ground level. The rope was tied solid to the tie at one end and the halter at the other. Gabby went berserk, bucking and kicking, and the railroad tie became airborne flying through the air like a missile. Scott was trapped in the small corral trying to dodge both horse and flying railroad tie. Miraculously, Scott survived, but he had to inhale an entire can of Copenhagen to calm his nerves.

That same fall, I gave Crunch to a good cowboy from New Mexico named Devin Kanapilly. One morning Devin got on the thirteen hundred and fifty pound, three-year-old, and the horse went to bucking. My three-quarter ton

Dodge pickup was parked not too far from the wagon, and Crunch, with Devin on top, bucked into the front of the pickup. The Dodge had a heavy-duty steel grill guard in front which saved the truck from being demolished, but the hit it took when the bucking horse connected with it moved the truck sideways twelve inches. We measured it.

Years ago I had a friend named Jack Dawes. Jack was a stepson of a famous old cowboy named Logue Morris. Logue had raised Jack tough. As a young boy, Jack learned what it was to be rode hard and put up wet. Jack grew up to be a big tough and rugged man. He was a noted fighter, whom I knew had backed down more than one tough guy. I roped with Jack at several big team roping events, and he had always been good to me. When he was young, he had done lots of cowboying but he took to operating equipment, trying to make that big money. One time Jack and I were visiting and talking about the cowboy way of life, and he told me, "I'll tell you, Ed, I like to punch cows! But I decided I wasn't tough enough to be a cow puncher. I can't stand the pain!" I think of Jack's, comment when I think of Tom Swede and Broken O or Scott Westlake dodging the flying railroad tie in the Keseha round pen.

ℰᏻᏣᎡ

Milo Dewitt was working at the Diamond A Ranch in the late '70s and had a string full of hard to get along with horses. He worked for the outfit a week, and every horse they led out to him bucked. He was getting them all ridden, and was making a hand, but was receiving a lot of criticism from the manager for the way he was handling the buckers. On about the seventh day, he mounted an outlaw who blew up and bucked high in the front end acting like he was going to flip over backwards. Milo pitched him a lot of slack in the reins hoping this would keep him from falling over backwards; he was also spurring him hard trying to get some forward motion out of the horse. In his attempt at staying on and not getting killed, he spurred the horse in the shoulder. "You can't get away with that on this outfit, partner," the manager hollered at him!

When the horse quit bucking, Milo stepped off and held the bridle reins out toward the manager. "Here, show me how," Milo told him. The manager gave him a dirty look and rode off. That evening, when work was through, the manager fired Milo.

Not long after that Milo came to work at Babbitts where I was working. The outfit had two outlaws they had acquired from another ranch, one named Bonnie and another named Clyde. I was riding Clyde and Bill Howell gave Bonnie to Milo. Right before Milo stepped on Bonnie the first time, Bill told him, "You can spur him anywhere you think you're man enough to! If you ride him, we'll give you a glass of whiskey and a steak! And don't worry, I'm not going to fire you!"

ଛୠ
The Old One
ଛୠ

A great many of the ranches in Mohave, Yavapai, and Coconino Counties are made up of rough mountainous terrain, and in many places, covered with thick vegetation, attributes that make gathering cattle difficult. The Supai and Hualapai people have lived for centuries in some of the roughest and most inhospitable landscape on the planet. Peach Springs, which is the only settlement of any size on the Hualapai Reservation, is situated in the headwaters of Peach Springs Canyon, a major tributary of the Grand Canyon. The Supai Village, the only inhabited place on the Supai Reservation, lies in the bottom of the Cataract Canyon, which is also a major tributary of the Grand Canyon.

If you travel on what is called the Supai Highway, which turns north off of old Route 66 about thirty miles west of Seligman, you'll end up at a place known as Hualapai Hilltop. The highway ends there on the very edge of sheer cliffs descending downward at an angle that would make a red-tailed hawk nervous. At the end of this lonely road is a set of corrals whose appearance does not do justice to their importance. Housed within this squalid set of pens that are made of a combination of pipe, quaking aspen poles, barbed wire, and heavy steel cable, a herd of overworked and sore-backed mules and horses are held captive. The corrals themselves have a floor of solid limestone rock bereft of any bedding save a few grains of sand or wet manure. Dry manure blows away immediately off the cliff's edge that drops suddenly from one side of the primitive structure. The trail to Supai Village leaves off the edge of the canyon rim a few steps from the corral gate, and from this point, all conveyance to Supai is footback, either your own feet, that will hopefully be well shod with your favorite brand of hiking shoe, or the feet of a mule or horse.

Supai Village is thirteen miles away. There are no cars in Supai Village, and the only way to get there is down this narrow and dangerous path. Occasionally a helicopter, funded through government subsidy, will land there to rescue a sick person or assist in some other emergency. Besides that, everyone and everything going to and from Supai is afoot or on a beast of burden. Every day the animals that rest in the corral at the end of the highway haul mail and supplies down into the canyon to the town where the Supai people live. Groceries are delivered with postage stamps affixed to the boxes that arrive packed in on a mule or horse. It's the law.

Where the Supai Highway, which is Arizona's Highway 18, leaves old 66, you are on the Hualapai Reservation. This road continues on north near the eastern frontier of Hualapai land, traveling very near Frasiers Well and finally entering the Diamond A Ranch forty miles or so north of old 66. Three or four miles inside the Diamond A Ranch, there is a nondescript two-track dirt road that turns off the Supai Highway and heads straight north. At this point, the highway itself is traveling east/northeast. If you follow this dirt road ten miles, you leave the Diamond A Ranch and enter Supai Reservation land. Although you won't know it by looking, when you cross onto the reservation, you are now on top of what is known as Long Mesa. Off to the west, a mile or two, is Little Coyote Canyon, and to the east, a mile or so, is Hualapai Canyon. When you travel continuing north another six or seven miles, the road will come very close to a cliff that is several thousand feet straight off. You can exit your vehicle at this spot and walk over to the cliff's edge, and there thousands of feet below you is the town of Supai, the ancient abiding place of the Supai people.

Very few people know of this spot, which to me is the most scenic place of all of thousands of square miles of what we call the Grand Canyon. Thirty miles to the northwest, and yet a lifetime away, is Mount Trumball rising out of the canyon bottom on the far side of the river, which you won't cross anywhere near here. As you stand here, you catch a glimpse of so many mesas and hilltops that you can't count them. Off to the north, you can see fifty miles of rock formations and cliffs that are part of Jumpup Canyon and Snake Gulch that flow south from Fredonia on the Utah border into the Colorado River, which hides from you a mere six miles away. You can see Sinyella Mesa, and the Cliffs of Kangaroo Headland, and the top of the Great Thumb. To the east are Steamboat

Mountain and Powell Plateau. Everywhere you look there are cliffs and buttes sticking up, and mesas, all of which are shades of yellow, white, red, purple, and ocher. The highest mountains far away are dark blue and black with pines, and junipers, and haze from dust in the air that is seldom washed clean. Long Mesa is a good place. There are no people there save the Supai who are trapped in government housing thousands of feet below on the canyon floor eating out of boxes with postage stamps on the outsides. The government subsidy checks also arrive like the groceries delivered via U. S. Mail on mules and horses that belong to the white man that has the contract to pack the mail down the thirteen miles of canyon trail.

The village of Supai is a mile or so down the creek from where Hualapai Canyon and Cataract Canyon come together. Cataract Canyon heads out some eighty miles to the south in the pine trees on the north slope of Bill Williams Mountain. Havasu Springs is near the confluence of these two drainages, and then a short distance downstream from the town of Supai itself is Mooney Falls where turquoise-colored water flows by the thousands of gallons per minute: a spot that is one of the most beautiful and spectacular in all of the world. But up the canyon going south from the village, the canyon bottom can be a dry waterless place except for a spring or two that only a few old-timers know about. During wet times, floodwater will come down the canyons in torrents of biblical proportions, and then a few months later, water upstream from Havasu Springs is almost nonexistent. It is a land of extremes: extreme beauty, extreme heights and depths, extreme flooding, extreme drought, and extreme hardship.

Charlie Wascogamie was born in the bottom of this place sometime around 1920. Possibly he didn't know his exact birthdate because my memory tells me he seemed uncertain about his own age. Perhaps his Indian stoicism thought it was nobody's business, it's hard to say for sure. There have always been Indian cowboys scattered around working on cow outfits all over the West. In northwestern Arizona most of the Indian cowboys have been Hualapai's or Supai's or crossbreeds of both tribes, and Charlie was working as the horse wrangler at the Diamond A when I went there to run the wagon in 1992. He stood about five feet eight or nine inches and weighed around one hundred sixty. He had a little bit of a belly on him, such as an old man will get, but not too much; and he was active and a very good rider. He had several horses in his string like the rest of the crew, but a certain little bay was his favorite. He called him Pony Soldier; the horse was a beautiful blood bay with a streaked-face and four white socks. He was short strided and pranced a little when he followed

the remuda, which numbered around one hundred head. Charlie had an old worn out roping saddle with dried up corners, the result of never seeing oil or saddle soap. Half of the saddle strings were rotted off, and there was no rope string, requiring Charlie to pack his rope in his hand all the time. All of this suited him fine, and he seemed happiest as he bounced along with his toes in Visalia stirrups that were almost too long for him. He wore a fleece-lined denim jacket that was never buttoned up all the way, and even on the coldest days, a small piece of his chest and neck were exposed. He never complained or tipped his hand giving me a glimpse of what his inner thoughts might be.

Dan Moore worked for the Vs for several years beginning in 1926, and in his book "Log of a Twentieth Century Cowboy" he comments about the Hualapai and Supai Indians that were in the area at the time. On numerous occasions, Dan Moore and other Three Vs cowboys were approached by old and infirm Indians who had been cast off by their own people and turned into miserable beggars, roaming around the Coconino Plateau, eventually dying of neglect. Charlie Wascogamie was born into and witnessed this behavior.

Most historians agree that the book "Nine Years Among the Indians" written by Herman Lehmann is one of the most, if not the most, accurate account of nineteenth century southwestern Plains Indians ever written. The great writer J. F. Dobie described Lehmann's book as being, "…the finest of the captive narratives of the Southwest." Herman Lehmann was a twelve-year-old boy when he was captured by a raiding party of Mescalero Apaches near his home by Fredricksburg, Texas, in 1870. His captors took him to New Mexico where he eventually became a favorite of an Indian chief and became an Indian brave himself. After nine years Mr. Lehmann was persuaded to return to his people where he experienced great tribulation returning to civilized life. Many years after being reintroduced into the White culture that he was born into, he wrote his book which describes in great detail living with Indians who had not been subjugated by white Americans. Herman Lehmann's book doesn't paint the Indians he lived with as having the phony nobility described by Hollywood and so many modern writers, nor does he describe them as bloodthirsty, but he does go into great detail about their struggle to preserve their culture. Their struggle was violent, even grossly violent, and their suffering was almost unimaginable. The book is an excellent window into the clash of two cultures at extreme odds with each other. The Supai Indians were very different in many ways from the Apaches and Comanches that Herman Lehmann knew and lived with, but in many ways they were the same. Like all American Indians, the Supai people lived in a way that would almost make one think they were of a different species, and yet they were not. They were as human as any white-skin that ever lived. The years between 1880 and 1940 were years of great transition for the Supai. Charlie Wascogamie was the only Supai I ever knew that was a product of that generation.

Like all cowboys that start young and stay at it, Charlie had instincts about animals, such as cows or horses, which

were uncanny. He had been born in the canyon and knew every inch of the Cataract and Hualapai Canyons and their tributaries. He knew where water was, and perhaps even more important, where it wasn't. He knew the trails in the bottom and the ones that would ascend thousands of feet and take you up and out to the top. Eventually his knowledge and range increased, and he learned the country on the Hualapai Reservation and the country on top and east of Supai and north of the Babbitt Ranch. He married a Hualapai woman and shared a home with her in Peach Springs as well as a home in the bottom at Supai. He was a man who could catch the wild horses and cattle. As the old cowboy saying goes, "He knew where to get."

Larry Leist became acquainted with Charlie in the '70s and worked with him, recognizing his smoothness in rough country and with bad cattle. When Larry went into business for himself running cattle on the Denny Ranch, he started working Charlie. Larry, with Charlie's help, ventured off into the depths of Cataract Canyon gathering wild cattle. The first time they went down, they used a little known trail on the west side of Cataract Canyon that topped out between Platinum Tank and Baldy Basin Tank. According to the elevation marks on the map I have of that area, the elevation on the canyon rim near Platinum is fifty-six hundred feet and the elevation straight off at the bottom of the canyon is three thousand feet. Horizontally that same distance on the map is less than a quarter mile.

On that trip, Larry and Charlie took one horse apiece, which they rode, plus Larry led a packhorse loaded with a minimum of camp supplies. At one point, going down, the cowboys had to negotiate a sharp corner with a large rock sticking out on the uphill side of the trail. The pack on the horse Larry was leading rubbed against the rock, pushing the horse off the trail. Luckily at that spot, the downhill side was a steep slope with loose shale type rock. The packhorse slid in the shale, but somehow they got him drug back up on the trail to safety.

When they hit bottom, they turned upstream, which was south. The canyon was very narrow at this point, from rim to rim less than a mile wide in places. The first day they made it as far as the bottom of Kirby Trail that descends from the east and tops out in the Box K Pasture on the Babbitt Ranch. Near this spot, at the bottom of Kirby Trail, was a cave in the canyon wall, and they made camp for the night. There were numerous well-preserved matates lined up in a row at the mouth of the cave.

The next day, they turned around and headed downstream pushing cattle before them and were accumulating a good number, including several big old steers and maverick cows. It was late spring and the waterholes were drying up and finding good camp water was a problem. Charlie knew the country and knew how to find water. At one spot, Charlie knew where a small amount of water would be dripping down from the canyon wall. The two men built a primitive dam with their hands and were able to accumulate enough water for themselves and their horses; although it took a while for the water to build up in their handmade reservoir. The cattle went thirsty. At another spot, when they were particularly dried-out, Charlie led them to a hidden place where there was a small deposit of water in a small hole. The surface had a deposit of scum, sealing it, almost hiding it, but underneath was a measure of good water. About the time Larry was going to take a drink, Charlie announced in a matter of fact tone, "This is a place where medicine men get water for their ceremonies! They say anyone else who drinks it will die." The two men stared at each other for a minute, and then Charlie said, "But I think we can drink here."

After several days they had to start camping in the canyon bottom to try to guard the trail because the big steers would attempt to get back in the night. Most of the cattle kept drifting downstream, but on several occasions, old steers snuck back in the dark, seemingly on tiptoes, wanting to go back; obviously recognizing captivity and not liking it. The next morning the two men tracked them and did whatever it took to turn them around.

A good many Supai Indians were good ropers, and the village of Supai had a community roping arena. They, in the past, had produced a yearly team roping event, and a few cowboys from Kingman and Seligman would ride down into the canyon to attend. That roping arena was the only corral of any size in the canyon, and when Charlie and Larry finally got to Supai with their herd, they penned them there.

Using Charlie Wascogamie as go between with any Indians he wasn't already acquainted with, Larry offered to buy any of the cattle they had gathered that someone wanted to sell. Larry and Charlie's roundup wasn't organized by, or approved by, or sanctioned by anyone. They just went down the trail and did it because they had the cajones to get it done. Quite possibly, it was the most thorough roundup that had taken place in Cataract Canyon in years. The menagerie they had surrounded with cleverness included every kind of cow-brute ever seen. Many were unbranded. Many still were branded the wrong way. Lots of mother cows were wearing one iron and the calf on her side wore another. There was plenty of Indian talk, Indian sign, and plain old finger-pointing and fist-shaking taking place. Larry and Charlie sat on the sidelines and took in the show, letting water seek its own level. They knew in time things would get sorted out.

In the end, Larry made a deal to purchase between seventy-five to one hundred head of cattle. (When he told me the story thirty years after the fact, he couldn't remember the exact number.) Somehow Larry got word to a friend named Mo Dwiggens who came down and helped him and Charlie trail the cattle he had purchased up Hualapai Canyon to the horse corral on top at Hualapai Hilltop. When they set out with the trail herd, Larry was concerned about the hikers and tourists coming down the trail causing trouble and scattering the cattle. But the big old steers, many of whom were quite old with age, took the lead, and any tourists they encountered were immediately intimidated and gave wide berth to the cattle.

When they finally topped out and corralled them, Larry began hauling the cattle to the Denny Ranch, eighty miles to the south. When he got a big old steer loaded, he would have to tie his head to the front of the truck, or he would turn and fight any cattle that were following him into the truck. Larry and Charlie worked their butts off, as the saying goes, but the venture was a success. Larry told me he couldn't have done it without Charlie Wascogamie.

Larry, with Charlie's help, eventually made several trips into the depths of Cataract and Havasu Canyon gathering wild Indian cattle and horses. Charlie acted as guide and interpreter, but his real expertise was cowboy. He knew every nook and cranny of the canyon country and was a good partner. He was an expert roper.

Larry brought Charlie out of the canyon and began using him on the Denny Ranch, thirty miles west of Seligman. Charlie was never loud or profane and to a stranger exhibited a typical Indian aloofness, but to someone he liked and was comfortable around, he opened up with an Indian-style dry sense of humor. His comments were brief and wouldn't be repeated a second time. One winter Larry had Charlie staying in a cow camp called Denny Five. Larry and his wife Jo Ann lived with their children at Hyde Park, a dozen miles away. One day Larry stopped at Denny Five to check on Charlie, and the two of them sat in the house visiting. Larry noticed pieces of charcoal from the woodstove that Charlie had placed in the windowsills and above the doors on the door jam. "What have you got going on there, Charlie? What are those pieces of charcoal for?"

Charlie looked at him and answered with a hint of whimsy on his face, "Those charcoals are there to keep the quidgidy away." Larry wondered what a quidgidy was and figured it must be an evil spirit. He remembered the waterhole that Charlie showed him in Cataract Canyon that was poison to everyone but the medicine men. "But I think you and I can drink it." Charlie had told him. Necessities, such as water to treat a severe thirst, sometimes overrule quidgidies and medicine men.

Larry and a good cowboy named Walt Robinson got a contract to gather wild cattle off of a ranch near Castle Hot Springs on the south side of the Bradshaw Mountains. There was no rougher country or tougher place to gather cattle anywhere on earth. Charlie had never been that far from home, but once he was horseback, he was in his element and made a top hand. But he had never been around big bad cactus like the kind that grew profusely in that area.

Larry had a real good bay horse that only had one eye; the other had been poked out with a stick in an accident when he was a colt. Charlie was riding the one-eyed horse one day as the men were riding together off of a very steep trail. They were at a spot where a sharp cliff dropped off the right side of the trail and the bay horse was cocking his head to the right, keeping his one eye focused on the cliff. The narrow trail came to a spot where a very large saguaro cactus rose up on the left side of the trail making the trail very narrow between cactus and the cliff's edge. As Charlie rode the one-eyed horse by the cactus, the horse got closer to the saguaro than Charlie wanted because he was concentrating on the drop-off to his right. Charlie instinctively reached out with his left hand to push himself away from the saguaro. He made the mistake of pushing hard against the cactus with the palm of his left hand, and as a result was severely impaled with saguaro spines. "Oh, my!" He jerked his hand back in pain and looked at it but rode on. No cursing, hollering, or blasphemy: simply one comment, "Oh, my!" Nothing more was said.

One time Larry and Charlie were gathering some trotty steers, and several of them took a run on them and the two men got separated for a short spell. Larry had roped one or two, tying them down and then went looking for the old Indian. He found him resting while sitting on a steer's side that was lying tied down. Another steer was tied down a short distance away. "I'm getting too old for this!" Charlie commented dryly.

Larry chuckled to himself thinking, "Yeah, you're old, but you obviously can still get it done." Two wild steers tied down a short distance from each other isn't an accident. Someone with skill has to be involved.

One time a cowboy businessman from Mojave County made a deal with Charlie to gather wild Supai horses in the bottom of the canyon. The man helped, but it was Charlie who knew where to trap the horses, giving them only a small escape route where a man could get a good run at a horse trying to get away. Charlie roped fifty or sixty horses, and they got the horses out to Hualapai Hilltop where they could load them. They trucked the horses down toward Kingman, and the man sold them. No one knew how much Charlie got out of the deal or if he even cared.

Charlie had been working on the Diamond A Ranch for several years when I went there in 1992. He was wrangling horses, and you wouldn't know by looking that he was a top cowboy. He didn't say much or show much expression or emotion. He did his job quietly and required no compliments. He puttered around camp in his own world doing little things to occupy his time. I would find where he had fixed a broken wire in the horse pasture fence or replaced a broken fence stave. His favorite kind of fencing material was yellow hay twine, and there were places all over the ranch where he had patched something with yellow twine. His chaps, saddle, and bridle were all patched up with twine.

He was especially fond of Pat Prosser and considered him to be his best friend and protector. He was friendly with everyone and might choose any individual to share some small piece of wisdom that he occasionally thought needed to be shared. One never knew why he conveyed his thoughts to one person one day and someone else the next, but these releases of valuable information were small and obviously intended to be cherished. But Pat, who was (and still is) an outstanding cowboy, was his obvious favorite. The old Indian was respectful but not friendly toward me. I was the new "boss" and, at least for a required testing period, was to be ignored except for official and therefore required business.

He immediately took a liking to my youngest son, Clay, who turned fourteen about the same time I took over as wagon boss. He referred to Clay as my little friend and would give him extra tidbits of the ancient wisdom he possessed. In the evenings after horses were caught, he would take Clay out and gather green limbs from appropriate plants and demonstrate how the old ones made bows and arrows. He would talk of the old ways and tales of wild cows and horses in the depths of the canyon.

One day during my first winter as wagon boss, we worked some cattle in the corrals around Pica Camp. The wagon wasn't officially out, so we had no wagon cook, and our tent and fly and all the official wagon regalia were rolled up and stored away for the winter. Pat Prosser and his family lived in one of the houses at Pica, and Charlie Wascogamie lived in the small bunkhouse nearby. My two boys, Everett and Clay, were helping as well as Randy Rutledge, Pat Prosser, and perhaps another man or two. I had just hired a Navajo Indian named Lee Dohi to build fence. I had known Lee for years when I had worked on the Babbitt Ranch north of Flagstaff. Lee built a lot of fence at Babbitts and was probably the best fence-builder I ever saw, before or since. Lee preferred to work alone. There had been another Indian, a Hualapai named Lawrence Matook, working as a fence-builder on the Diamond A for a long time. Lawrence was big and fat, and a surly individual, and was quite lazy. He was mad at me for hiring the Navajo who was working circles around him.

On this particular day, Pat's wife Debbie cooked us a good lunch, and around noon all of us cowboys were seated around the table eating. Lawrence Matook and Charlie Wascogamie had acquired a bottle of firewater somewhere and had been having a private powwow at Lawrence's camp, which was a small camp trailer set off in the distance away from the other houses. About halfway through the noon meal, I heard the back door of Pat and Debbie's house open, and someone stepped inside and approached the table. I had my back toward the door and didn't see who entered, but the person walked up to my backside and leaned over almost brushing my cheek. It was Charlie. He was quite drunk. "Ed!" He exclaimed in a commanding tone, "Lawrence, he's going to quit!"

Without looking up I answered, "Okay, Charlie. That's fine." He straightened up behind me and stood there silently for a moment, and then I heard his footsteps retreating out the back door. I sensed my answer and lack of concern had surprised him.

In about two minutes, I heard the door open and footsteps coming toward me again. Charlie leaned directly over my right shoulder and loudly exclaimed, "Ed! Lawrence, he don't want to quit no more!"

I deliberately chose to be stoic like an Indian, and without expression said, "Okay, Charlie, that's fine with me." By this time, Pat was mad at the Indian's behavior and ordered him to get out of his house. I stayed out of it and kept my mouth shut.

A few minutes later, we all finished eating and got up and headed out the back door and found Charlie and Lawrence waiting outside. They were glassy-eyed and weaving. Lawrence was swelled up like a cow that had been dead eighteen hot hours and gave me a mean look. I was the first one outside with Everett close behind me. Clay made the exit in third place, and as he walked past the drunk Indians, Charlie waved him over and said loud enough for all to hear, "Clay! Me and you, we're pretty good guys! But them two," pointing at Everett and me, "they wipe their feet too much!"

Jimmer Fancher was another of Charlie's favorites, and he called him Whim. When Jimmer came to work for me, I asked him to try and get some use out of a big bay four-year-old bronc in the remuda named Snuffy. When I took over as wagon boss, there was a boy who had Snuffy in his string but wouldn't ride him because he was afraid of him and for good reason. Snuffy stood 15.2 and weighed close to twelve hundred, and the bone in his forehead was similar to cast iron. He had no plans on being compatible with humanity. He wanted to buck, and as he got older, he got better at it; eventually having a career as a dependable 21 point saddle bronc in Scott McDaniel's bucking string, but this was in his formidable years.

Jimmer's father, Ben, was as good at making a hand on a rank bronc as anyone close to my age. As one old-timer put it, "There's just something about those Fanchers. They're cowboys." Jimmer gave Snuffy a good go for his money and could and would ride him; but the horse was a true hard-mouthed meathead who did not want to be a saddle horse.

One day in the winter, we were roping and castrating some big six hundred pound Braford bulls. The outfit had about eight hundred Hereford cows and Brahma bulls running in Last Chance Pasture, in the northwest end of the Aubrey Valley. We had left a lot of the male calves with all their hardware when we branded beings someone in charge thought they would bring a lot of money as herd sires. No one wanted them, so we eventually castrated them. Clay, Everett, Charlie Wascogamie, Pat Prosser, Jimmer, and I were heading and heeling them and cutting them. Jimmer was an excellent roper, but old Snuffy wasn't cooperating. He was riding the horse in a snaffle, and it was obvious that pulling on a bridle rein was like lifting an anvil, but less responsive. Jimmer was doing a lot of missing and was almost in tears he was so frustrated. We got down to the last bull and Jimmer was in pursuit and the tension was high. He missed several loops, and then the big bull ran into a corral corner, and Charlie rode up to him on Pony Soldier and dropped a loop around the bull's neck without even swinging. Jimmer was mad enough to bite a nail in two. "That's my best shot, Whim," Charlie said casually.

One very cold morning in February of '94, I drove into Pica about sunup. Charlie was standing in the middle of the driveway between the corrals, barn, and the three houses. He looked like a deer in the headlights of a car. There were several of the people who lived there standing in the distance, and they seemed to be hiding from the old Indian. I drove into the middle of the situation, and Charlie hurried over to my pickup wanting to talk to me. He was stirred up and acting like I was suddenly his best friend. It was obvious he had been drinking. His shirttail was out and his denim jacket was unbuttoned. His hat was on his head resting sideways and looked like it had been used for a pillow. He told me that Pat and everyone else around camp was mad at him.

Pat was trying to get his company pickup started and the cold-blooded Ford wasn't wanting to cooperate. I asked Pat what all the fuss was about, and he explained to me what had transpired. Charlie found some firewater and got very drunk the evening before. He usually stayed away from liquor, and in the year and a half I had known him, I only saw him drunk one other time, when Lawrence Matook wanted to quit. But that night he got into the bottle in a big way. From the sound of things, he probably found a second bottle. Finally in the middle of the night the quidgidies came calling and Charlie traveled back to the old days and began doing battle with every evil spirit that ever came up out of the Canyon. Perhaps some Peach Springs quidgidies came calling also. Charlie got some eagle feathers and nailed them over the doors and windows of the small bunkhouse, along with bits of charcoal from a fire. Evidently, the quidgidies flew past the feathers and charcoal and landed heavily on Charlie's shoulders. Maybe the old medicine men had heard he had allowed Larry Leist to drink from the sacred hole in Cataract Canyon. Someone in the bunkhouse had a .22 caliber automatic rifle, and Charlie found it along with a good amount of ammo. If the feathers and charcoal wouldn't work, perhaps lead and gun smoke would, and the old Indian opened up with everything the Remington had to offer. He shot at the feathers, he shot at the charcoal, and as the other man in the bunkhouse made a quick exit, he shot holes in the ceiling. He went outside into the cold darkness and danced to soothe the evil spirits that vexed him, and then shot at them with the rifle. The bullets missed the quidgidies but bounced off of corral posts and the barn, while everyone in Picatown hid under their beds, praying to God who had not heard from some of them in a good while. Finally, he ran out of bullets and stood in a crazed stupor somewhere between the old ways and a future he didn't belong to.

Pat had retrieved the rifle and berated him back to reality and to the fact that his days as a Diamond A cowboy were over. Pat ordered him to roll his bed and get his stuff together because at sunup he was taking him to Peach Springs.

After talking to Pat for a moment, I got back into the cab of my Dodge diesel pickup to warm up and let the situation play itself out. Pat had his Ford ranch pickup started, and after he scraped the frost off the windshield, he threw Charlie's bedroll and saddle in back and ordered the old man to get in. As they drove past me, I noticed the old one looking straight ahead, confused, with the look of a petty criminal on his face. He didn't wave.

I could have intervened. I was running the outfit, and I could have pulled rank and rescued the old man and took him off to stay at one of several cow camps on the ranch many miles away. But I didn't; after all, he had always been Pat's boy. I was the new one who wiped my feet too much. I look back and wonder why I didn't take advantage of his knowledge. I had thousands of uncounted cattle to gather, and he could have helped me tremendously. But he was old, and Pat was his favorite, and I ignored him. We do that to the old ones, our parents or old hands who know more than we do, or who may not be impressed by our presence. We toss them into the creek like a wooden stick and watch as they float over the rocks and rapids, and then as they pass under the shade of a tree, they round a bend, and they are out of sight. Gone forever.

Pat drove his pickup out the gate of the stockade that surrounded the buildings at Pica Camp. He headed toward old Route 66 three miles to the south, and when he got there, he turned west toward Peach Springs, twenty miles away. I never saw the old one again. Oh, my…

ℰᏣ

Postmortem on a Dead Horse

ℰᏣ

Most of the local folks around Seligman call the Aubrey Cliffs, the Pica Rim, and the large valley below it, the Pica Flat, but on a map, it is called the Aubrey Cliffs. The Cliffs, or Rim if you prefer, are a high limestone promontory that rise up one thousand feet from the valley floor and run at a general north by northwest angle for thirty miles, starting at Chino Point, four miles west of Seligman. The Aubrey Valley, or Pica Flat, are one and the same and cover about two hundred fifty sections; the lion's share of which is within the boundaries of the Diamond A Ranch. The Cliffs rise up off the sandy valley floor at a sharp angle which eventually reaches eighty-five or ninety degrees. In many places there are limestone rim rocks that are completely vertical for twenty feet or more, and there are multiple examples of this phenomenon between the valley floor and the top of the rim, one thousand feet higher. There is one major canyon dissecting this geographical wonder: it is called Road Canyon. Named thus, I suppose, because of the well-traveled road going up its bottom. This road is the main route between Pica Camp and Rose Well, twenty-three miles to the north. There is one other canyon, called Crater Canyon, that invades this natural boundary, and it is about ten miles north of Road Canyon. There is nothing more than a cow trail going up and down Crater Canyon.

We pulled the wagon out the day after Labor Day the fall of '93 and had a good crew. Pat Prosser, Jim Marler, John McGrew, Tom Reeder, Jimmer Fancher, Cody Dinsmoure, Cody Cochran, Jason Mueller, Bruce Barker, Steve Webb, Truman Ruston, Rick George, Butch, and a buckaroo named Shane were all there. Charlie Wascogamie, the old Hualapai Indian was wrangling horses. Al Smith from Texas had asked for the cooking job, and beings no one had a better idea, I gave it to him. Al worked hard at it and did better than average, especially when you consider he had no experience cooking for a bunch like that in such primitive conditions.

We camped at I Tub in the Reed Cashion Pasture to start out with and gathered cattle in that area, including lots of snakey ones in Reed Cashion and the Buck Tank Pasture. Around the middle of the month, we moved camp to Keseha and began gathering the country around there, starting in Black Mountain. One morning, probably the first day we worked out of Keseha, we left camp trotting south into Black Mountain and kept going until we reached the rim of the Aubrey Cliffs, seven miles south of camp.

We reached the top of the Cliffs a few minutes after sunup on a cool morning. The wind was blowing, as it usually is on a precipice such as this, and a few clouds made us think a storm might be threatening. I suppose every cowboy who ever rode up to the edge of the Cliffs has stopped and stared into the distance at any number of vistas available. Off below us at least one thousand feet and a couple miles to the west was Lemonade Tank and about six miles to the west-northwest was Pica Camp. A good stone-thrower or outfielder for a pro baseball team could throw a baseball and it wouldn't hit terra firma for a long time. The whole crew sat on their horses saying nothing, enjoying the scenery for several minutes. Finally, needing to get something done besides sightseeing, I looked at the buckaroo Shane and pointed to the Lemonade Dirt Tank on the valley floor. "Shane, you see that dirt tank and water lot down there?" I asked. "That's where the holdup is going to be, and I'm going to drop you off first. We'll go on, and I'll drop someone else off a quarter mile down the country." Everyone was staring at me, listening as I spoke, and I turned north and trotted along the edge of the Cliffs. Several men started chuckling to themselves, but no one laughed too loudly. We trotted along for a couple hundred yards, and then I stopped and everyone looked back at Shane who had not moved but was leaned over the brow band looking for a way off. I waited for a minute and then hollered, "Shane! Come back, Shane!" I waved at him, motioning him to catch up to us. "I was just kidding; we're going to make a drive this other way back toward Keseha."

One afternoon, when we first moved to Keseha, I needed to drive out to the north end of the ranch and do something. I don't remember what, I just remember driving out onto the Cataract Plains twenty or thirty miles north of camp for some reason, and I took Shane and Butch with me.

Butch was a big man, about forty-seven years old at the time, and had what could be described as a caustic personality. He was from Kansas, originally, but had cowboyed around over several states, mainly Montana, Nebraska and South Dakota. He had also herded sheep a fair bit, or so he said, and was proud of it. Working with sheep was no sin as far as I was concerned, but I knew nothing about sheep and therefore did not think of myself as a good judge of sheepherders. Butch rode an A fork saddle with a center fire rigging but packed sixty foot of rope with a horn knot braided into it: not exactly what a cowboy would call a normal set up. I only saw him rope one cow, and it was ugly; an event truly worth watching. One time Butch and I were in the drags of a herd and were riding along talking. We got to talking about intelligent people and what makes a person intelligent. He mentioned IQ tests and the Mensa organization and seemed to know all about it. "So how high on the scale is a really intelligent person?" I asked him.

"Well, the Mensa people scored a man with an I Q of 162 once." Butch replied.

One hundred sixty-two or seven hundred meant nothing to me. It all seemed relevant if you put numbers on it, especially if you considered I knew nothing about the Mensa people or I Q tests in general. But I didn't want to sound stupid about such an important topic, so I nodded my head in mock understanding and, trying to be a good conversationalist, asked, "How high is your IQ, Butch?"

"One hundred fifty-seven. Albert Einstein's was one hundred sixty," he replied.

I had counted several large herds of cattle, one being over three thousand head, but figured my IQ to be much lower than one hundred fifty-seven, so I hoped he wouldn't ask me what it was. I had not been introduced to Mr. Mensa.

Butch, Shane, and I accomplished whatever we had set out to do and turned back south riding in the cab of a Dodge diesel pickup. The sun went down when we were still ten or twelve miles from camp, and I remember being very tired. Butch and Shane were doing all the talking and, up to that point, had kind of buddied up during the several weeks we had been working. They both wore wide-brimmed flat hats. I had my mind on ten million things and wasn't paying much attention to their nonsense. Somehow their conversation got around to sheep, and Butch started telling Shane about the big sheep outfits he had worked on.

I listened as Shane started kidding Butch about being a sheepherder, and within a sentence or two, he called him a gunsel sheepherder and started slapping his leg and laughing with great gusto. Butch retorted, "I'll tell you what, you sorry #%^&*, I'm a better hand then you'll ever be!"

"Ha! Ha! Ha! You fat old @#*&%^, you're nothing but a gunsel sheepherder!"

"I'll tell you one thing, you sorry little @#$%^&*, I'll kick your sorry little ass all over the place, you sorry little @#$%^&! The best hands I've ever known were sheep men!"

"Ha! Ha! Ha! You're nothing but a stupid gunsel sheepherder!"

"Stop this truck! I'm going to drag this sorry little whelp dog outta this truck and kick his sorry little ass!"

I kept driving knowing the gate going into the Keseha holding trap was only a half mile away. Butch was getting louder by the minute and making more lethal threats that now included the shedding of blood and making sure the dumb buckaroo's lineage would be forever cut off with a sharp knife—literally. I now had the headlights on because it was dusk. I had remained silent, chuckling to myself at first, but after several minutes of listening to their cursing and threats, I grew weary. I wanted to get to camp and lie down in my teepee and go to sleep. Butch had been screaming at me for five minutes to stop so he could kill the boy from Northern Nevada, who was twenty-five years his junior. Finally, we drove up to the gate and the

Dodge pickup rolled to a stop. I stared straight ahead, and the cussing and threatening continued but no one touched a door handle. I sat there. I seriously considered crying. Suddenly I was twice as tired as I had been two miles down the road. The screaming continued but they wouldn't get out.

"GET OUT AND OPEN THE DAMN GATE!"

They stopped screaming and stared at me. Shane started pouting. Butch grabbed the door handle, almost ripping it off the inside of the passenger door, and stepped outside, and quickly slammed the door very hard. Perhaps, he had changed his mind about wanting the youngster outside with him. He stomped into the headlights and unchained the gate and swung it open. I drove through and kept driving to the wagon a quarter mile away and went to bed. Butch had to walk the last quarter mile into camp.

ᏩᎯᎯᏣ

We worked in Black Mountain for several days and gathered enough big weaner calves to fill several trucks but deposited them in a holding pasture between camp and F Tub. Then we started gathering Trinity Pasture. The east side of Trinity rose in elevation considerably higher than the west side and had several small mountains as well as canyons and lots of pinion and juniper trees and cliffrose, which in places grew very thick. There were cattle in Trinity that had not been gathered in years. The first morning, we trotted and loped to the far southeast corner of the pasture behind Trinity Mountain to the east. We were about ten miles from camp when we split up with plans to make a drive into the Trinity Dirt Tank at the foot of Trinity Mountain on the north side.

I kept the drive tight, dropping men off no farther than a quarter mile apart and sometimes only a couple hundred yards. There were lots of spoiled cows running in the trees that would come toward noise instead of running away from it and would try to sneak back between men and get away, so I wanted the cowboys close together. We made it into Trinity with a good bunch of cattle, probably thirty or forty head, but there were a half dozen cows that didn't want to stop; and Pat Prosser, Jim Fancher, Cody Cochran, and I had to do lots of fast riding to get ahead of them and stop them. But even though we got them checked, they merely turned around and ran back the direction they had come from. Not all of the crew had made it into the holdup and cattle were still trotting into the holdup ground, coming from the southeast. Most of the cattle slowed down and became manageable with the exception of six or eight of the leaders that turned back in front of me and headed back running to the north side of the big dirt tank and looking for a hole to escape through. After being turned by me, they charged toward Cody Cochran, who was flanking for me, but he ran at them slapping his chaps, and they turned into the herd again another time. Buckaroo Shane was flanking for Cody and was late showing up, and when he did, he just lollygagged around not paying attention to what was going on. In his defense, poor Shane had never been exposed to fast cattle and rough brushy country and didn't even realize a bunch of cattle were trying to escape. But the cows didn't care whether Shane was awake or comatose, and when they realized he wasn't riding fast and ready to plug a hole, a bunch of them bolted and ran by him like he was standing still; well, he was standing still, and he watched them depart. Cody Cochran ran crashing through the trees and rode around Shane, and when Pat Prosser came to me from the other side, I followed suit, trying to assist Cody in turning the escaped cattle back into the holdup. Not knowing what to do, Shane simply watched us crash about through the rocks and brush. Cody, with a little help from me, got everything turned back into the holdup except one

big crossbred, brindle-colored cow that at the last minute made a right turn and ran behind Shane, missing him by thirty feet or so; and she ran full out down the draw below the tank dam, going northwest. I was going as fast as I could, off to her right, trying to turn her; but I could tell she wasn't going to turn anymore. Cody Cochran was behind me a few yards when the cow hit the bottom of the rocky draw. I was still off to the right twenty yards, figuring I would catch her down the country one hundred yards or so when an opening, or good place, offered itself. Pretty soon, I heard the cow bellering and tree limbs breaking and could see through the brush that Cody had roped her around the neck. He was a good enough hand he didn't need an opening to offer itself; he roped her going full tilt in the brush. We got her wooled around and led her back to the herd that was now pretty settled down.

All the men had made it into the holdup by then, and we sat there for a minute letting our horses blow. I rode over to Shane and tried to explain to him the art of getting around trashy cattle and holding them up. I suppose he was embarrassed, being hand enough to know he had moved way to slow. I also suppose I could have handled the situation in a kinder and gentler fashion, with more sugar and less vinegar. Probably I should have kept my mouth shut. Hindsight, from twenty years later, is always more clear than having salt in your eye in the midst of a battle.

The next morning, we left Keseha as it was starting to get light, trotted east through the horse pasture, then through a gate into the Rogers Pasture, and down the fence a mile or so, and stopped, and went through a gate entering the Trinity Pasture a mile and a half west of Cook Dam. I was riding a four-year-old bay colt someone had named Beaner. Quite a moniker to curse some individual with, but I'm superstitious about changing horse's names, so I decided he would have to wear it. Beaner had been started by a young man among the crew named Jason Mueller, who was a very fine young man. The company had sent Jason to California to train colts for the ranch under the tutelage of a certain character named Jack, who was considered by the manager to be a horse guru. Jack had spent ten years in San Quentin for murdering an innocent man who made the mistake of looking like a fellow he was mad at. Prior to San Quentin, Jack had been the manager of a lettuce shed near Salinas and a dock worker at the Oakland Port of Entry; but after his time in San Quentin, he had taken up horse whispering.

Jason was a good boy and very talented and could ride about anything, but he would never move or do anything on a colt. He was tall and thin and could slip up on a colt with no effort, and once there, he never moved. He would glide along, keeping his arms close to his sides, and could stay on a horse for hours with the horse being unaware that a man was anywhere around. He wasn't a man that liked to rope and, therefore, didn't mess with a rope much when on a colt. California Jack didn't believe in roping on anything under ten years old. The long and the short of it was, the colts Jason and California Jack produced had never been sacked out much.

Beaner had goated around a little when I got on, but it didn't amount to much, but when we entered Trinity, he was still grabbing his hind end and acting skittish. I had only been on Beaner one other time and then only for a few minutes. We were making good tight drives and working with a holdup and not missing a lot of cattle, but the flip side of that was, we were running a lot of old spoiled cows into our holdups and getting to rope something was commonplace. I knew Beaner had never been roped on and possibly had never even had a rope taken down or swung on him, so I figured it was time he started learning. As someone was off opening and shutting the wire gate so we could all ride through, I took my rope off the string that held it to the fork of my Scott Dieringer saddle. Just the untying of my rope got Beaner shook up, and when I held it out to my right side a little and started to build a loop, he grabbed himself and threw a fit. I held the rope in my right hand and lifted it high and wide, and brought it down slapping my heavy shotgun chaps. That was too much for the bay colt and he took off. It's been my experience that the best way to cure a runaway horse is to turn 'em loose and let 'em run. After expending a lot of energy and accomplishing nothing, they usually don't run off again. Rather than try and pull Beaner around and stop him, I pitched him the slack and kept slapping my chaps with my coiled up rope.

Beaner ran like a bat out of hades for about a quarter mile with me waving my rope around making sure he could see it, and every once in a while, I slapped my leggings and squalled good and loud like an Indian. I figured before the day was out I would probably need to catch a wild critter, so school was on as far as I was concerned. After about five hundred yards, Beaner and I ran through a spot that was particularly rocky, which was hardly noticeable because there wasn't an acre of ground within ten miles that didn't have a semi-load of malpai rock laying on the surface. But as we raced along, the colt stumbled and went down nose first at a great rate of speed, and I was thrown out in front and to the right creating a considerable dust cloud. I skidded and bounced, and for a moment feared for my life, but bounced right up as my crew loped up staring through the cloud of dust. I bounced up quicker than Beaner, and when he did get up, he held out his right front leg with a loose hoof dangling in space. The front leg was completely broken exactly halfway between his knee and pastern.

We were at least three miles from camp and no one had a gun, and I wasn't sure there was a gun or other means of civilized euthanasia at camp had I sent someone back

to retrieve such a thing. I had Tom Reeder and another cowboy, it seems like it was Jimmer Fancher, but I'm not sure, pull Beaner down and hold him, and I cut his throat with a sharp pocket knife. It was over in seconds. So now the wagon boss (me) was afoot. I asked Bruce to loan me his horse and told him to just lie in the shade of a juniper tree all morning. He was riding a big Belgian horse named Moose, and we switched saddles. I had ordered the cook to bring us a lunch at noon to the gate we had just rode through and where the wreck with Beaner had started. The horse wrangler, Charlie Wascogamie, was supposed to show up with the cook with a change of fresh horses for all of us, so Bruce would be able to get mounted again after a good morning's nap.

We all took off again, with me riding big ol' Moose, and loped southeast toward the high mountain between Jones Tank and Trinity Peak. When we finally arrived at the spot where I planned to start the first drive of the morning, I thought we were short a man but reminded myself that I had left Bruce stranded several miles back. Then I realized that Shane was missing also. Several men said that Shane had got farther behind as we trotted along and had finally stopped, turned around, and started riding back toward camp.

We made three or four good drives setting up a holdup of cattle we had gathered and got settled down. We moved our holdup several times to a new location and had a good successful morning's work. Around noon or a little after, we ended up with all the cattle we had gathered down near the gate where Bruce had been napping, and the cook and horse wrangler were waiting with a lunch and fresh horses. I asked Al Smith, the cook, if he had seen Shane, and the question made Al beam with happiness as he was one who loved to share information, especially juicy information. He explained that Shane had come riding into camp about eight thirty and had unsaddled his horse, turned him loose, and commenced rolling up his bed and teepee and loaded it all up with his saddle on an extra company truck. He took time before driving away to have a cup of coffee with Al and tell him what a horrible person I was. After changing the subject for a minute or two, Al remembered that Shane also loaded up a brand-new flower-carved saddle made by John Herron that belonged to Truman Rustin. I asked Truman if he and Shane had made a deal to trade saddles, and Truman replied that, no, he and Shane had discussed a saddle trade but nothing had been finalized. I made the comment that it appeared to me that Shane was a saddle thief, to which Truman nodded in the affirmative.

We needed to trail the cattle we had gathered on to the shipping trap on the north side of the Keseha shipping pens that were probably three miles distance. We also needed to do a little sorting on them before turning them loose for the night. We got done and back to camp about three thirty, and I gave orders to Pat Prosser, who was my jigger boss at the time, to catch horses and do what was necessary to prepare for the next day's work.

I jumped in my Dodge pickup and headed toward Pica with intentions on hunting down Shane and the borrowed saddle. I had no idea where Shane would have ended up, but I was going to try and find him. My pickup, as well as several others around the ranch and three or four of the houses, had a two-way radio in it, and I called asking anyone if they knew of Shane's whereabouts. The head maintenance man's wife, who lived at Pica, said Shane had passed through Pica earlier in the day but did not know where he headed. The manager wasn't answering his radio, which was unusual, but his wife was answering the one in their home at Hoffman Camp on the edge of Seligman. She claimed that she knew nothing of Shane's whereabouts, but I didn't believe her. I found out later that she and Shane had several long conversations on the radio. Two-way radios are bad about letting anyone who's listening in on what's happening.

When I got to Seligman, I talked to someone who had seen Shane headed south toward the Double O Ranch, fifteen miles south of town. I drove into the Double O headquarters with the sun almost ready to go down and found the truck Shane had confiscated sitting in front of the bunkhouse. I parked my pickup next to the missing one and stepped out and walked over to the stolen truck and reached in back and picked up Truman's saddle and threw it in the back of my truck.

Shane came running out of the Double O bunkhouse followed by three or four Double O cowboys, including the boss Bunk Robinson, who is a good hand and a fellow I always liked. Shane ran up to within ten feet of me and stopped, and the Double O boys did the same. For a moment, Shane stared at me with gritted teeth but said nothing. Finally Bunk spoke up and kind of chuckled and said, "What's going on, Ed?" I believe we shook hands.

"Just taking Truman's saddle back." I said as I kept my gaze fixed on Shane. For an awkward moment, we all stood there staring at each other, Bunk being the only one who was able to notice the humor in the situation. After a quick stare down, I got in the Dodge and drove back to Seligman.

When I got to town, it was just after sundown, and I stopped to spend the night at the mansion with my family. The next morning I found out that about the time I was leaving the Double O headquarters, fifteen miles south of Seligman, the manager's wife, along with a delegation of ranch wives she had recruited, showed up at the wagon camped at Keseha and demanded that a couple cowboys drive them out to view Beaner's corpse. The designated cow hands did as they were ordered and were also questioned, as was the whole crew, about the particulars of the horse's parting.

A day or two later, I couldn't find a bridle of mine that had been hanging on a nail above where my saddle laid against a railroad tie corral fence. The bridle was a homemade twisted-wire snaffle that I had made in the shop at Spider Web ten years earlier. The snaffle hung on a homemade headstall made out of latigo leather that I had cut myself and had a pair of heavy latigo reins. About ten days later, we moved camp to Rose Well, and after being there a week or so, Al Smith got a letter from Shane who had migrated back to Nevada. The letter was short, containing one main sentence that said, "Tell that @#$%^&*, Ed, if he wants his missing bridle, to look in the bottom of the Keseha outhouse." Sure enough, it was there.

ഇൻ
Nonsense and Other Misunderstandings
ഇൻ

We were camped at Keseha in the fall and had loaded four trucks full of five hundred pound calves and were riding back to the wagon to eat lunch. The shipping corrals at Keseha were a quarter mile away from the barn with a small arroyo and a few cedar trees in between. We had the wagon parked off the northwest corner of the barn, about fifty yards distance, with teepee tents set up all around, some of them being twenty yards from the wagon and cook tent and others a hundred yards away. I was in the lead as we rode out of the shipping corral gate, and Devin Kanapilly rode up alongside of me and said, "You wanna race?"

Before I could accept his challenge, he whipped his horse into a dead run, which wasn't very fast because the horse was a dullard with no athletic ability. Devin's next actions caused me to freeze in my tracks. As the bay horse took off, Devin jumped around in the saddle and started riding backwards. He had tied his long latigo reins together, but had the tails of the reins in his hands, and was whipping the horse across his rump, and was laughing at me as the horse ran out of control toward camp. I loped along, keeping up, thinking I might need to rescue him out of his harebrained scheme but was afraid to run fast and pass him thinking I might cause the horse to injure him. Devin knew riding backwards and laughing at me would give me a brain freeze, and he whipped the horse into camp racing through the teepees with the whole crew loping behind and laughing uproariously. The stunt scared me to death, making me think I was going to have to haul another man to the hospital.

ℬⅭℛ

Scott Westlake had a brown horse called Luigi that was a particular slow learner. The horse wasn't gentle, but not athletic enough to be a good outlaw; he was somewhere in between, being, in general, very aggravating to get along with. We were camped at Number Five out on the Plains and had made a drive in the morning and after eating lunch had caught fresh horses with plans to gather more cows in the afternoon. Scott had called for Luigi, and after saddling our horses, we were all going to load them in gooseneck trailers and haul out to some remote location. My pickup was hooked up to a sixteen-foot gooseneck that would haul five horses. I loaded mine and three others in the trailer and waited for Scott to load Luigi last. Luigi didn't want to load, although there was still plenty of room for him in the trailer. Clay had loaded his horse right in front of Luigi, and he stepped around behind the brown horse and tried to coax him in as Scott pulled on the lead rope, whispering to him. Pretty soon, I and several other men were behind the horse helping Clay try to herd him through the trailer gate. A couple of us put our arms together and tried to lift his butt up and push him in. Nothing we were doing was working. This wasn't our first go round trying to teach Luigi to load. Luigi didn't learn anything the first go round. We had a lot of work to do, and we were burning daylight, and soon everyone on the crew had used up their personal bit of advice, and none of it worked. Luigi stood at the back of the trailer's open gates with his front feet eighteen inches from the end of the trailer and would not get in.

I slammed the trailer gate shut and latched it. I asked Scott to hand me the lead rope that was attached to a stout halter on Luigi's head, and when he handed it to me, I tied it solid to the end of the trailer with about four feet of slack. I turned to Scott and ordered him, "Get on!" And without pausing, I turned and marched to the pickup and got in and started the diesel engine. I suppose my mind was somewhere else because I didn't notice what was happening behind me. Scott was standing at the rear of the trailer muttering to himself, "I'm not getting on that horse! I'm not getting on that horse!" Clay and several men were standing near Scott laughing at him as he kept repeating, "I'm not getting on that horse!"

Finally, Clay, who knew how to interpret my orders, informed Scott, "He meant for you to get on the back of the pickup." Clay led Scott to the back of the truck and directed him to get in as Scott said, "I wasn't going to get on that horse!"

When everyone got loaded, we headed down the dirt road leading Luigi behind. I drove as fast as I thought the horse could run for about a mile and then stopped. We tried to load him, but he was still dummied up, so I said, "Get on!" Scott loaded right up this time, and I drove on another mile, a little faster. This time he loaded. Four or five days later, we tried to load Luigi again, and he refused to load but loaded after one long run behind the truck. After that second application of the leading technique, Luigi would load himself anytime he heard a trailer gate rattle, whether someone wanted him in or not.

ℰↃℭ

Brad was a good hand, and a man who was always ready to deal in mischief, and beings he was well practiced at the art of mischief and foul deeds amongst his brethren, he became expert at it. But being prolific at pulling pranks on one's friends can also result in becoming the target of the same.

One afternoon in the fall, after we had moved to Rose Well, I sent three or four men to help Brad, who was my jigger boss at the time. I had given orders to Brad to move some cows a short distance in the vicinity of Keseha Camp, which was fifteen miles south of Rose Well. After lunch at the wagon, Brad and the four men loaded their horses in a gooseneck trailer and headed south. Among the men that Brad took with him was a boy named Stan, whom the crew had nicknamed Stinky Stan because of his aversion to bathing. Brad made a regular habit of tormenting Stinky Stan and never missed an opportunity to do so. After completing the task I had assigned Brad and his men, they loaded their horses in the gooseneck and prepared to return to Rose Well. As you leave Keseha, you drive through a gate, and Stan got out and opened it, and then Brad drove the pickup and trailer through and stopped, and Stan closed it behind the truck and trailer. When Stan started walking toward the truck so he could get back in, Brad put it in gear and started driving. Stan began to hurry, trying to catch up, as Brad stuck his head out the truck window, laughing and hollering, "Hurry up, Stan! Hurry up and get on!" Soon everyone was laughing as Stan ran behind the gooseneck trailer trying to catch up.

About the time Stan ran out of air, Brad slowed down a little and hollered, "Jump on the trailer, Stan!" And so Stan jumped on, and fifteen minutes later, Brad came crashing into Rose Well with Stan hanging on for dear life attached to the rear end of a speeding stock trailer. Stan's muscles were twitching from stress, and Brad continued to slap his legs and guffaw for an hour.

A few days later, Brad was holding court inside the big cook tent while everyone was waiting for the cook to holler chuck. The entire crew was gathered round as Brad gesticulated and expounded on some adventure he had once been a part of. Among the crew was a Texan named Doug Nolan, who was about fifty-five years old and hailed from Rotan in Fisher County. Doug was a small man about five feet five and sported a big walrus mustache, and his wide-brimmed black hat had a pooched out "Yosemite Sam" style. He was one of those people whose wit was subtle, but also had that important ingredient of timing. The young men on the crew loved him because he made them laugh.

As Brad continued on with his outrageous story, he had everyone's attention except Doug Nolan's, who quietly stepped outside the tent without anyone noticing. Brad and several other men were seated on a homemade bench made out of a two by twelve inch pine plank that was held up by rickety legs on its ends and was sitting against the tent wall. Brad and the other men had their backs against the canvas wall, while most of the crew sat across from them against the other side of the tent and watched Brad as he talked. Suddenly, there appeared a man's hand, and then the attached arm, directly underneath Brad's body. The hand and arm were sliding along the ground underneath the canvas tent wall. Everyone in the tent saw the hand except Brad, who was talking loudly and enjoying ownership of a captive audience. The hand snuck forward like a snake in a slow and groping movement that seemed to be searching for prey. Momentarily, the hand came slowly off the ground moving upward in a deliberate fashion, appearing to have confidence in attaining its destination. The men watched in wonderment at the hand, and beings Brad was nearing the punchline of his story, he thought they were all watching him in awe of his ability to communicate. Presently, the hand positioned itself for the deathblow, and with the speed of a diamondback, the hand struck upward in a violent fashion, and the fist and long fingers belonging to Doug Nolan grabbed Brad by the testicles and began squeezing and pulling downward. A great sucking sound exuded itself out of Brad's talking head, and he tried to stand up but the hand squeezed harder on the jewels it held captive, and Brad became paralyzed with his Levi pockets being two inches off the pine board. His eyes ran out of his skull on a stem and stared straight ahead at the crew that rolled on the floor screaming in laughter. Just before Brad passed out, due to a lack of oxygen, Doug Nolan let go and started running.

Around that same time, I was able to accompany my family to a high school rodeo, which both my boys were competing at. They were held about once a month at various locations throughout Arizona. While sitting there in the grandstand, I visited with a friend named Larry Finch, who was a chiropractor, practicing in Kingman, Arizona. Larry's daughter was competing at the same rodeo. I mentioned to Larry that I was suffering from a severe case of stiff neck, and I was barely able to turn my head to the right, a condition I had suffered from for years. Larry offered to give me an impromptu examination and, upon completion of it, informed me that he could fix me right up. We departed the grandstand and headed for the contestant's parking lot. Larry instructed me to stand up with my back against the nose of my horse trailer, and then he wrapped his left arm with my Levi jumper and held it between my shoulder blades and the side of the horse trailer, which was made of sheet metal. He instructed me to relax and stand straight and still, and then he put the palm of his right hand against my sternum. "Relax and be still," he repeated! And then with the swiftness of lightning, he pressed into my sternum with a forceful thrust. His actions were executed in such a professional manner that I felt nothing, absolutely no pain! Instantly my neck and back felt better than they had in weeks, if not months. I was completely free from pain.

Several weeks later, Brad walked into the cook tent about four in the morning leaning forward and groaning with pain. "What's the matter, Brad," I asked?

"Oh, it's bad! I'm down in the back so bad I can't straighten up!"

"Where does it hurt?"

"Oh! Uh uh uuuhh! Oh! It hurts between my shoulder blades!"

"Well, shoot!" I exclaimed. "I can fix you right up!" I took my Carhardt coat off and wrapped it around my left forearm and instructed Brad to lean up against a tent pole that was in the middle of the large cook tent. I told him to relax and be calm, just the way Larry Finch had instructed me. "Now, stand up straight, and I'm going to fix you right up!"

Brad stood as straight as the pain he was experiencing would allow. I gently laid the palm of my right hand against his sternum, right at the bottom of where his ribs were connected at the bottom of his chest. "Now relax, Brad!" I told him one more time, and then with a forceful shove, I tried to sink the palm of my right hand into his chest cavity.

Brad's knees turned to mush, and he fell like a fallen redwood and landed face first onto the dirt floor of the cook tent! His forehead was resting in the dirt and great sucking sounds came wheezing out of his esophagus. Margie Fancher, who was cooking breakfast, dropped the spatula that she was using to turn bacon and sat down because she was laughing so hard. "You killed the #~`@$%^&*#%~! She exclaimed and started coughing because she was laughing so hard.

"Brad, are you all right," I asked? Suddenly, I was filled with fear and anxiety because Brad lay prostrate, face down, and could not speak, but continued to make guttural sounds like a large beef that had been killed by the cutthroat method. I realized I had been foolish to think I could reproduce Larry Finch's medical procedure. Finally, after ten minutes, Brad drug himself out of the cook tent and lay down in his bed. He couldn't work for seven days.

At the next high school rodeo, I told Larry Finch what I had done. "You did what?" He screamed at me, "You idiot! You could have killed him! Don't ever do that! You could actually kill someone! Do you understand?" Yes, I understood, I assured him, and I even admitted that the whole affair had scared me. But Margie Fancher was in a good mood for a whole week after witnessing it.

୫୨୦୧

One afternoon Brad, Lee Pehl and several men were lounging around the B.S. fire visiting. Somehow the conversation became centered around cowboy's hats. One fellow mentioned he liked one brand of hat and someone else related how he liked a different brand. And then they began talking about what size they wore. "Well, I wear a seven and three-eighths, long oval," one man said.

"Well, I wear a six and seven-eighths," another said.

"Well, I tell you what!" Brad said. "I wear a seven and an eighth, long oval!"

"Oh, Brad! You don't know what you're talking about!" Lee Pehl said as he looked at Brad from the opposite side of the fire. "You wear a seven and an eighth, SQUARE OVAL!"

୫୨୦୧

Rodeo cowboys and cowboys who make their living on a ranch are two separate breeds but historically shared the same great-grandparents. A hundred years ago many of the cowboys and cowgirls who became rodeo stars were also top hands out on a ranch somewhere. Slowly the two job descriptions and related requirements have become separate entities with little in common, but a great many cowpunchers are rodeo fans and admire the skills and expertise rodeo stars exhibit in the rodeo arena. That is especially true of the bronc riders and ropers. Jake Barnes and Clay O'Brien Cooper are two of the greatest ropers in rodeo history. They, being teamed up together, have been world champions a total of seven times. They have won virtually every award a team roper can win, and in 1995 they were sitting on top of the world and were known as the very best in their field of endeavor. But, alas, all things come to an end eventually, and those of us who were rodeo fans began hearing rumors that Jake and Clay were going to retire. They were both younger than me, and I did not consider myself to be old by any stretch of the imagination. I had first seen Clay Cooper rope twenty years earlier at the big Fourth of July roping at Mormon Lake, south of Flagstaff thirty miles. At that time, he was just a young teenager but could out rope everyone that was there including several men who went on to be world champions themselves. He was, and still is, an icon; and at the time, I couldn't imagine why he would retire. Besides what else could he do?

One afternoon the manager showed up at Rose Well, where we were camped, bringing a load of groceries with him, and after unloading the groceries and putting them in the proper place, the manager poured himself a cup of coffee and sat down in the big cook tent. I poured myself a cup also and sat down. Scott Westlake was present, and the three of us had a congenial conversation about nothing important. No one else was present. The manager and myself had been having some difficulty seeing eye-to-eye on certain matters, and I welcomed the opportunity to just sit and visit in a pleasant manner without butting heads about something concerning ranch business and cow work.

Things were going smoothly and our talking was even mixed with small doses of laughter and several smiles and grins. I was appreciative of Scott's presences, thinking that it probably diluted the atmosphere, which of late had become clouded when the manager and I were alone. We talked about this and then talked about that, and then one of us said something about a rodeo he had attended once, and someone else mentioned a good saddle bronc rider he was acquainted with, and we all shared a rodeo yarn or two. Presently, the manager mentioned the rumor going around that Jake Barnes and Clay O'Brien Cooper were retiring.

I said, "No, they'll never retire!"

"Well," the manager continued, "I heard from a good source that after the Finals this year, they're going to hang it up!"

"Well, I don't believe it!" I answered.

"Well, I heard after all those years they're just tired of going down the road, and they are going to quit!"

"Heck, they can't quit." I said. "What are they going to do?"

"They tell me, they've made so much money they don't have to do anything."

"Oh, baloney!" I continued with authority, "Everyone has to do something. They will be surprised how fast that money will run out." Scott sat silently listening while holding a can of Copenhagen in his hand.

"I don't know, but I've got a friend who knows them, and he says they're quitting. They aren't going down the road anymore!"

"Heck, they can't quit!" I replied, trying to decipher this dilemma in my mind. "What are they going to do? They don't know how to do anything but rope and rodeo! They don't have any other job skills! Well, shoot, they've never done anything except rope and rodeo. They don't know anything else about nothin'!" I paused for a moment trying to think this out. "Well," I went on, "I guess if nothing else, they could go get a job managing some big ranch somewhere."

Scott slapped himself in the face with an open can of Copenhagen and inhaled the contents in one gulp. He jumped up, keeping the tobacco can in front of his face, and ran out of the tent, and disappeared. Right on his heels the manager exited the tent muttering something about needing to go somewhere. Wonder what the heck's wrong with those two fellas? I thought to myself.

ଗଠ
Tom Reeder
ଗଠ

Tom Reeder came to work for me at the Diamond A when the wagon pulled out in the spring of '93. He showed up at my house and asked me for a job rather than go through higher channels of management. He wanted to work for me. We were old friends. I had first met Tom in 1974 when I went to work for Bill Howell on the Babbitt Ranch. Tom worked for Babbitts for many years starting in the early '60s.

Tom had grown up in Texas and Oklahoma where his dad had cowboyed and rodeoed. Boots O'Neal told me that when he was a young boy Tom's father, who also was known as Tom, had the reputation of being one of the best bronc riders in the country. He was both good in the arena and out on the ranch. The elder Reeder worked on some of the bigger ranches in the Panhandle country

such as the Matadors and JAs. At some point in time, he migrated to Oklahoma, and Tom the junior spent much of his childhood there.

When Tom (Jr) was a teenage boy, his dad put him on a bus and sent him, along with a saddle that was stuffed in a tow sack, to Elko, Nevada. Evidently, it was time the boy learned to make it on his own, and being fifteen hundred miles from home, or anyone he was even remotely acquainted with, seemed like a good idea to the old man. The boy had a bad taste in his mouth for Nevada the rest of his life. The trip up north didn't help his relationship with his father either.

When Tom was around twenty, he landed in Northern Arizona where he spent, with the exception of several short trips back to Texas, the rest of his life. On one of these forays back to Texas, Tom worked for a spell at the big Waggoner Ranch near Vernon. While driving down the highway near Vernon, he was stopped by a Texas state patrolman for having a taillight out. The traffic cop asked Tom to produce his driver's license, and Tom handed him the license, which was from Arizona. The patrolman asked Tom where he lived, and Tom replied that he was working for Waggoners. "You need to get a Texas driver's license, boy," the patrolman chastised him! Tom drove to the ranch and rolled his bed and went west to Arizona and stayed there.

Tom worked for several outfits in Northern Arizona including Babbitts, the Double O, and the Diamond A, but probably spent more time at Babbitts than anywhere. He was dependable but was never a cowboy the boys talked about while sitting on barstools on Whiskey Row. Tom never had what you would call flair. His expertise with a rope was adequate but not exceptional, and he was never known as a good bronc rider. But he was a student in the art of cowpunching and flair or not, he made a hand. He took pride in it. Tom was an outstanding cowman, and in that way was ahead of most cowpunchers I've known.

He had, like many of his kind, a weakness for liquor. If he had done without for a good spell, the mere sight of a beer can would set the muscles on his cheekbones to twitching. He stuttered, and when his speech impediment caused a roadblock in his communicating, he would lift his hand and start pointing, trying to help whoever was listening. If the stuttering spell was a particularly bad one, he would start blinking and pointing at the same time. When he consumed two or three beers, he became quite opinionated, and if he downed a dozen, his opinions about whomever he was with might get negative; but usually he would laugh when drunk, and he stuttered when he laughed just like when he talked.

Sometimes Tom's mouth would get him in trouble. I found him one time standing by his truck in the parking lot of the old Tusayan Bar south of the Grand Canyon

National Park. He was mad and muttering to himself. "What's wrong, Tom?" I asked. To which he replied that the fellow who owned the bar, whose name was Pete, had just thrown him out. Pete, the bartender, was a little cocky character who had a little guy complex, and he and Tom had been involved in several previous disagreements.

Tom went on to explain that he had entered the beer joint and sat down at the bar. When Pete walked up behind the bar and asked him what he wanted, Tom told him, "GGGivve mmee a hhairccut!"

"What the heck you talkin' about? This ain't no barber shop."

"Yeah, III hhheard ttthhis wwwas a cclipjoint!"

Pete ran around to Tom's side of the bar and grabbed Tom and escorted him out the door. When Pete released his handhold on Tom's collar, Tom turned and said, "My sshadow wwill nnevver darken yyyour ddoor again!"

Tom was well liked by his cowboy mates who ignored his snide comments that he made when he was drunk. Sometimes his friends would get mad at him, or tired of him, but they respected him—most of the time. He would test your patience.

One time about the fall of '72, Tom was working with the Babbitt wagon. Jeff Prosser was there also, and the crew was camped at Tin House, about fifty miles north of Askfork. Jeff had a pickup at Tin House, and one evening he decided he would drive up and see Elmer and Nellie McDonald at Number Five, about thirty miles north of Tin House. Tom wanted to go along accompanied by a bottle of VO Whiskey. They arrived at Elmer and Nellie's camp after dark and found Elmer and Nellie glad to have company. Camp Number Five on the Diamond A was a long ways from anywhere, and you don't get much company when you live there. They drank coffee and visited, and then they drank whiskey and visited. And then Tom got to smarting off about something Elmer said, and then Jeff felt embarrassed because Tom had insulted his friend, so he gathered Tom up and headed back to Tin House. Tom kept drinking and smarting off, and by the time they reached Tin House, Jeff was madder than a hornet. He grabbed Tom by the throat and drug him into the bunkhouse and laid him on his own bedroll that was rolled out on the concrete floor. Then he rolled the bed up with Tom lying on the top, and he put the leather bed straps around it and buckled them up as tightly as possible. One of Tom's hands and a foot was sticking out on one side and part of his cowboy hat and his eyeglasses were visible from the other end. From inside the bedroll, you could hear muffled pleas for help. Jeff wouldn't allow anyone to answer Tom's call. The next morning, Tom emerged wrinkled but sober, with no memory of how he had managed to roll himself up in his bedroll. No one said anything. By breakfast Jeff was laughing but wouldn't answer any of Tom's questions.

When I met Tom, he was married with two small children and was living at the Harbison Camp on the Babbitt Ranch. We worked together for several years, and then he got a job running a ranch south of Flagstaff, forty miles. Tom could probably run a ranch for someone as good as anybody because he was a good cowboy who knew how to handle cattle correctly and was an excellent cowman.

Somewhere about here, Betsy, his wife, got tired of the whiskey, or maybe she got tired of Tom; but for whatever reason, she up and pulled out. She took the girl, who was the oldest, and Tom kept the boy. He was a good one, and Tom worshiped him. Tom stayed as straight as he could while the kid was still at home. He bought a horse trailer and hauled the boy to some ropings and high school rodeos. He was let go by the people he was running the ranch for, so he just took the boy cowboying wherever he found a job. They worked together at the O RO Ranch and several others. Tom sent him to Babbitts one spring for a spell, and I worked with him there. He was quiet and very reserved but likable. He made a hand and everyone liked him. He was a boy a dad could be proud of. Somehow he finished high school, and then he joined the Army. He told his dad that's what he wanted to do.

Not long after Pete, which was what Tom's son's name was, went to the Army, Tom came to work for me. I was very glad to have him. He had worked around a lot of good crews, and he knew how a crew should function. He would go on a bender once in a while, but he kept the drinking down to a low boil. He was loyal to me and loyalty from an old-timer was worth a lot in a crew of predominantly younger men. He knew how to work big bunches of cattle and that's mainly what we did: gather, move, sort, brand, and ship one big bunch after another. He made a hand and I appreciated it.

Occasionally his drinking would be a problem, but I treated it like a bad headache, hoping it would go away after a while. Once when we were camped at Rose Well, he got really drunk. Several of us were sleeping in the small bunkhouse there, while most of the crew stayed in their canvas teepee tents. There were two bedrooms in the Rose Well bunkhouse, and Tom and my son Clay had their beds rolled out on the floor in one room, and I was staying in the other one with someone else. Tom was drunk and being pretty obnoxious one evening but finally passed out around eight, and we all tried to go to sleep. About the time I was falling asleep, Tom woke up and hollered, "OOOOWWWEE! OOOWWEEE! OWW!" He sounded like a sick wolf. "OOOWW! OOOWWWWWE!" He'd squall and then he'd say, "Ed's mad, ain't he, Clay! Ed's mad, ain't he? Well, that's fine, I like a mad Ed! OOOOOWWWEE! OOOOOOWWW!" And then he would fall asleep, but every thirty minutes until about three in the morning, he repeated the same scenario. "OOOOOOOOWWWWWE! Ed's mad, ain't he, Clay? Ed's mad. Well, that's fine, I like a mad Ed. OOOOWWWW!" The next morning, he couldn't remember anything but he knew he had been socially unacceptable.

One weekend during the winter, I went with my family to a high school rodeo somewhere in southern Arizona. Everett and Clay were entered, and I was able to go and watch, which was a special occasion because on many weekends my wife and boys traveled to the high school rodeos without me, and I stayed at the ranch and worked. After a weekend together, we got home to the mansion on Picacho Street late Sunday evening. While my wife and Clay packed suitcases into the house through the back door, Everett and I unloaded Kid and Scooter, the rope horses, and made sure they were fed and watered. Not too long after entering the house, Clay and Jean Ann came rushing out the back door in animated conversation with each other. Jean Ann motioned me closer and said, "There's someone in our bed!"

"What in tarnation?"

"There is a body on our bed covered up by the bedspread."

"Well! Who is it?" I demanded.

"I don't know. It's covered up and I can't tell." I walked through the back door and down the hall to our bedroom and there he was, his right arm and hand dangling limply off the bed, his fingertips reaching the floor. His right leg was bent at the knee and the lower half of his leg hung to the floor. He was lying on his back, and before passing out, he had grabbed the bedspread and pulled what he wasn't laying on over the upper half of his body. No part of his head was visible. There was a black hat laying on the floor.

I knew who belonged to the body. I recognized the black cowboy boots, and the hat, even the wrinkles on his hand. It was Tom. He had been at the Black Cat Saloon, probably all weekend, and had let himself into my house. He had passed on, but not to death, but to the land of alcohol unconsciousness. In some twisted cowboy way, I felt honored that he considered me to be friend enough to crash on my bed. Evidence showed that first he had tried the couch in the living room. His eyeglasses were laying on the living room floor just under the edge of the couch where he had first tried to rest, but he had become cold and had migrated to the bedroom and the bedspread. Evidently his legs weren't cold just his chest and head.

Tom hadn't worked for me more than six months when Superman bucked him off on that fateful day when Barney Prosser was hurt bad and hauled to the hospital in a helicopter. For several months, Tom was on industrial compensation insurance and could do nothing. He almost went crazy. He was too far from town to hang out at the saloon and too broke to stay liquored up.

When the doctor finally said he could go back to work, he was given a small electrical device that was supposed to hasten healing. The device was a small square box that held batteries and had a number of wires several feet long with suction cups on them that he was supposed to attach to his skin near the shoulder and collarbone that had been broken. In the evenings, when work was through, Tom would come to the campfire that was always seventy feet outside the cook tent. He would take his shirt off and sit on a big stump, naked from the waist up, with electrical wires attached to his torso, supposedly sending healing impulses to his frail old body. He would smoke the ever present cigarette and stutter and talk while the kids on the crew stood off in the background giggling about his sagging skin and bony elbows.

One time when we were camped at Rose Well, Tom was in the bunkhouse in the evening and for some reason had disrobed with the exception of his BVDs that were two sizes too big. His legs shot downward out of his shorts like two sticks. He was waiting his turn to take a shower and shave in the only bathroom provided for cowboys on the biggest cow outfit in the state of Arizona. He had found a small stash of alcohol somewhere and wasn't concerned about his appearance. The bunkhouse sits on the side of a hill with the only door being on the downhill side with three high concrete steps leading up to it. A cowboy came walking up the hill carrying a change of clean clothes and a clean towel rolled up hoping to find room in the much-used bathroom. He walked briskly up the steps and quickly opened the door and ran head on into an almost naked Tom Reeder. "AAAAAAHHHHHH!" He threw the towel, shaving kit, and clothes into the air and fell backward rolling down the stairs and continued rolling down the hillside screaming as he rolled along, "Golly, Tom! Put your clothes on! You scared me! You look just like ET!" With an unconcerned look on his face, Tom turned and walked back into the center of the dilapidated cowboy abode wondering who the heck ET was.

For a spell, we had a cook who was nothing more than a town kid fresh out of high school. His grandparents lived across the street from the mansion on Picacho Street and talked me into hiring him, claiming he wanted to be a cook. Boiling water was a challenge to him, especially on a woodstove resting on a dirt floor. The crew nicknamed him the Vampire due to his white hair and almost opaque white skin. His demeanor was similar to a member of the rock group K.I.S.S. He was scary in his likeness to a body laid out in a satin-lined coffin. One morning I walked down to the cook tent looking for a hot cup of coffee to warm me up. It was cold outside and we, like always, had a big day ahead of us. Several men were sitting in the tent staring into the lantern-lit dimness of morning. I walked up to the cook stove, which was cold, and looked at Vampire who sat on a five gallon lard bucket staring into a cavern of nothingness. A large skillet lay on top of the stove with numerous slices of bacon laying in it being still white as if ice-cold. I lifted the lids to the two large coffee pots and thought I could see ice floating amidst the coffee grounds. I walked around to the front of the stove and took the lid handle and lifted a round lid from the top of the firebox and peered in to see a small flame whispering in the middle of a few scant pieces of kindling. Breakfast was supposed to be ready in fifteen minutes. I questioned Vampire about his readiness, and about his knowledge of what well-done bacon looked like. He stared at me as if hung over after a night of revelry during a K.I.S.S. concert. He continued sitting and staring at nothing. I opened the firebox on the woodstove and began stuffing pieces of cedar into it, and then with a lid off the top of the stove, I took a gallon of diesel that was kept in camp to assist in the starting of fires and turned it upside down into the firebox. Woosh! Woosh! Woosh! Woosh! The stove began sucking wind, trying to supply oxygen for the burning diesel. It began to dance up and down on the axle and sixteen inch tires on which it rested. Woosh! Woosh! Woosh! Woosh! The Vampire woke up out of his comatose stupor and tried to run out of the backside of the tent but stopped when I forced him to start cooking breakfast. A good cowboy named Mike McLaughlin came walking down the hill toward the cook tent and saw flames shooting thirty feet into the sky out of the chimney sticking through the roof of the large tent. As he stepped through the tent flaps into the lantern-lit interior, he asked, "What's for breakfast, Ed?" I was turning bacon that had started sizzling. "Well," Mike continued, "whatever it is, I bet it will be done." Vampire quit that afternoon.

Tom offered to cook. His shoulder wasn't doing real well, and he was looking for a way to make a hand. He was worried about losing his job. Being a broken-down old man with nowhere to go can lay heavy on an old guy's mind even if he doesn't want to admit it. I gladly took him up on his offer. When you have fifteen men that you are working hard for ninety days at a stretch, a cook was a necessity.

Tom did his best. It wasn't great but it was hot, and it was on time. He was clean, and he knew the drill, having spent more time around cow camps than anyone on the crew, including me. He made one serious mistake: he was loyal to me, showing me the respect due a leader. He had little rapport with the manager, or his wife who kept the keys to the commissary; a thing of equivalence to having the key to the backdoor of the White House. She was powerful. Tom's tongue was stuttering but full of mischief.

Along about that time, I requested a company check to buy a few dollars' worth of porcelain coffee cups for the wagon. The crew was bad about leaving cups outside around the campfire and then losing them. I was told by the manager that the company wasn't going to buy my crew any more coffee cups. At that same time, I put in an order for groceries for the wagon, and when they arrived, the sum total of what was brought fit into a box eighteen inches square. We were camped at Sixteen, which was a ninety mile trip back to town going down the Supai Highway. I drove down after work in the afternoon and managed to appropriate a pickup load of groceries to take back to the wagon. Beings it was late, I spent the night at the mansion with my family and then headed back to the wagon leaving home around three in the morning. The two gentlemen who owned the cattle were scheduled to show up at breakfast, along with the manager, to ride with us for a day. This only took place about once a year.

I got to the wagon about four thirty and stepped into the tent to the sound of frying beef and the smell of coffee. Tom stood behind the stove with a large fork in his hand and a Marlboro hanging from his lips. Several men were sitting on the dirt floor or on wooden stumps drinking coffee. We always kept a small table on the left side of the tent as you stepped inside. On top of the table set a drawer out of the chuck box that held tin plates, coffee cups, and knives, forks and spoons. Next to it was another small drawer with sugar, salt and pepper, and whatever simple condiments might be available. I walked to the table to get myself a coffee cup and noticed an old three pound Folgers coffee can that had white paper taped around the outside. The plastic lid that came with the coffee can had a large slot cut in the top of it causing it to resemble a piggy bank. I picked up the can and in the dim lantern light read the words that had been written on the paper. Donations for Coffee Cups had been printed on the paper in bold writing. I set the can down and looked at Tom. His cigarette twitched as if he was nervous, or perhaps he was stifling some laughter. "YYeahh, yeah, yyyeah, I I I thought we might take up a collection." I started to tell him that his joke was a bad idea, and then I thought I would keep my mouth shut. I poured myself some coffee to the sound of pickups driving up and men getting out and walking and talking as they approached the tent. Tom lit another cigarette.

They entered, the three of them, the men who owned the cattle and the manager, all smiles and salutations going around to all hands. The two men, whose cattle we worked so hard to herd about and make sense of, had always been good to me. I greeted them with a smile and told them the coffee was hot. They had been to the wagon before and knew where the cups were and stepped toward the small table with the drawer on top, and then they spied it. One of the men picked up the Folgers can, turned offering plate, and silently read the words on the white paper taped to the outside, Donations for Coffee Cups. "What's this?" The man demanded as he stared first at the manager, and then at me, and then at Tom. At first no one spoke. He held the can out and began to speak again when Tom started talking, "TTThhee ooutfit cccan't afford ttto buy cccups, ssso I fffigured to gget ddonations." Tom held his ground, cigarette dangling from his stuttering lips, standing behind the hot stove. I rested my cowboy boot on the tongue of the cook stove that stuck out through the center of the tent. I took a drink of hot coffee and felt detached from the situation. I always figured a man should do whatever he's big enough to do. This was Tom's show, and I decided to let him ride it out. The manager began trying to explain the difficulties of managing a ranch selling several millions of dollars' worth of calves while simultaneously having to keep a bunch of cowboys furnished with coffee cups they refused to keep track of. Somewhere in the back of my brain, I heard the sound of someone pounding with a hammer. Pounding nails. Nails in a coffin. A coffin for Tom, and a coffin for me.

Tom was gone before roundup was over.

ဆာ

Gathering More Remnant

ဆာ

Babbitts C O Bar Ranch, Winter, 1989

The CO Bar Ranch bordered the Navajo Reservation for forty miles in the vicinity of Gray Mountain, forty miles north of Flagstaff. Wild Indian horses and cattle were a constant nuisance, and a Babbitt cowboy could always find some Indian livestock to run back to the reservation if he didn't have something else to do. Babbitt cattle getting out on the reservation was also a problem; although not as much because the overgrazed condition of the reservation wasn't very inviting to a cow.

One cold, windy day in the middle of the winter, I made a big circle out on the reservation north of the lava beds that flow north from S P Crater. There was a big dirt tank on the reservation in that area known as Gordy Dam, and nearby was a set of corrals that bore the same name, made out of cedar posts and good Quaking Aspen poles. I had my youngest boy, Clay, with me, and he was about eleven years old. I don't remember what I was riding, but Clay was riding a very good bay horse named Beaver.

Somewhere out north of Gordy Dam and several miles north of the Babbitt boundary fence, we found six yearling Babbitt heifers weighing about five hundred fifty pounds. We pointed them south and trailed them to a gate a little east of the lava beds. The wind was blowing at a pretty good clip, and there was no danger of anything getting overheated.

The gate we intended to put the cattle through had an old abandoned cattle guard on one side that had not been used in many years, and the barbed wire fence was strung over it. Off to the west side of the old cattle guard was the wire gate that was used by anyone passing that way. There were also pieces of an abandoned car and other curious items of refuse laying in the general vicinity of the gate. Paper and plastic sacks that had held wine bottles were blown up against the fence stays and bushes, creating an unlimited supply of boogers to make the heifers not want to walk through the gate.

We drove the yearlings up to the gate with the wind blowing, and sacks shaking in the wind, and tried to put the cattle through. They weren't wanting to cooperate. We waited patiently and let them stare. We tried to force them. We drove them toward it from both directions, east and west, approaching the gate sideways. Nothing seemed to work. Then, on one of these attempts at putting the cattle through, a heifer took a run and lit out for parts unknown, and beings I was mounted very well and cinched up, I roped her very quickly. The country was wide open, so roping something quickly was a non-issue. Driving the cattle a mile or two east to a different gate never crossed my mind, or at least my selective memory doesn't remember it. I drug the heifer through the gate in short order while Clay held the rest of them against the fence.

"Come on and heel her for me, Clay."

"I don't have a rope."

"What? Where's your rope?"

"I forgot it and left it in the saddle house."

I decided it was time for a responsibility lesson. I jerked the heifer down and got my rope off and then went and roped another and drug her through the gate. And then I roped a third one, and after retrieving my rope off number three, I rode up to Clay, and handed him my rope, and told him it was his turn. "You rope the other three." I said.

Clay rolled up on Beaver and roped one around the neck and led her through the gate. After going fifteen yards, he turned Beaver's head toward the heifer who was bouncing around on the end of twenty feet of rope. "What do I do now?" Clay asked me as I watched from twenty yards away.

"I don't know, but you need to hurry up because you got two more to rope!" He figured it out real good and had a big smile on his face when it was over.

$$\mathcal{EO}\mathcal{C3}$$

Diamond A Ranch, 1994-1995

The famous Arizona cowboy Dave Ericson has a saying that goes, "A great cowboy is one who can go into another man's country and beat him at his own game." I would say that Dave's aphorism is accurate. Every part of the west has situations and methods of operation unique unto itself. In the old days, cowboys in the Southwest were noted for their skill and speed with a rope, which evolved from their need to rope and doctor cattle with screw worms that infected any bloody sore such as a peeling brand or freshly castrated steer. The cowboys in Northern Nevada became famous for their trigger-reined cow horses that they rode with spade bits. An Arizona cowboy was likely to practice his roping in his spare time, while his counterpart in Elko County spent his spare time training his colt to slide and spin. Cowboys from the Texas Panhandle are famous for riding cutting horses trained to cut a cow with the rider dropping his hand on the horse's neck and applying no pressure to the bridle bit. Cowboys from up north, from places like Montana and Wyoming, were noted for their bronc riding skills. Many an argument has started because two hombres from different parts of the West claimed their skills were more important or useful than those of their counterparts.

The rough and rocky country of Central Arizona has a history of producing cowboys that are expert at gathering wild cattle in bad and dangerous places. Many places in the world have livestock gone wild and in need of being gathered. There are wild and trashy cattle in the swamps of Florida and Louisiana, the brush country of South Texas, and the vast wilderness areas of Australia. The thing that makes Arizona unique is that you have brush and trees to deal with, but you also have to contend with some of the roughest, steepest, and rockiest mountains found anywhere. There are many legendary wild-cow-gatherers, some of whom are modest, and others who will tell you they are the best, but the ones who are successful at getting the job done, all have one thing in common, they show up for work. To apprehend the one, or the many, that got away, you have to get up early and come home late. Nobody ever gathered the wild ones while sitting on a barstool or an easy chair; it's long, hard, and tedious work; and along the way, you will have as many bad days as not. But you get up early and you go at it again.

In the fall of '92, there were at least five hundred unbranded yearling cattle running on the top country on the Diamond A Ranch. From what I saw and later gathered, there were close to another three hundred that were two years old or older. If anything, these numbers are conservative. Besides the big steers in Shafer, there were a few others scattered around, mainly in Trinity, Buck Tanks, and Big Chief.

The winters and springs of '94 and '95 were dry

enough that we were able to get around and really knock a hole in the number of remnant cattle, many of whom had never been part of an accurate tally. Every cowboy on the ranch got involved helping gather, brand, and take a tally on these cattle. When the wagon was out and working during fall roundup, we did our best to leave as few cattle ungathered as possible. Because in the winter some of the cowboys had responsibilities in the camps where they stayed, such as Camp Sixteen, Camp Five, or Pica, they didn't have the opportunity to help gather these remnant cattle as some of the rest of us did. This had nothing to do with their ability to make a hand, it just meant they were busy doing other things on parts of the ranch where remnant cattle didn't exist.

The lion's share of the remnant cattle gathered during those two winters were gathered by Jim Marler, Scott Westlake, Clay Ashurst, Mike McLaughlin, and me. Pat Prosser, Brad Meade, Steve Webb, Devin Kanapilly, and Baldy also helped a lot but were not always available. The winter and spring of '94, Jim Marler and I did nothing but gather uncounted cattle running on the top country. Many days we had Clay's help. Then during the winter and spring of '95, it was Scott, Clay, and I working together. We had old Banjo, the Catahoula dog Walt Robinson loaned me. I tried numerous other dogs, but none of them were much good. Banjo was hardheaded and sometimes difficult to control, but it was uncanny how he could find a cow. Many times the dog would "wind" or smell cattle sometimes from a mile and a half away, and he would take off and go to 'em! Once he found a bunch of cows, he would go to barking, and he would hold them up. A cow or some other kind of big critter that didn't want to stop would have Banjo hanging on by an ear or nose, and if the cow brute kicked him loose or scraped him off on a tree or big rock, he would just attack and get a hold with his teeth and huge jaws and do battle again. When he got hot, in the course of battle, and his blood got to running, Banjo quit listening; and more than once, we went to bed so hoarse we couldn't talk because we had screamed at the dog so much. We loved him anyway. He was a meathead, but he was good help.

On the side of a limestone ridge, three miles north of Seligman, there was a huge letter S painted in white that could be seen from town or the interstate as you drove by. The country that lies between the town's big initial and town itself was a nice, open piece of country known as Hubbard Pasture. But when you climbed on top of that ridge above the big white S, you were in one of the hardest pieces of country to gather on the ranch. It was Buck Tank Pasture, and the south side of it was one big thicket full of cedars, pinion pines, and cliffrose plants, some of which were twelve feet high. (cliffrose, Cowania Mexicana, or quinine as some people call it, is a beautiful evergreen plant with pretty white flowers that bloom in the summer. Cattle as well as deer browse on the bush, especially in wintertime or droughts. It has a sweet yet pungent odor and prefers to grow in limestone.)

One day, Scott, Clay, and I were riding on a limestone ridge about a mile north of Seligman's famous white S. We were in the middle of a cliffrose thicket where the plants were way over our heads. We couldn't see fifteen feet. The cliffrose trunks were six to eight inches in diameter, and as strong as iron, and grew no more than a foot or two apart. We had entered the thicket following fresh cow tracks. Banjo was with us walking along and looking bored, and then suddenly, he lifted his nose in the air, and sniffed, and took off to our left. Within two or three seconds, he was raising a ruckus, and some cows were bellowing. We plowed our way through the cliffrose, a distance of no more than sixty feet, and there was Banjo with a half dozen cows held up. The brush was so thick we couldn't see the cattle and were fixing to ride passed them when Banjo smelled them and took off running.

In the fall of '94, when we had several hundred cows

get through the drift fence that ran east from Rose Well and separated Lower Sandstone from Midway and Broken Axle, Cole Moorhouse and some men got most of the cattle gathered before the wagon pulled in that fall, but a few were still running on the plains. We needed to get the calves gathered so we could ship them, and later that winter, I spent several days doing this. One day in particular sticks in my mind. I left Pica before sunup pulling a sixteen-foot gooseneck trailer that was six feet wide. I had a good gray horse that Randy Rutledge had broke, named Powderface, saddled and loaded in the trailer. I drove out into the Midway and Broken Axle Pastures, and when I spied a big weaner calf, I would unload Powderface and run and rope the calf. By then some of the calves weighed over six hundred. I would load one, and then put it in front of the divider gate and then load my horse in the rear. After several hours of repeating this process, I had the front of the trailer full with no room for more. After that, I would rope a big critter, jerk it in the trailer, and tie it down so I could load my horse without the cow brute escaping. When I got a couple tied down, I started leaving them standing, but tied to the inside of the trailer by their necks. Finally there was only room for Powderface, so I loaded him and then waded off into the crowd and untied all the calves that were either tied down or necked to the side of the trailer. I had twelve big calves plus my horse in the trailer when I got back to Pica about sundown. That was one of the most enjoyable days I've ever had.

In the middle of Trinity Pasture, there was a dirt tank in a steep canyon that was known as Jones Dam. On the south side of Jones Dam was a long hog-backed ridge with the slope on the north side toward Jones Tank and the south side toward Trinity Tank being very steep, almost too steep to ride up. But the slope going up from the west was not too steep, but several miles long. At the top, you were as high as Trinity Mountain itself but, for some reason, the ridge had no name.

One day in the afternoon, Scott, Clay, Jake Bowser, and I made a drive into Jones Tank and got several head of cattle held up. We left Jake holding the small bunch of cattle, and I went north, making a circle by myself; and Scott and Clay rode around to the west side and then turned and rode up the westward slope of this high ridge going east toward the top. We had already made several runs getting around some fast cattle, and by the time the two cowboys reached the top of the ridge, their horses were tired. They stopped and unsaddled, letting their horses cool off and catch their wind. As they stood there resting, they looked off the steep north slope and spotted a bunch of cattle, about a half dozen, halfway down, between them and Jones Dam, a half mile away and five hundred feet lower. Among the cattle was a black baldy cow that had escaped from us on several occasions, and Scott and Clay could tell by watching her that she was watching them, and she was getting nervous. In the bunch with her was a very large animal, much bigger than her, and smoky grey in color. They figured it was a big steer. The black cow could probably smell them, or see them, or both; and they knew she was going to blow out of there pretty quick, and she was a half mile away with a very steep slope between them. They saddled back up and started toward her. There was no sense trying to sneak around from another direction and ambush her because she was already aware of what was going on and was experienced at giving cowboys the slip. It was just as well to attack head on, try to keep up, and do battle somewhere in the distance where there was better ground. They had Banjo and another dog and hoped the dogs could hold them up. They mounted up and descended at a fifty degree angle with lots of brush and trees to get in their way, and the black baldy cow took off leading the rest of the pack with her. Banjo took off, and before long, he was barking but the sound of breaking tree limbs and rolling rocks meant nothing was slowing down.

Scott rode out wide, to one side, trying to get in front of the cattle, and Clay stayed behind trying to overtake them from the rear. By riding at breakneck speed, Clay caught up with the bunch, which had decided to turn slightly uphill. The dogs were trying to get a hold of an ear or nose, but this bunch was experienced at getting away and simply rolled over the top of old Banjo, and gave no quarter. After a long run, Clay rolled up on the big smoky-colored critter, which turned out to be a steer weighing at least fifteen hundred and standing over fifteen hands. When Clay came to a spot where he figured he could make his move and get the steer roped, his horse had nothing left to give him, that last quick burst of speed to get a loop on him. He had thirty feet of rope, and his horse, a red roan named Rebel, wouldn't get closer than thirty-one feet. Scott showed up, and his horse was completely wasted also, and they followed the steer, who stayed just out of shooting range until they finally gave up. Their horses were completely done in, Banjo was beat up and bleeding, and the black cow and smoky steer escaped. Sometimes you get whipped no matter how hard you try.

There were a few places on the ranch that barely got touched, such as Robbers Roost, which was a high promontory rising up from the bottom of the Aubrey Valley on its north end. If you were on Route 66 near the Pica Camp turnoff, and you looked straight north twelve

miles, Robbers Roost rose up like a sentinel and was a landmark known by everyone in the area. The Hualapai Reservation fence goes over the top of this butte, and only the southern tip of it was on the Diamond A side of the fence with perhaps two or three sections of the top of it being on the Diamond A side. Around the 1ˢᵗ of December in '92, six weeks after I took over as wagon boss, we made a drive on top of the high point. We had just moved camp from Rose Well to Pica and were going to gather Last Chance Pasture, which Robbers Roost was a part of, so I thought working the top of it would be a good place to start. No one on the crew had ever heard of someone leading a crew of men up there in an attempt to gather any cattle. No one on the crew claimed they had ever been on the top, and several rolled their eyes when I mentioned venturing up there.

At the foot of Robbers Roost on the east side, and about a quarter mile off the Hualapai Reservation fence, was a dirt tank that had plenty of water in it at that time. Indian Well was about two and a half miles northeast on the fence. There were lots of cow tracks leaving the dirt tank going uphill toward the top of the Roost. I didn't know the country on top, but no one else did either, so I struck out leading everyone uphill like I knew what I was about. I left Al Smith and another man at the dirt tank, instructing them to "set up a holdup" and telling them we would run cattle toward them. We rode to the top following a cow trail that was powdery from being well used. We climbed at least a thousand feet, traveling a couple miles distance and reached the far side. There were about twelve of us on top plus the two men on holdup at the dirt tank below. We split up, and I sent Pat Prosser to the reservation fence, and I took the outside around the rim of the Roost on the south side, with the rest of the crew spread out between us. There was the worst cliffrose thicket on top I've ever seen, with the plants being twelve feet high and sometimes higher. They were extremely thick, and you had to claw your way through them at a snail's pace. There wasn't a lot of country up there, so we were pretty close together, and before long there were cattle moving out in front of us. A great deal of the time, I was able to move fast, being near the rim rock and the thicket's edge, and I could see fifteen or twenty head of cattle running downhill in front of us. I figured if I could see that many, there were two or three times as many cattle that I couldn't see. I was feeling good, thinking we were really accomplishing something. I tried to pace myself moving slightly ahead of the crew where I could keep the cattle turned toward the fence and our holdup, but not so fast that I would leave a big gap behind me. For quite a while, I couldn't see anyone because of the thicket but watched the leaders of the cattle moving downhill in front of me. Things moved faster as we tipped downhill, and finally men began emerging out of the rocks and thicket. I began to lope, running through the limestone rocks, hoping to reach the men on holdup and help them. When I was two-thirds of the way to the bottom, I could see cattle running out into the valley, past the dirt tank and my two holdup men. I whipped my horse into a dead run, trying to reach the holdup where surely there was a wreck taking place. But when I got to the dirt tank, Al and the other cowboy were astraddle their cowponies and perched on the top of the earthen dam watching the last of the cattle run past them on the fence a quarter mile away. The leaders were already a mile and a half away, running in the sand on the valley floor.

"Al! What the heck's going on? Why didn't you try and stop the cattle? You just let them run by you!"

"Did you want us to stop them? I thought you just wanted them to go out onto the flat."

"I told you to set up a holdup here at this tank!" I replied, "Didn't you hear me say, holdup?"

"What's a holdup?"

Slowly I was learning that I needed to explain things a little better, especially to some people. I never rode up on

Robbers Roost again, not because I didn't want to, I just never had the time. Perhaps we gathered some of those cows the next morning, but I never knew for sure.

Throughout 1993 there was little real change in the number of untallied cattle on top due to the wet winter, but when the wagon wasn't out, we pecked away at it. But finally in the winter of '93 and '94, we made major dents in the number of uncounted cattle. Even then there were places on the ranch that I never rode through in a thorough manner. I never made it back on the top of Robbers Roost, and there were places along Aubrey Rim in Big Chief Pasture I never became familiar with and only remember riding down into the bottom of Crater Canyon once or twice. But still, we were relentless in our pursuit of cattle running in all the pastures on top throughout the early months of 1994. Finally, about the time we threw a crew together and started spring roundup in late March 1994, tracks were getting hard to find. At least a person could drive in a pickup all over the top and ungathered cattle didn't stand there mocking you as you drove by. I didn't know for sure, but from the looks of the sign, I thought there was less than a hundred fifty head of cattle left on all the four hundred square miles that was known as the top.

We threw the roundup crew together the last week of March and started gathering the Cataract Plains and trailed cattle south to brand and, subsequently, drift them farther south to summer pasture on top. It seemed like a cruel conundrum to say we had gathered all the remnant cattle off the top country through the winter and then turn around and fill it back up again in the springtime. It was job security, or so it seemed at the time; and in my mind, it was a good mystery because I enjoyed the constant search for ungathered cattle more than I enjoyed the wagon.

In the fall of '94, we were able to gather the top cleaner than the two previous falls that I had been there. We had a good cowboy crew including some good young men who were getting to know the country, and we were making better drives, using a holdup in the rougher, brushier country. The cow count from spring to fall and year-to-year was coming out right, and we were gathering and shipping close to the same number of calves I claimed we had branded. Things were making sense as far as the cow work was concerned.

In May 1995, about halfway through the spring roundup, one of the two partners who owned the cattle showed up at Seligman and stayed for a day or two. While he was in town, he stayed in a house catty corner to the mansion on Picacho Street. The wagon was camped at Rose Well, and we were branding; but I drove home several nights a week and returned to the wagon early the next morning. One day while the owner was in town, the manager sent word to me that the owner, whom I really had very limited contact with, was hosting a little party and had requested Jean Ann and I be present. A couple representatives from his bank were also going to be there.

In the early afternoon, I drove into town and got slicked up, and we walked across the street to the big boss's living quarters. He had a barbeque grill fired up on the patio out the back door and was grilling rib eyes. There were only a half dozen folks present, but the owner, who was a nice man, was in a festive mood. The horrible drought of 1996 and the disastrous cow market that followed were hidden twelve months into the future. The man cooked juicy rib eyes and talked happily about the cow business. There were two cases of very expensive Cabernet Sauvignon sitting on the kitchen floor, and he made it known, they had not been bought to be stored in the closet. After turning the rib eyes, he pulled up a chair at a table where the manager and his wife were sitting with Jean Ann and me. He talked happily for a moment to everyone in general and then looked at me with a smile and said, "Did you know that we have gathered five hundred more cows than we knew existed?" I nodded my head in the negative and, out of the corner of my eye, noticed the manager and his wife staring off into the distance. The man then got up and took the rib eyes off the grill, and we all ate steak and drank Cabernet.

That next fall in October of '95, we were gathering Trinity Pasture, and one afternoon Scott, Clay, and I went to the east side of the pasture, against the Sevens Ranch fence, and were trying to find some cattle we thought we had missed earlier that morning. Against the Sevens Ranch fence there was a high malpai ridge, thick with cedars and very rocky; and in places the fence between the two ranches was almost nonexistent, and there was evidence that cattle were going back and forth. On the west side of this ridge, which was only a quarter to a half mile wide, there was a very deep canyon with steep and rocky sides. The canyon was south of that high ridge where the big smoky-colored steer escaped Clay and Scott, and south of the deep canyon was Trinity Dirt Tank that sat at the foot of steep Trinity Mountain on its south side.

We had Banjo with us and made a pass along the high ridge against the Sevens Ranch fence, but we found nothing; and then, always searching for a new vista, we rode up to the edge of the deep canyon to our west and gazed off into the bottom. And there, a half mile away, and five hundred feet below us, were what looked like a half dozen cow brutes. One of the cows made the mistake of bawling, and Banjo heard it, and perhaps even smelled them; but in any case, he descended the canyon wall in a dead run. There was nothing left for us to do but follow the dog that was in full attack mode. He was gathering remnant whether we wanted to or not. We fell off the slope as fast as possible with rocks rolling, but long before we hit bottom, we could hear Banjo barking like hades, and cows bawling just as loud. We soon caught up and found four or five cows and a couple big calves weighing five or six hundred pounds. The cows were not ones we recognized and were acting like some of the last holdouts of a bygone era.

We got around them, hoping to hold them with loving kindness, but when they realized we were humans that were helping the dog, they got really nervous, and soon they splattered. One red cow, who was four or five years old, separated herself, and ran downstream by herself; and beings I was the nearest to her escape, I put up hot pursuit. I was riding a fine bay roan horse named Fooler, and I was cinched up and ready, or so I thought. It had been colder than normal, and I had on a heavy Eddie Bauer parka, and by the time we reached the cows, I was sweating from

being over-clothed. I jumped ol' Fooler into a run like he had been eating corn, thinking I would have the cow caught within eighty feet. As I rushed past the first cedar tree between me and the cow, a limb from the tree jerked my loop out of my hand as the cow caught another gear. Fooler ignored my lack of skill with the rope and ran up on the cow, and about the time my second loop was built, we crashed between a couple cedar trees and an algerita bush, and my loop was jerked out of my hand a second time. As I hung on for dear life with Fooler running all out through trees and brush, I realized I was hyperventilating, and although the heavy Eddie Bauer coat had been ripped by a snag, I was sweating heavily. The cow ran on, and finally after I built a loop in my nylon rope a third time, I threw at the cow and missed. The brush was getting thicker, and when Fooler crashed between two pinion trees, another large tear was made in my heavy parka. The hole and extra air it let in didn't cool me off. I was still sweating profusely! Where was that durned dog when you needed him? Sometime between my fifth and sixth loop, the cow ran out of air and fell down, and me and Fooler almost ran over her. I stepped off the horse, whose sides were heaving, and pulled the cow over on her side and tied her hind legs together with a pigging string. Man, I thought, talking to myself. You are a heck of a hand!

I rode back up the canyon to where I had left Clay and Scott, which was a distance of a half mile. I ran onto Clay who was sitting on a rock letting his horse cool off. I inquired as to where all the cattle had gone, and Clay answered, "Well, I've got three tied down, and I think Scott caught a couple; and as soon as my horse blows for a minute, I was going to go looking for him." Smart aleck kid!

Clay got mounted, and we rode up the canyon a ways and found Scott, who was on his horse that was a known outlaw, and he was staring down his rope, which was tied to the saddle horn on one end and a big Brahma-cross cow on the other. There was a cedar tree, about six feet high, in between them; and it was obvious the cow and the horse were both sulled up pretty bad. About the time we came into view, the outlaw horse decided to give up, and he lay down. No matter how hard Scott urged him, he had decided it was quitting time. Scott stepped off hoping his new Don Butler saddle was going to survive the wreck. We managed to get the cow heeled, and then tied down, so Scott could get loose from the big cow, and then he was able to get the outlaw up, and loosen his cinches, and let the horse blow for a while.

We cooled off for several minutes and discussed how we were going to get all the cattle up and moved to a corral somewhere before sundown, and then we heard Banjo barking way off in the distance to the west. The sound was very faint, but it was obvious he had a cow brute cornered somewhere. We took off and found the dog a mile and a half away at a big steel water trough on a pipeline. The place and trough were known as Middle Water, and we rode up and found Banjo on the ground outside the trough that was round and twelve feet in diameter. He was barking at a six hundred pound steer that was belly high in the water, in the center of the trough. The dog and steer were both soaking wet, and occasionally Banjo would plunge into the water to attack the steer that would then submerge his head down into the water to protect himself. The steer was very glad to see us and was more than willing to cooperate in any way we desired. We got back to camp late that night.

ഇൻ
Cowboy Lost
And Then Gone
ഇൻ

Santa Fe Trail, 1840s

To the men and women who won the west, a horse was a tool to be used. That's not to say, they didn't like them, or appreciate their beauty, or make great efforts at training and understanding them, because many of them did; but a horse was a thing to be used. Contrary to what twenty-first century horse whisperers with television shows would like you to think, horse worship in the nineteenth century western frontier was overshadowed by sweat, saddle sores, harness galls, and sun-bleached horse carcasses that lay alongside the trail. Many a horse was ridden to death by a man desperate to reach a certain destination, or perhaps more important, a man equally desperate to escape an impending situation. The westering man loved a good horse, but a good horse to him was a horse he could use. And if need be, wear out.

There are many famous stories of men and horses who accomplished great feats of endurance and stamina in the old West. Probably the most famous of these is the story of Felix Aubrey's famous ride from Santa Fe, New Mexico, to Independence, Missouri, in 1847. To many, the story is known as the "Legend of Little Aubrey's Ride." Felix Aubrey was a Canadian of French extraction who landed in New Mexico after following beavers and trade goods southwest from Winnipeg. He worked and traded with well-known trappers including Beaubiau and Maxwell. Little Aubrey, as he was sometimes called due to being slight of build, was a successful man and shrewd trader. He also was a noted character who was willing to take on a challenge or wager.

In August 1846, another man of note whose name was Tobin made a voyage from Santa Fe to Independence, Missouri, in eleven days, which at the time was considered almost unthinkable. Upon completion of this feat of endurance, Mr. Tobin became something of a celebrity. Felix Aubrey recognized an opportunity to elevate his stature and boasted that he could travel the same route and cut the time by at least a third. Soon people around Santa Fe were talking and offering to put up money against Aubrey's claim. Aubrey wagered five thousand dollars of his own money but also laid down his own rules.

It was agreed by him and those who had called his bet that he had to follow Tobin's route, which was the well-established Santa Fe Trail. But he could use any amount of horses he wanted and switch mounts when he chose.

To win the bet, he had to travel the distance in seven days and eight hours. Felix Aubrey sent horses, one at a time, eastward with wagon trains bound for Independence, Missouri. The trains had come west with supplies for Santa Fe citizens and the garrison of soldiers stationed there. Though loaded with some trade goods, the supply trains traveled faster on the return trip eastward because they packed less weight. Little Aubrey sent six different horses with six different trains and figured he should start his ride when the trains were positioned at a spot he envisioned to be appropriate for a horse change. Considering the absence of communication capabilities, the potential for the entire event turning out to be a logistical disaster was enormous. Without a doubt, to those who called Felix Aubrey's bet, the man must have seemed to be a poor businessman, if not downright crazy.

For the first stage of the trip, Little Aubrey rode a beautiful blooded mare known to have tremendous stamina. The mare's endurance was sorely tested because she and Felix didn't catch the first wagon train, which was traveling faster than Felix expected, until they had traveled a ways north of Wagon Mound, and one hundred fifty miles north of Santa Fe. He stopped long enough to switch his saddle from one horse to the other and drink a large amount of coffee and water. He mounted with some food in his hand and ate as he rode on.

Besides issues like meeting up with six different wagon trains to change horses, and dealing with hunger, thirst, and fatigue, there was the very serious threat of hostile Indians. A raiding party of Indians usually avoided a large wagon train but considered a lone rider an easy target, even if his tired horse was a fast one. Felix rode on and miraculously met up with each of the wagon trains and fresh horses near the various spots he had predicted. On the entire trip, he only stopped to sleep three times and then for no more than several hours. Five days and fourteen hours after leaving Santa Fe, little Aubrey rode into Independence, Missouri, two miles west of present day Kansas City. He rode seven different horses a total distance of eight hundred thirty miles. Including the time he stopped to rest, his average rate of speed was six miles an hour. He averaged riding each horse one hundred eighteen miles in less than twenty hours per horse. No one knows for certain how many hours he actually stopped to sleep, but subtracting that unknown number makes his journey even more incredible.

There is no record that any of Felix Aubrey's seven horses died as a result of his amazing feat, which gives even more credence to his skill as a horseman. A dead horse would have done the man no good; but on the other hand, he couldn't have accomplished what he did had he not pushed them close to the end of their endurance. He did not spare the spur or the whip. Regardless of what some modern horse lovers might think, Felix Aubrey had his mind on the five thousand dollars he was going to win and not the health of his horse.

ℰ⋑ℭℛ

Diamond A Ranch, 1990s

It was late October, and we were camped at Rose Well gathering cows off the top country and shipping about six truckloads of calves a week. The calves were weighing around five hundred fifty pounds; it had been a good year. One morning we left camp at daylight and traveled south in a trot, going up Rogers Draw, gaining elevation as we went. About eight miles south of Rose Well, we arrived at the old Red Lake Camp. The old camp house, where so many old cowboys had stayed over the years, was still standing but in need of repair. The old corrals as well as the horse pasture were laying down on the ground unable to hold anything more than the ghosts of memories past.

It was very cloudy and cool with a damp wind blowing out of the southwest that smelled as if it was blowing off of a rain on the Big Sandy River, one hundred fifty miles away. We split up there at the Red Lake Camp, with Jim Marler taking four or five men west toward the Owen Dam Pasture fence, and me taking the rest east toward Brushy Tank. The plan was to drive a big swath of country straight back into Rose Well with the center of our drive being the bottom of Rogers Draw. At the start, we were about four miles wide, with our drive narrowing the closer we got toward camp. The country at that place was scattered with low hills and cedar breaks, thick patches of pinon, cedar, and cliffrose in places, and intermittent spots of open space that might be several hundred acres in size.

I moved along at a trot and lope, dropping men off and pointing them toward Rose Well at intervals of a quarter to a third of a mile. About the time I started bending my horse back to the north, I dropped Cody Cochran, who was the last man I had left, and explained to him that my course would soon be north by northwest. At the moment we parted, a man's visibility was around ten miles with lots of good landmarks showing themselves in every direction, and the drainage of Rogers Draw being easy to make out. Things went smoothly for about a half hour, and Cody flanked to me on several occasions, and received cattle from me, and pointed them toward the man on the opposite side of him and, subsequently, the center of the drive. And then the bottom fell out of the sky, and it started raining. For about thirty minutes, it rained at a rate I guessed to be about two inches per hour, and then it backed off to a slow drizzle. Where an hour earlier you could see for miles, you now were lucky to see three hundred yards. Beings no landmarks were now visible, everything looked the same, with every tree, bush, or open space appearing to be no different than ten thousand others in a fifty mile radius of where we were. I felt comfortable in my bearings, although the land and sun were hidden by clouds, because I had been in that country many times before; but I was paying very close attention to what I was doing and was hoping the sun would show itself momentarily. It did not but, instead, continued to rain at different rates, sometimes heavy for a few minutes at a time, and then backing off to a sprinkle for a while.

After an hour of seeing no one, I had accumulated a few cows that were moving along in front of me in the rain. Finally I ran into Steve Webb, who was the man on the opposite side of Cody from me. Steve and I talked for a moment, and then he told me he had not seen Cody since the rain started. A man getting out of place on a big drive in brushy country during a rainstorm was nothing out of the ordinary, and Steve and I separated and kept moving north toward Rose Well. We bumped into each other several more times before the drive reached the gate going into the corrals at camp, and each time I inquired about Cody, with Steve having not seen him. About the time the leaders of the cattle we had gathered began walking through the gate, it quit raining, and an occasional patch of blue sky appeared. Within ten or fifteen minutes, the entire crew showed up, except Cody whom nobody had seen in several hours.

Everyone was soaked, even though most of us had rain slickers. Beings a breeze had replaced the cold rain, we were shivering, so we loped to the horse corral, unsaddled and changed horses, finding a fresh horse waiting for us in the corral. We walked to the wagon to eat lunch, and drank some hot coffee, and tried to warm up. From where the wagon was set up, it wasn't hard to see up toward Rogers Draw, and we all kept looking that direction thinking Cody would appear shortly. We had fresh saddled horses nearby in case we needed to go out and help him pen some cows he might be trailing into camp. And so as we waited and gazed south, we ate a hot meal, and drank hot coffee, and sat around the big B.S. fire.

At first the fact that Cody had failed to show up when and where he was supposed to was nothing that anyone thought much about. Every cowboy who ever participated in work such as we were doing had a story or two to tell about being lost and turned around, myself included. But as time ticked away, and Cody didn't come riding into camp, I began to wonder. By one thirty in the afternoon, I was thinking I better start looking. It had quit raining about eleven thirty, and there was an occasional patch of sunlight showing through, if not continually, definitely every ten or fifteen minutes. Visibility had returned to at least several miles.

I sent several men south, horseback, with instructions to fan out on each side of Rogers Draw, cutting for sign as they went. Jim Marler and I loaded our horses in a gooseneck and drove in the mud to Red Lake and unloaded near where we had all split up early in the morning. We trotted east toward Brushy Tank cutting for sign as we moved along. Jim was an outstanding tracker and no doubt better at that art than I, even though I was no slouch either. But trying to pick up a horse track in the mud may not be as easy as one would think. Had Cody passed through our path while it was raining as hard as it had, his tracks would be hard, if not impossible, to pick up. Every indentation in the ground, such as a cow track, was full of water, even though the rain had stopped several hours before, and any track made in the first hour of the rain would have been completely wiped out. We traveled a long way to the east, and then split up, one of us going north and the other going south, and we agreed to meet back at the truck and trailer in an hour or so.

Neither of us saw anything that might get us on the correct path. It was now getting close to four o'clock, and I decided it was time to push the panic button. I got on the two-way radio that was in my pickup and touched base with someone at Rose Well and was told that Cody had not showed up there. Then I radioed the manager, who was in Seligman, and informed him of my dilemma, and the two of us discussed what, if anything, should be done. Neither one of us thought Cody was hurt or in any great danger, but we were getting concerned. He decided to call the sheriff's department and get the search and rescue people to head toward Rose Well if possible. He said he would also see if someone, like the Arizona Department of Public Safety, might have a helicopter available. He said he would call and give me details as they became available. Jim and I loaded our horses and drove back north to Rose Well.

About the time we pulled into Rose Well, I got word, via the two-way radio, that a D.P.S. helicopter was at that very moment flying toward our camp and would land and pick me up on the road a half mile south of Rose Well. I needed to be waiting for them. Within minutes of parking my truck at the appointed spot, the chopper came flying in and promptly landed. An officer in uniform jumped out and asked if I would mind getting in and showing them the route they should take that would have the highest percentage chance of finding the missing cowboy. As I got strapped into the big chopper, they told me they only had thirty minutes worth of fuel before they would have to touch down, deposit me back to mother earth, and then return the bird to Flagstaff, eighty miles away. I definitely got the message that I needed to make the most of the thirty minutes worth of aviation fuel. I instructed them to fly south over the same route we had ridden earlier that morning. When we got to Red Lake, I told them to keep flying south toward Cooke Dam on the Trinity Pasture fence, another eight miles away.

I figured the most likely scenario was that Cody had become disoriented during the hard rain, and because of the lack of visible landmarks, he had gotten turned around and headed the wrong way. We had just moved to Rose Well a few days earlier, and he had never been in any of the country where we were now working and did not know the lay of the land. But I also knew there was a possibility he was on the ground and injured due to his horse falling on him or some other mishap. The horse he had been riding was gentle, so I ruled out the possibility of him being bucked off. I also feared the possibility of my friend being struck by lightning. For an hour or so that morning, there had been a number of lightning strikes in our vicinity, and all cowboys know what lightning can do. When the chopper got to Cooke Dam, I asked the pilot to fly west over Keseha, and then turn back north flying over the north Keseha shipping trap; and then when we got to Red Lake, we turned east and flew over Brushy Tank and circled Murphy and Johnson and then on north toward Sullivan Tank, which was three miles east of where I had last seen Cody. From there we went west over the location of our last encounter with each other and continued on to the Road Canyon road hitting it very close to B Tub. Then we zigzagged from the road to Rogers Draw going north as we flew. When we got close to the spot where they had picked me up, the pilot said they were low on fuel, and my time as a passenger had ran out. We had accomplished nothing, and now it was getting close to sundown.

I gave instructions to Jim Marler and the crew to catch horses for the next day, saying we would continue gathering cattle just like my schedule was written down; but I was apprehensive. As the crew caught horses and did chores around camp, I drove up and down several roads churning up mud and worrying. At dusk the manager showed up, and we discussed our options, which amounted to about nothing beings it would soon be dark and cloudy with no chance of a moon or stars to navigate by. We decided to build a huge bonfire along the road a mile and a half south of Rose Well, hoping it would serve as a beacon should Cody be able to spy it from a distance while wandering around in the night. Not long after we got our fire started, the Coconino County Sheriff's Department Search and Rescue team started arriving pulling trailers loaded with

ATVs. By the time they were unloaded and ready to go, it was pitch-black. None of the men and women belonging to the search and rescue team knew the country any better than Cody, and about all I could tell them was that he was out there somewhere—pointing into the cold and wet darkness. The good folks in the rescue team took off in various directions, and the manager and I threw lots of wet wood on the fire and waited for something to happen. Something came in the form of nothing, with the exception of the search and rescue folks stopping by once in a while to ask questions about the lay of the land. Transferring locations on a map into reality in the darkness was a difficult task. I tried to be helpful, but my biggest means of feeling like I was doing my duty was throwing more wet wood on the fire. At times I dozed while lying on the wet ground, but for the most part, it was a long and extremely dull night.

At dawn the search and rescue folks congregated, and some of them loaded their gear and headed back to Flagstaff, and then several new members of their organization showed up to replace those who needed to depart for whatever reason. Jim, the foreman of the maintenance crew, arrived with a couple men from his crew, and the manager sent them toward Black Tank, instructing them to travel through Lower Sandstone Pasture and Farm Dam and then turn south toward Black Tank Camp, which was fifteen miles southeast of Rose Well. By the road going through Farm Dam, it was a distance of twenty-one miles from Rose Well to Black Tank. I saddled up with my cowboy crew and went south of Rose Well in search of more cows. The search for Cody had now outgrown me, and I figured that wandering around in the trees and brush might produce results as much as anything else that was happening. It was anyone's guess where Cody was.

About 8:00 a.m. we finally struck pay dirt when Jim, the maintenance man, found Cody five miles north of Black Tank riding north toward Farm Dam. He had never before been closer than fifteen miles to that place. He was tired and hungry, as was his old bay horse, but other than that, he was fine. Someone was sent with a pickup and gooseneck trailer to pick him up, and the suspense was over. When I and the rest of my crew arrived back at Rose Well with the herd of cattle we had gathered, Cody was there heartily feasting on anything the cook would dish out to him.

He told us that shortly after he last saw me it started raining hard, and directly he encountered a couple cows that took a quick run on him in what he thought was the wrong direction. He spurred his bay horse into a run to get around and turn them toward camp; his horse slipped on a big flat malpai rock and fell down on his left side. The horse went down hard, and the fall addled Cody, and he lay there for a minute waiting for his head to clear. Then Cody mounted his horse and started riding before he realized that in his addled state his glasses had fallen off. It was raining in earnest by this time, and visibility was next to zero, and Cody rode hard thinking he was now way behind the drive. But he rode east instead of north. He kept riding and searching with no help from the sky because the sun was hidden, and he had never before been anywhere near where he was. By the time it quit raining, he was miles east of where he should have been. He hit a draw and followed it downstream thinking it was Rogers Draw and it would take him to Rose Well, but instead it was the big canyon that drains east and down into the Black Tank Camp. About sundown he rode into Black Tank, unsaddled the bay horse, and turned him loose in the corral, and then let himself into the old camp house a few yards away. There wasn't a stitch of groceries in the house, but he found some matches and was able to build a fire. About the time he was making his fire, the manager and I were making our big bonfire twelve or thirteen miles to the west.

Early in the morning, he headed north of Black Tank

on the road going toward Farm Dam, and several miles north of Black Tank was where Jim found him. His horse was give out and missing some hair on his belly where Cody had spurred him; but both of them would be fine after a meal and a little rest. By the next morning, Cody was raring to go.

Cody grew up around Abilene, Texas, where his grandfather, on his mother's side, was an old-time Texas cowboy and horseman whose specialty was training calf horses. His grandfather had never been a well-known competitor but was very proficient at riding colts and rode them well into his eighties. He had been like a father to Cody, and Cody would have died for him. Cody's father was a successful professional calf roper who competed at the pro level for many years, but really wasn't a cowpuncher or ranch cowboy, merely a rodeo athlete. Because of his father's association with the sport of rodeo, Cody grew up around it, and like his father, he learned to rope calves in the arena at an early age. His father was competing in the '70s and '80s, and Cody's peers were young boys like Joe Beaver, Fred Whitfield, Cody Ohl, and Stran Smith. He competed in high school rodeo at the same time as they did and others like them.

Cody's father qualified for the National Finals Rodeo in 1987, which in itself is a dream come true for a rodeo hand. Beings I was an avid roper and rodeo fan, I was always asking Cody about his experiences growing up around a great rodeo athlete like his father. I asked him about various well-known rodeo hands that he had grown up with. I wanted him to tell me stories about being at different pro rodeos he had attended.

Finally one day after I had quizzed him about something pertaining to professional rodeo, he looked at me and said, "You know, Ed, I'll tell you, I really don't like rodeos or being a rodeo cowboy." I suppose I looked shocked, and then he went into further detail. "I'll tell you, the year my dad made it to the Finals, my mother worked three jobs to pay for my dad going down the rodeo road full-time. That same year, I qualified for the High School National Finals in the calf roping, which is very difficult to do if you are from Texas; and we were too broke for me to go. All the money we had went to keep Dad going down the road so he could win enough to make the Finals. I went to Vegas with my dad when he competed at the Finals, but my mom stayed home and worked. My dad won fifteen thousand dollars there at Vegas, but he also drank a lot of beer and chased a lot of women. When we got back home to Abilene, we were broke; so my mom kept working three jobs so he could go some more." I looked at him and could tell that somewhere inside there was a lot of pain. He went on, "I love to rope, but I hate the rodeo lifestyle. I've seen what it does to families. I watched my mom work for years for nothing except to pay for more entry fees and beer. I don't want to be a rodeo hand; I'd rather be a cowpuncher like you and my granddad; yeah that's what I want, I want to be a cowpuncher!"

Two days after Jim found Cody wandering north of Black Tank, we shipped six loads of calves. One of the owners of the operation, who lived in California, came out with the manager to weigh the calves and watch us do our work. Everything went smoothly, and we had the trucks loaded by noon, and we all headed to the wagon to eat lunch. We sat around camp for a while and visited after lunch with everyone joining in the storytelling and having a good time. Charlie Wascogamie had trotted out to wrangle horses, and when he got them gathered, we all walked to the horse corral and proceeded to catch horses. Several men had plans on shoeing a horse or two beings the wagon had been out now for six or seven weeks, and many horses in the remuda needed to be reshod.

About the time we had finishing eating, the manager's wife had showed up delivering some groceries to the wagon, and she stuck around visiting, especially with the California owner whom she was fond of. After catching horses, I was busy putting new shoes on one of the horses in my string. The remuda was still hanging around close to the horse corral, and as I worked at nailing shoes on my horse, I noticed the manager's wife and the California owner walking through the horses acting as if they were looking for something. I was thirty yards away, and on the opposite side of a cedar picket corral fence, and somewhat hidden; and I watched, wondering what they were doing. Suddenly, the manager's wife seemed to find something that interested her, and she motioned for the Californian to come and look at what she had found. I was puzzled at their actions until I realized she was pointing at the ribs of the old bay horse that Cody had been riding when he got lost several days earlier. She was pointing at his sides where a small spot with no hair existed as a result of Cody's spurs. I was too far away to hear what was being said but could tell that she had become quite animated as she shook her finger and talked to the gentleman we all worked for. Oh brother!" I thought to myself. I wonder where we will go with this situation.

We worked around camp all afternoon, shoeing horses and other duties that needed caught up on. About sundown I got in my Dodge truck and drove south to the mansion on Picacho Street to spend the evening with my family. My wife and two boys and I caught up on some family time for an hour or so, and then I showered and went to bed about eight o'clock. I planned on getting up at three thirty to start back up the hill toward Rose Well.

I had just dozed off to sleep when the phone rang. It was the manager, and he wanted to talk about the missing hair on Cody's old bay horse. I explained as best I could that Cody had ridden the horse harder than usual as a result of being lost and trying to find his way back to camp. He countered my explanations saying the outfit didn't approve of animal abuse, and spurring the hair off a horse's ribs was unacceptable. So I countered back that the horse did have a reputation for being lazy, and Cody had been operating under extenuating circumstances. He began talking in a louder voice and told me there was no excuse for animal abuse. Silently I wondered what he thought about human abuse, like expecting me to mount good men on horses like Broken O, Beaner, Gabby, or Snuffy, and then go gather and make sense of ten thousand cows on over eleven hundred square miles of fallen down fences and corrals. I offered up the thought that I was thankful that Cody wasn't injured. When I said that, he snapped. "I won't put up with this @#!$~%^&*!! I am not going to put up with this @~`#$%&~**!! I will not put up with this any longer!" I lay on my back in bed and held the phone six inches away from my ear and listened to him scream. Suddenly, I felt old and tired. Very tired. He continued, "You better get a hold on this @#~``~$%^&**!!"

"Okay!" I told him, and then he hung up the phone. I lay in bed and wondered why a cow outfit would put more value on a fifty dollar horse than on a man's life. Was a two-bit horse worth more than a real good young cowboy who woke up every morning wanting to make a hand? I was as down as a man could be. An old-timer I had worked for had a saying, "I'm lower than whale manure!" Well, I thought to myself while I contemplated my dilemma. I'm lower than whale manure! Suddenly I thought, It ain't worth it. I give up! Piss on it! I picked up the phone and dialed Hoffman Camp, and the manager answered the phone. "Write me a check to pay Cody off, and I will be over and pick it up in fifteen minutes."

I got up at three thirty in the morning, left the mansion, and drove out to Pica, then north to Rose Well with Cody Cochran's last Diamond A paycheck folded up and deposited in my shirt pocket. After breakfast, while everyone headed to the horse corral to catch horses, I called Cody aside and handed him his check. It's funny how a man can know something is coming and yet be surprised at the same time. I don't remember him asking why, only standing there looking at me. Not mad, just hurt. I stood looking at him and was mad and hurt, but mostly ashamed. There was no need for this to happen except the fact that I had caved in to the powers that be. I felt like a coward. I told him that I had just talked to Vic Howell over at the Babbitt outfit, which was true, and Vic had told me they were short a man on their crew.

"Go over to Babbitts, and they will hire you, and they will like you, and appreciate you! This outfit doesn't deserve you," I told him as he stood there looking at me. "They like good cowboys over there."

I turned and walked to the horse corral and roped myself a horse, and when I got my saddle on him, I led what was left of my crew out into the cedar trees in a high lope.

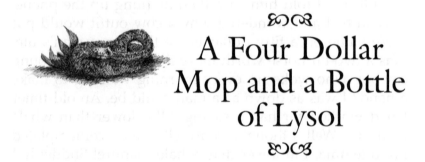

೫೦ಛ
A Four Dollar Mop and a Bottle of Lysol
೫೦೮ಜ

I have good memories of my days at the O RO Ranch, south of Seligman thirty miles, for many reasons; one of which is the beautiful headquarters known by old-timers as the Oaks and Willows. I lived there one winter and the following summer, and the place was one of the prettiest spots in Arizona. Charlie Greene, the old gentleman who owned the outfit, lived in a mansion down the road a mile and a half; and his old house had the distinction of having seven fireplaces scattered throughout its rambling space because of Mr. Greene's desire to heat with wood, which was plentiful. Charlie was a good man who cared for those who worked for him, and one way he showed it was that he always fed you good, or rather, better than good. He also furnished the single men, which was what most of his crew were, with a nice place to live when staying in camp and not out with the wagon during roundup. The bunkhouse at the Oaks and Willows was the nicest I ever lived in, and I've lived in quite a few. It had a small yard, fenced in with several big trees, and a wide, screened-in porch where a cowboy could sit and ponder things that cowboys ponder, some of which are deep but many more you would consider shallow. There was always a good cook installed there to keep a man's belly full, which aided in the art of pondering. There was also a spacious bathroom with several commodes and two shower stalls, plus a bathtub. Across the floor from the showers was a cabinet which held several nice sinks backed by a very large mirror where a single boy could see to do a good job of shaving the fuzz off his chin in case he was planning to venture into Prescott, sixty miles away, to see some girl he had been pondering while sitting on the screened-in porch. When the O RO wagon pulled in around Thanksgiving 1971, the bathroom was full of dirty cowboys scrubbing a fall's worth of crud from their filthy selves. One of the cowboys was Roy Olsen who reveled in the bathtub full of hot soapy water, and while he lay in it soaking up the civilization it provided, he smoked a big cigar and grinned from ear to ear.

I remember in detail the old wagon boss Whistle Mills shining all aspects of the bathroom, from the washbasins to the commode, with a clean towel in his hands and whistling a tune as he worked. I have no memory of Whistle asking me, or ordering me, to contribute to the shining of something as base as a toilet. My only job was to break horses to ride and gaze at my shadow as I bolted across the prairie on a hackamore bronc. I had great admiration for Whistle, but my memory loves him more because I know now that a great deal of his leading was done by example. He gave few orders but got much accomplished. Perhaps he didn't think I was smart enough to clean a toilet.

The Diamond A Ranch when I was wagon boss only had one bunkhouse, which was at Rose Well, that was equipped with bathing facilities where a man could bathe if the notion stirred him in that direction. When I first showed up, I was appalled at the filthy condition the bunkhouse was in and started a three year fight to bring it to a level of acceptability. Remembering Whistle, I got down on my knees and scrubbed the base of the commode more than once, hoping the idea would catch on. Toilet cleaning has scarcely been a thing in vogue amongst cowboys, and it continued to be an uphill battle while I was there, but several men rose up and did their part to help, among them Devin Kanapilly and Scott Westlake, both as good a man as I've ever been around. Baldy was especially good, perhaps because of his years living in the "institution," which teaches a man humility amidst base and lowly conditions. I greatly appreciated those who helped keep our camp something we didn't need to be ashamed of.

Late in the fall of 1995, I stopped at the general store on the west end of Seligman, where the ranch had a charge account and charged a cheap mop priced at $3.99, and a six ounce bottle of Lysol. I went home to the mansion to spend the night and returned to Rose Well early the next morning taking the mop and Lysol with me to assist in the art of bathroom cleaning, a thing in which all great wagon bosses should be experts. At least it seemed that way to me.

Several weeks later, around the first week in December, I was relaxing at home in the afternoon. The wagon was officially in for the winter with all the cow work done except the task of gathering remnant. I was sitting in the glassed-in front porch, or entryway, enjoying the sunlight coming through the large windows, and I was buck stitching a pair of chaps that I was making for a friend named Sam Gould.

As I sat there, enjoying a little bit of home life for a change, the manager's wife pulled up in her crew cab Ford pickup and stepped out directly outside from the window where I sat. She had a yellow piece of paper in her hand and appeared to be hunting someone who needed their throat cut. She marched around the side of the house toward the back door. Deliberately, I concentrated on my leather work, hoping someone else's life was in danger. I heard Jean Ann say come in and buried my thoughts in the art of stitching two pieces of leather together.

Presently, I heard a voice raised in the kitchen, several walls away, and someone loudly proclaiming, "I don't furnish mops to employees' wives!"

"What are you talking about?"

The voice reached a crescendo, "I DON'T FURNISH MOPS TO THE WIVES OF RANCH EMPLOYEES!"

Then I heard my wife calmly say, "Go talk to Ed, because I don't know what you are talking about." And then the walls of the house began to tremble, and I wondered if perhaps we were experiencing an earthquake. Soon the one who held the yellow piece of paper appeared in the doorway staring at me with fire in her eyes. I held a chap leg in my lap as I remained seated, and hidden beneath the leather leg, my hand clutched a needle-sharp marlin spike that was eight inches long. It had been given to me by Buck Smith and was made out of a tine from an old horse-drawn hay rake that had been used at the old O RO Ranch at Naco in Cochise County. I've been told, by those that know such things, that hog butchers use a similar tool to kill hogs by stabbing them in the heart. I took stock of the difficult situation, and it appeared she did not have a gun or a sharp knife but, rather, was armed with nothing more than the yellow paper.

"What are you doing, charging a mop at the store?"

"I bought it to…" at that point, she interrupted.

"The ranch doesn't furnish mops for cowboys' wives!"

"I didn't buy it for my wife! I bought it to clean the

bathroom at Rose Well!"

"I DON'T FURNISH MOPS!" She held out the yellow paper, which was a receipt from the general store, and she shook it at me. My trembling hand clutched the marlin spike that was still hidden under the chap leg.

I sat there contemplating the intricate details of making Arizona bellbottom leggings while I ignored her, which was unwise because her twitching increased while holding the receipt and shaking it at me; and then she stormed out the front door, making the foundation of the house shake. She walked around to the other side of her truck to get in, and as she did so, Target, her ring-eyed, man-eating dog stared at me while sitting on the passenger side of the pickup seat.

Several weeks later, Scott, Clay, and I gathered a stud named Bull Max and a band of mares that he had run with all year in the Hubbard Pasture, on the edge of Seligman, on the north side. We ran the stud and his band of mares and colts into the shipping pens at Hoffman, east of town a mile or so. We were going to wean the colts and get Bull Max separated to be kept up at Hoffman all winter and fed grain so he would be fat and healthy come springtime. We ran the herd of horses into a big square corral, about one hundred twenty feet in diameter, and tried to cut him through a gate into a different corral, but he wasn't wanting to be separated from the mares. The manager and his wife walked out from the house where they lived, which was a couple hundred yards away. They intended to take pictures of the babies so they could be registered with the A.Q.H.A. They waited and watched while we made several attempts at cutting the stud through the gate, but he ducked by us and escaped each time.

Bull Max was halter broke and actually quite easy to handle when you got him caught and settled down, and I figured once I got a rope on him he would lead into the other corral easy enough. So I stepped off and cinched my saddle tight, and then remounted my horse, and built a loop in my nylon rope. The horse I was riding was a three-year-old sorrel named Chief that I had only ridden once or twice. Someone else on the cowboy crew had ridden him a few times through the fall roundup. Bull Max came circling around the corral from my left and ran behind me, between me and my horse, and the corral fence, and when he came around on my right side, I jumped Chief forward, took two swings, and roped the stud around the neck. Bull Max weighed eleven fifty and Chief weighed nine fifty at the most, and when I dallied, the stud hit the end of the rope very hard. When Chief felt the jerk, he blew up and jumped about as high as a horse can jump, and while he was going up, the stud whirled around and faced us for a second throwing a lot of slack in my rope. About the time Chief and I were at the top of his high buck-jump, the stud whirled back around and hit the end of the rope a second time. It all happened fast, and everything was fine until the stud hit us that second time. I was still dallied and in the saddle, but the weight of the stud against the weight of the colt, who was in midair, jerked the colt through the air like a huge hammer had hit him. In the process, I came off, with a whiplash effect, and was slammed face and chest first on the corral floor that was as hard as concrete.

I've been bucked down many times, but this was the worst in my memory. I lay on my stomach and tried to suck in some air but could not make my lungs function. My chest was seized up, and try as I might, I could not either push air out or pull air in. I was paralyzed and couldn't even scream or groan in pain. I lay there in an odd state of calm thinking how strange it was to not be able to breathe. I was not afraid, but the question ran through my mind, How long can one live like this? I lay on my stomach contemplating the dilemma of lungs that were not functioning, and I turned my head to the right with my mouth round and sucking like a goldfish out of water, and just about the time my eyes crossed, I saw her staring at me as she sat thirty feet away with a Polaroid camera in her hand. Perhaps it was her visage that jolted my system back into functioning, and with a great, tremendous gasp, my lungs brought life back into my body. With life came great pain. I had never hurt this badly before—ever. I thought my back was broken along with numerous ribs.

I lay there for a moment hearing someone ask, "Are you all right?" Hell no, I'm not all right. I thought to myself, but I knew that it was the cowboy way to deal with one's own problems, so I began scraping myself up off the ground. I felt like an egg with a broken yolk that someone was trying to salvage out of a hot frying pan before the yellow part turned hard. I felt yellow all over. I got up and crawled back on Chief but have no memory of what took place after that, except I know we finished what we needed to do.

I had Clay and Scott drop me off at the mansion on Picacho Street and asked them to take my horse on out to Pica where I kept my horses when the wagon wasn't out, and I went into the house. I asked Jean Ann to drive me to Flagstaff so I could see a doctor. My back had seized up with a stiffness that has never gone completely away, and I suspected I had some cracked vertebrae.

The emergency room physicians looked me over thoroughly, including numerous x-rays of my spine, a full dose of pokings and proddings, and several pages of paperwork. After detailed study of the x-rays and all the data they had compiled, the doctor in charge informed me that I had "acute thoracic trauma." Fearing the worst, I asked the doctor what that meant.

"It means you are really sore," he answered.

"Yes! But for a while I couldn't breathe!"

"Yes, well, you see, occasionally that happens. Your diaphragm went into a spasm as a result of your severe fall, and it was pushing upward, and as a result, you could not breathe, that's true," he explained. I felt relieved that he didn't think I was exaggerating. "But," he went on, "that only lasted for a few seconds, causing you some consternation, but really you were never in any real danger. I will give you a prescription for some pain reliever."

I wonder, I thought to myself, if there is a pain reliever for damaged pride? I get bucked off harder than I ever have in my life, and I can't even get a cracked rib out of the deal. I walked back to my pickup looking straight ahead because I was incapable of turning my head sideways.

I kept working, but for a few days, I could only move slowly. When I rode, I kept my horse throttled back to a slow trot. We had a very large bunch of calves penned up in several large corrals at Pica and were feeding them hay, awaiting some future date when they were to be shipped. About the time I got bucked off, these calves started getting sick, and for a couple weeks, we were doctoring quite a few. Scott and I were riding through them one very cold morning, a day or two after I came down with thoracic trauma, and were roping and doctoring them. Scott would rope them around the neck, and I would heel them due to the fact I couldn't ride a horse fast enough to catch a calf by the head, even a sick calf. On this particular day, there were a half dozen pretty college girls at Pica because the California partner had donated some ranch colts to the Cal Poly horse breaking program. The girls were perched on the top rail of the fence watching Scott and me rope and doctor sick calves. Scott roped a calf by the neck, and as I threw at the calf's heels and missed, I overheard one of the college girls say, "It's too bad that old man has to continue working in the cold, beings he's so crippled up!" I was forty-four years old, and by golly, that's a long ways from being old. I was riding Chief again, and when I heard that remark, I mustered up enough courage to spur him good and hard, and momentarily we broke into a slow lope. Old man! I thought to myself, I'll show her! And I rolled up to the sick calf and roped him by one hind leg above the hock.

By the end of January, my back was somewhere near normal, and things were rolling right along. Clay was busy working on his junior year of high school using a correspondence course. School wasn't hard for Clay when he put his mind to it, so he was whipping through a year's worth of school in a few months, and would be then able to come back to work for me fulltime. Everett had spent a semester in college and was back at the Babbitt Ranch, where he had spent most of his childhood, and had a job breaking horses. He had his PRCA card and was riding saddle broncs at as many pro rodeos as he could get to.

On the morning of February 1, 1996, I was up at 4:30 a.m. and was sitting in the kitchen, with its canary yellow walls, drinking coffee while Jean Ann cooked breakfast. At exactly 5:00 a.m. the phone rang, and I got up to answer it. It was the manager who had been gone to Phoenix for a week where he and his wife had attended the company's annual budget meeting. "Ed, I need you to come over here to Hoffman. I need to talk to you." I hung up the phone, got my Carhardt coat and black cowboy hat, and went outside, and got in my Dodge pickup. It was decidedly cold, about five above.

I drove up to Hoffman and saw the house was dark except for the kitchen, which also served as the office. When I knocked, he answered saying, "Come in." I entered, and there he stood with his back against the wall, the fax machine on his right, and the darkened doorway that led to the living room to his left. Target, the man-eating dog, sat on his haunches abreast of his left leg that filled a new pair of Levi's. In his right hand, he held two pieces of paper, which he held out to me motioning me to take them. I took the papers and looked at them, realizing they were two paychecks. "Ed," he said, "we're letting you go and giving you an extra month's wages severance pay."

I stared at the checks for a moment and then looked at him, measuring the distance, and then looked at the dog who sat staring at me through his one black eye. I turned my gaze toward the darkened doorway and wondered if she was there in the shadows, with a loaded gun. I turned and walked toward the door leading to the porch, and when I touched the doorknob, he spoke, "Ed, we are not firing you because you haven't done a good job. Actually, you've done a hell of a job; we're firing you because we don't like you!"

Damn! I thought to myself. I thought everyone liked me.

When I got back to the mansion, Jean Ann and Clay were eating breakfast. "What's up?" My wife asked.

"I just got fired," I replied.

"WHAT?" You got fired?" Really?"

"Yeah!"

She jumped up and started dancing. "We're fired! Thank You, God. I won't have to live in this house in town any longer! Thank You, Jesus!" My wife danced off into the living room clapping her hands and singing hallelujah. Clay sat watching, laughing, and then returned to eating his breakfast. Jean Ann called from the other room, "Clay, go outside and start bringing in boxes!" I sat down with a hot cup of coffee and stared at the canary yellow walls. Jean Ann passed through the room coming from one direction and exiting through another door, running in excitement. I stared at her as she passed by, and then she disappeared in a flash, but in a second, her head and shoulders appeared as she leaned backwards through the door and looked at me and said, "It's all right, honey; you'll get over it!"

We rounded up boxes, and personal horses, and made plans, and did the things you do when you move. I've moved a lot in my life, but I'm still not proficient at it. Amidst all the confusion of packing and making phone calls, I was able to say goodbye to several of the good men who worked for me. Baldy, who had left the ranch and moved to Wikieup, came through town and stopped by, and we had a good conversation.

The day before we left town, Cole Moorhouse came driving up to the mansion and knocked on the back door. Cole was still staying out at Camp Five and had worked for me for two years. He had made a hand and had stayed sober, even though he never received a copy of the company rule book. He had been glue that had helped me keep a crew together after seventy, eighty, and ninety days without a day off. I was happy that he thought enough of me to come by and say goodbye.

"You shoulda' never got involved in ranch politics, Eid!" He said, putting and i between the E and d in my name with his slow Texas drawl. We talked for a while, drinking coffee and telling a few stories of days gone by. Presently he stood and shook my hand, with a cigarette drooping out of the corner of his mouth; and walking slightly stooped over as he had for twenty-five years, he walked out the back door.

I got up and began arranging boxes to be loaded the next day, and Cole walked two blocks south to the Black Cat Bar and went to drinking.

Watershed

ℰℭ

In August 1996, we were living in southern Arizona, and one hot day, Jean Ann and I decided to take a leisurely drive to Nogales. I had not been to the famous border town in over twenty years, and Jean Ann had never seen the place, so off we went with a carefree attitude. One thing I wanted to accomplish on our trip was to visit the Paul Bond boot shop thinking I might be able to buy a pair of handmade boots right off the shelf. I had been to the Paul Bond factory in 1974 when it was located downtown on Morley Street in a small storefront shop with a very small crew of employees working in the back of the building. On arrival to Nogales, I learned that Paul Bond's was now located out near the interstate in a big new building that set on its own little hill and resembled a big two-story barn with rustic and western appointments all around. A very noteworthy step upwards indeed.

We entered the store, which was vast, and airy, and smelling of new leather and other sweet aromas. Upstairs, in a sort of open balcony, were located workplaces where talented artisans were busy with their hands creating beautiful cowboy boots, which are things akin to oil paintings by famous artists like Bill Owen or Rembrandt. When we entered, I spied a tall young man who was busy waiting on other customers and was obviously in charge of running the store. He was well over six feet tall with an expensive beaver hat on his head, creased to perfection in the style known as "Gus," and sported an extra wide ribbon circumventing the crown. He was wearing a new and shiny pair of Paul Bond boots, with tops that were no doubt twenty inches in height, with jeans stuffed down inside. The boots had high, under slung heels, at least two and three-fourths inches high, which added to the man's impressive stature. He also wore an expensive-looking cowboy shirt with too many pearl snaps to count unless you were able to run them through a gate, two by two, like a herd of steers. To top off all this grand attire was a groomed and cultivated beard and mustache, the last of which held no less than a tablespoon of the finest wax. I knew him by reputation to be a gentleman known as Spider Daley. He had spent some time in Northern Arizona cowboying at the O RO Ranch, and Scott Westlake and several other cowboys I knew were acquainted with him, and they had told me that of late he had been promoted to the management position at Paul Bond's. He, nor the boots, nor the mustache, had seen the dust of an Arizona cow camp for some time.

I had the advantage over him because I had heard he was employed in the position he presently held, and his substantial height and cultivated style had been well described by several who knew him. He could tell by my way that I was no dude, and the sunburnt hide and dusty hat that was sprinkled with cow dung suggested I might be a man of the open spaces, but he was unsure of my identity. We watched each other, the two of us, like two old bulls in a large corral that afforded them room to avoid battle, but near at hand enough to paw the ground and make bull-like noises. My wife and I browsed for a long spell looking at many pairs of boots, belts, and all sorts of leather goods. I watched different boot makers as they busied themselves in their handiwork, and in general we enjoyed ourselves in the beautiful store, just soaking up the atmosphere. Spider Daley never spoke, and he seemed to circle the store, always on the opposite side from me and watching, but busying himself with other customers. Finally I chose a pair of boots, and Jean Ann chose a pair also, and I walked to the counter with the merchandise in hand. Spider approached, and I laid the desired boots on the countertop and produced a credit card, which I handed to him. Up to this point, nothing had been said between us. He looked at the card and then seemed to freeze. For some seconds, he stared at the card and then at me, and then at the card, and began to roll a toothpick around in the corner of his mouth. I decided to play the best poker hand I could muster and began to stare at him like he was a pillar of salt or some other rare item of historical value. He, too, had obviously decided to act out his role in as dramatic a fashion as possible. Finally he spoke, while still holding the credit card at arm's length. "I've heard a lot of bad stuff about you!" He added to that exclamation point by raising his eyebrows and cocking his head ever so slightly, which was obviously a request for an answer. I gave him none. I had worked with Charlie Wascogamie, numerous other Indians, and poker players, and had learned to look and act like Kawliga the wooden Indian much better than he. Eventually I wore him down with silence, and he ran my credit card through the electronic device, and Jean Ann and I departed with two pair of new Paul Bond boots. Spider Daley had entertained me better than any cinema or stage show I might have attended. I drove down the streets of Nogales reveling in the deliciousness of our encounter.

What amount of cow camp legend or barroom gossip would prompt a man to gaze at another man's name on a credit card like it contained poison or the combination to the Da Vinci code, one can only imagine. When the legend becomes the truth, print the legend.

After close to twenty years, I know the truth and whereabouts of some of the characters I've written about.

Cole Moorhouse lived a few years after we worked together at the Diamond A but slowly became crippled by advanced emphysema. He found refuge on a ranch, south of Seligman, which was run by Beano Kimball, who was kind to him, giving him a place to live, (as well as several other old-timers). Eventually Cole ended up on life support in a hospital in Prescott, and I was told by someone who knows that one night when things were black, his nurse exited his room momentarily, and when she returned, Cole had unplugged himself and was gone.

Tom Reeder continued cowboying around Northern Arizona, working for people who appreciated his talents and especially his knowledge about a cow. He would have liked to have slowed down more than he did, but retirement for those who move frequently, in an industry that isn't known for retirement security, requires that you work or ask for handouts. Thankfully, Tom was never forced to ask for handouts, and besides, there were several who appreciated his knowledge.

Tom worshiped his boy Pete, and the boy was a shining star in the old Texan's life that he greatly appreciated. Pete joined the Army and married a nice girl who came from a military family in Carolina, and their union produced grandkids for Tom to be proud of. And then there came the day in 2004 when Tom received word that Pete Reeder was killed in the streets of Baghdad, Iraq, in the line of duty. It was a hard pill for Tom to swallow, but he took it better than anyone guessed he would. He continued to work and make a hand and packed his memories of Pete without disgrace. In 2006, Tom was working on the Double O Ranch, south of Seligman, and one day he and a couple other good hands were in pursuit of a yearling steer, when Tom's horse stumbled and fell on him, killing him instantly. Like Pete, he was killed in the line of duty.

Charlie Wascogamie continued working when he needed money if someone he liked offered him a job cowboying. Time and money didn't mean a lot to Charlie. Peach Springs and the reservation was a place where superstition, jealousy, and half-truths can get a man in trouble; especially if you've made someone mad. Charlie was falsely accused of molesting a young girl, who was encouraged to lie about the old man, and he was drug off to jail and sat in silence awaiting a trial. Charlie knew nothing about the judicial system, he only knew about horses and cattle, and the hidden places in the canyons and hills where wild beasts might be apprehended. He sat and listened to a court-appointed attorney who promised him that everything would be all right. The attorney, without explaining to Charlie what he was doing, acquired a plea bargain for the old Indian whom he had promised to represent. The attorney got his fee for misrepresentation, and Charlie spent a year in prison for a crime he didn't commit. The Old One went to be with his fathers about fourteen years ago.

John McGrew went to Elko to work in a gold mine and live on a road paved with asphalt.

The last time I heard anything about old Truman, he was in Deming, New Mexico, and had a rich girlfriend. Some things never change.

Jimmer Fancher, or "Whim" as Charlie Wascogamie called him, married a beautiful blonde gal who is solid as a rock, and Jimmer has a couple ranches leased and a herd of cows with his brand on them. He and his wife have a little girl who is a jewel. Good for Jimmer.

Baldy, who never dreamed of slowing down or retirement, was always talking about learning to fly. No one paid any attention to him, thinking that a man living below the poverty line on cowboy wages could ever pay for something that radical. Baldy started out playing around with gyrocopters and wrecked a couple and walked away. Old Bud Lehman, who would fly me around the Diamond A Ranch looking for remnant, took a liking to Baldy and began helping him in his pursuit of a pilot's license. Baldy got his first airplane from Bud, which was an ancient taildragger that had been locked up in a shed for years. They made it air worthy and Baldy began flying it. He began building airplanes in his house, with people laughing at him, wondering how he would get them outside. He was smart enough to disassemble them enough that he could fit the pieces out the front door. Today, in spite of everyone's skepticism, Baldy is a certified aircraft technician, and a licensed pilot, and owns several planes of his own. I don't know if it's true, but I've been told that he flies a plane like he rides a horse. Yee Haw!

Mike Landis retired to a little patch of land adjacent to old Route 66 on the western edge of the Aubrey Valley. He had a comfortable little house with a wood stove and plenty of nails on the wall to hang his silver-mounted Grijalva spade bits. Out back he built a little horse corral and a saddle house and, for a while, was content living like that. But Mike was always motivated, and he acquired a contract to cook for tourists who were traveling down into Peach Springs Canyon. To add to the cowboy cooking, he told flavorful cowboy stories and soon a college was paying him to give lectures labeled as "Western Heritage." He was a hit. He also leased a ranch and bought himself some Longhorn cows that he gathered while riding his favorite mustang. He was successful and stayed busy until emphysema finally crippled him. He died in the spring of 2014. Mike was true to his calling to the end. He never wore a ball cap and was never without a cowboy hat. The last time I saw him, he had on an expensive pair of handmade boots.

Alvin Wagner and Hazel stayed at the Sevens Ranch until sometime in the late seventies. I think it was 1976. He continued to make a hand through numerous changes of management, and perhaps an accomplishment that was equal to making a hand was his ability to keep his sense of humor and wit.

Alvin worked with Mike Landis the entire time Mike

held the Diamond A wagon boss job. Technically Alvin worked for Mike, and to my knowledge, he was not one to undermine another man's authority, but like most old-timers, he possessed strong opinions about cattle, horses, and cowboys, and the correct way to mix those ingredients. He could be sharp of tongue, but the twinkle in his eyes helped ease the pain and clot the blood of any wound he might inflect on someone.

Alvin was not a man who drank alcohol to excess but might occasionally have a drink or two with a friend. One night he and Mike Landis were taking turns buying rounds at the Black Cat Saloon in Seligman. Mike, at that time, was building a new chuck wagon for the Double O Ranch that he was running. This was after both the men had quit working at the Diamond A. Mike was very proud of the chuck wagon that he had produced for his roundup outfit at the Double O. He never worked over four or five men at the Double O Ranch and had ordered the wagon to be built smaller than most chuck wagons a person might see around the West. It had one axle and two wheels.

On this particular evening, Mike went into an excessively long dissertation about the genius of his wagon's design, which he was responsible for. Finally Alvin tired of listening to Mike's bragging and told him in a blunt manner. "Mike, I was born in a wagon over there out east of Tucumcari. I've been around wagons my whole life and could drive a team of horses hooked to a wagon before you were born!

Mike set his whiskey glass down on the bar and raised his hand, but before he could make words accompany his gesticulation, Alvin went on. "Mike, I'm telling you! Every wagon I ever saw had two axles and four wheels! Your wagon you keep bragging about has one axle and two wheels. A wagon with one axle and two wheels ain't a wagon, it's a cart! You're not a wagon boss, you're a cart boss!"

Mike walked out of the bar without noticing the twinkle in Alvin's eyes. Later they patched things up.

Alvin had accumulated some Kern County Land and Cattle Company stocks that he traded for Tenneco Oil stock when Kern County sold out to the oil company. He saved his money, and when he retired, he and Hazel bought a small house in Seligman and lived in harmony until she got sick and died. Alvin lived to a ripe old age and wore his black hat and red bandanna and smoked cigarettes long past the time they should have killed him. He had a twinkle in his eyes and a keen mind right up until he died at a very old age.

I hear tell that Brad Meade is running the wagon at the O RO Ranch. They say he's doing a good job, and the cowboys like working for him, working cattle in the old-time way. I don't think Bubba or his sister are working there.

Scott Westlake came by to help Clay and me load the U-Haul our last day in Seligman, which is not to be compared with helping us gather wild cattle, except perhaps Banjo's tension in the heat of battle and mine in the heat of wanting to get loaded and get gone.

Scott stayed at the Diamond A for a while after I left and then cowboyed around Arizona on various outfits including a return to the Diamond A for a part of the winter and the spring roundup of '98. And then later on, while working on the Babbitt Ranch, Scott and Bill Howell's granddaughter Victoria decided they were meant to be a team, so they got hitched. They now have three daughters and counting, and they all work together on everything from sorting the mare bands that run on the Cataract Plains, where they live, to raising goats for 4H kids to show.

Cody Cochran went back to Texas and married his childhood sweetheart, and he cowboyed around several ranches from Abilene north to Turkey. Eventually, he went to work at the Four Sixes at Guthrie and worked alongside my old friend Boots O'Neal. Cody worked at the Sixes for several years, and occasionally he called me, and we told cowboys stories. He and his wife Jennifer began attending a church at Roaring Springs, and in time Cody began getting involved in ministry in a small way. One day, out of the blue, he called and said he wanted my advice. He explained that there was a small church at Anson, Texas, that needed a pastor. The congregation consisted of a total of six elderly people, all having one foot resting on a banana peel. He asked me what I thought about him taking the job as pastor, to which I replied, "You're crazy!" He took the job anyway, and within a year, he had eighty people attending the church, within two years there was a hundred and fifty. Somewhere near four hundred, he quit counting, realizing numbers weren't as important as people. He told me one time that his church was filled with country people who drive there from at least nineteen different communities. They don't have a church background and are not religious but rather are "unchurched." Cody gathers them in like mavericks. He preaches like he cowboys. His old grandfather, Donald Rutledge, who raised him, still rides a horse and draws a paycheck well past his ninetieth birthday.

ഇOQ

Someday, if you take the time, you could go to that spot in the middle of Trinity Pasture at the base of that high ridge that lies south of Jones Tank and north of Trinity Peak, and you could ride to the top. It is a long gradual climb, and you will ascend a thousand feet or more. When you reach the top, the bottom of your Levis will have sweat stains on them, on the inside of the legs, where they hang down below your saddle fenders. When

you get there, you can unsaddled your horse and let him blow and cool off for a while.

It's a good place, and one from which you can see far enough to reflect on many things. If you look off to

the north by northwest sixty miles you can see Mount Trumbull on the north side of the Grand Canyon. And then when you turn and look to the northeast one hundred seventy miles, you can see Navajo Mountain on the east end of Lake Powell in southern Utah. To the east ninety miles are the San Francisco Peaks, the highest in Arizona, and south by southeast ninety miles is Mingus Mountain, and fourteen degrees west of that and the same distance, you can see Granite Mountain between Prescott and Skull Valley. About fifty-five miles south by southwest, you can see Mount Hope in the middle of the Grant on the O RO Ranch's east side, and then twelve miles west, the Mahon Mountains rise up on the O RO's west side. Finally, ninety miles to the southwest the Hualapai Mountains will complete the circle.

South of that ridge in between where you are in Trinity and Granite Mountain, Kit Carson almost starved to death when he passed that way in a drought and game was scarce. East of that place, Frank Banks and Bill Howell led many a crew of cowboys and, with their help, created lots of dust clouds, working large roundups of Hereford cattle. Whistle Mills was in the distance to the south around Camp Wood chasing mavericks, as was old Ben and Little Ben Fancher. Tom Dolan, Ed Brown, Demas Yoder, and Slim Guilliam have been on top of that ridge, as well as countless other good hands that time has forgotten.

If you stay there long enough, and you remain quiet and watch, you might see the big smoky-colored steer that got away from Scott and Clay because their horses were give out. Perhaps your horse will have caught his air, or maybe someone will show up to help you. Maybe the big smoky steer won't appear because he died without ever being gathered. It doesn't matter: there will be another because they are not all gone.

But the battle
for the
mountains and
cattle
Seem to bring
out the best in
a man
I'll find a new range to ride
and new knots to tie
In a country where Cowboys are King
I turn my tail to the wind
And the old Double Diamond
and disappear into the Sage

Made in United States
Troutdale, OR
11/23/2024

25163883R00176